KW-482-127

MEMOIRS OF THE LIFE
OF
SIR WALTER SCOTT
BART

BY
JOHN GIBSON
LOCKHART

VOLUME V

CHAPTER XXXIV.

PROGRESS OF THE LORD OF THE ISLES. — CORRESPONDENCE WITH MR. JOSEPH TRAIN. — RAPID COMPLETION OF THE LORD OF THE ISLES. — "REFRESHING THE MACHINE." — "SIX WEEKS AT A CHRISTMAS." — PUBLICATION OF THE POEM, — AND OF GUY MANNERING. — LETTERS TO MORRITT, TERRY, AND JOHN BALLANTYNE. — ANECDOTES BY JAMES BALLANTYNE. — VISIT TO LONDON. — MEETING WITH LORD BYRON. — DINNERS AT CARLTON HOUSE.

1814-1815.

By the 11th of November, then, The Lord of the Isles had made great progress, and Scott had also authorized Ballantyne to negotiate among the booksellers for the publication of a second novel. But before I go further into these transactions, I must introduce the circumstances of Scott's first connection with an able and amiable man, whose services were of high importance to him, at this time and ever after, in the prosecution of his literary labors. Calling at Ballantyne's printing-office while Waverley was in the press, he happened to take up a proof sheet of a volume entitled "Poems, with notes illustrative of traditions in Galloway and Ayrshire, by Joseph Train, Supervisor of Excise at Newton-Stewart." The sheet contained a ballad on an Ayrshire tradition, about a certain "Witch of Carrick," whose skill in the black art was, it seems, instrumental in the destruction of one of the scattered vessels of the Spanish Armada. The ballad begins:—

"Why gallops the palfrey with Lady Dunore?
Who drives away Turnberry's kine from the shore?
Go tell it in Carrick, and tell it in Kyle—
Although the proud Dons are now passing the Moil,[1]
On this magic clew,
That in fairyland grew,
Old Elcine de Aggart has taken in hand
To wind up their lives ere they win to our strand."

Scott immediately wrote to the author, begging to be included in his list of subscribers for a dozen copies, and suggesting at the same time a verbal alteration in one of the stanzas of this ballad. Mr. Train acknowledged his letter with gratitude, and the little book reached him just as he was about to embark in the lighthouse yacht. He took it with him on his voyage, and, on returning home again, wrote to Mr. Train, expressing the gratification he had received from several of his metrical pieces, but still more from his notes, and requesting him, as he seemed to be enthusiastic about traditions and legends, to communicate any matters of that order connected with Galloway which he might not himself think of turning to account; "for," said Scott, "nothing interests me so much as local anecdotes; and, as the applications for charity usually conclude, the smallest donation will be thankfully accepted."

Mr. Train, in a little narrative with which he has favored me, says, that for some years before this time he had been engaged, in alliance with a friend of his, Mr. Denniston, in collecting materials for a History of Galloway; they had circulated lists of queries among the clergy and parish schoolmasters, and had thus, and by their own personal researches, accumulated "a great variety of the most excellent materials for that purpose;" but that, from the hour of his correspondence with Walter Scott, he "renounced every idea of authorship for himself," resolving, "that thenceforth his chief pursuit should be collecting whatever he thought would be most interesting to *him*;" and that Mr. Denniston was easily persuaded to acquiesce in the abandonment of their original design. "Upon receiving Mr. Scott's letter," says Mr. Train, "I became still more zealous in the pursuit of ancient lore, and being the first person who had attempted to collect old stories in that quarter with any view to publication, I became so noted, that even beggars, in the hope of reward, came frequently from afar to Newton-Stewart, to recite old ballads and relate old stories to me." Erelong, Mr. Train visited Scott both at Edinburgh and at Abbotsford; a true affection continued ever afterwards to be maintained between them; and this generous ally was, as the prefaces to the Waverley Novels signify, one of the earliest confidants of that series of works, and certainly the most efficient of all the author's friends in furnishing him with materials for their composition. Nor did he confine himself to literary services: whatever portable object of antiquarian curiosity met his eye, this good man secured and treasured up with the same destination; and if ever a catalogue of the museum at Abbotsford shall appear, no single contributor, most assuredly, will fill so large a space in it as Mr. Train.[2]

His first considerable communication, after he had formed the unselfish determination above mentioned, consisted of a collection of anecdotes concerning the Galloway gypsies, and "a local story of an astrologer, who calling at a farmhouse at the moment when the goodwife was in travail, had, it was said, predicted the future fortune of the child, almost in the words placed in the mouth of John MacKinlay, in the Introduction to Guy Mannering." Scott told him, in reply, that the story of the astrologer reminded him of "one he had heard in his youth;" that is to say, as the Introduction explains, from this MacKinlay; but Mr. Train has, since his friend's death, recovered a rude *Durham* ballad, which in fact contains a great deal more of the main fable of Guy Mannering than either his own written, or MacKinlay's oral edition of the *Gallovidian* anecdote had conveyed; and—possessing, as I do, numberless evidences of the haste with which Scott drew up his beautiful Prefaces and Introductions of 1829, 1830, and 1831—I am strongly inclined to think that he must in his boyhood have read the Durham Broadside or Chapbook itself—as well as heard the old serving-man's Scottish version of it.

However this may have been, Scott's answer to Mr. Train proceeded in these words:—

I am now to solicit a favor, which I think your interest in Scottish antiquities will induce you readily to comply with. I am very desirous to have some account of the present state of *Turnberry Castle*—whether any vestiges of it remain—what is the appearance of the ground—the names of the neighboring places—and, above all, what are the traditions of the place (if any) concerning its memorable surprise by Bruce, upon his return from the coast of Ireland, in the commencement of the brilliant part of his career. The purpose of this is to furnish some hints for notes to a work in which I am now engaged, and I need not say I will have great pleasure in mentioning the source from which I derive my information. I have only to add, with the modest importunity of a lazy correspondent, that the sooner you oblige me with an answer (if you can assist me on the subject), the greater will the obligation be on me, who am already your obliged humble servant,

W. SCOTT.

The recurrence of the word *Turnberry*, in the ballad of Elcine de Aggart, had of course suggested this application, which was dated on the 7th of November. "I had often," says Mr. Train, "when a boy, climbed the brown hills, and traversed the shores of Carrick, but I could not sufficiently remember the exact places and distances as to which Mr. Scott inquired; so, immediately on receipt of his letter, I made a journey into Ayrshire to collect all the information I possibly could, and forwarded it to him on the 18th of the same month." Among the particulars thus communicated, was the local superstition, that on the anniversary of the night when Bruce landed at Turnberry from Arran, the same meteoric gleam which had attended his voyage reappeared, unfailingly, in the same quarter of the heavens. With this circumstance Scott was much struck. "Your information," he writes on the 22d November, "was particularly interesting and acceptable, especially that which relates to the supposed preternatural appearance of the fire, etc., which I hope to make some use of." What use he did make of it, if any reader has forgotten, will be seen by reference to stanzas 7-17 of the 5th Canto of the Poem; and the notes to the same Canto embody, with due acknowledgment, the more authentic results of Mr. Train's pilgrimage to Carrick.

I shall recur presently to this communication from Mr. Train; but must pause for a moment to introduce two letters, both written in the same week with Scott's request as to the localities of Turnberry. They both give us amusing sketches of his buoyant spirits at this period of gigantic exertion;—and the first of them, which relates chiefly to Maturin's Tragedy of Bertram, shows how he could still contrive to steal time for attention to the affairs of brother authors less energetic than himself.

TO DANIEL TERRY, ESQ.

ABBOTSFORD, November 10, 1814.

MY DEAR TERRY,—I should have long since answered your kind letter by our friend Young, but he would tell you of my departure with our trusty and well-beloved Erskine, on a sort of a voyage to Nova Zembla. Since my return, I have fallen under the tyrannical dominion of a certain Lord of the Isles. Those Lords were famous for oppression in the days of yore, and if I can judge by the posthumous despotism exercised over me, they have not improved by their demise. The *peine forte et dure* is, you know, nothing in comparison to being obliged to grind verses; and so devilish repulsive is my disposition, that I can never put my wheel into constant and regular motion, till Ballantyne's devil claps in his proofs, like the hot cinder which you Bath folks used to clap in beside an unexperienced turnspit, as a hint to be expeditious in his duty. O long life to the old hermit of Prague, who never saw pen and ink!—much happier in that negative circumstance than in his alliance with the niece of King Gorboduc.

To talk upon a blither subject, I wish you saw Abbotsford, which begins this season to look the whimsical, gay, odd cabin, that we had chalked out. I have been obliged to relinquish Stark's plan, which was greatly too expensive. So I have made the old farmhouse my *corps de logis*, with some outlying places for kitchen, laundry, and two spare bedrooms, which run along the east wall of the farm-court, not without some picturesque effect. A perforated cross, the spoils of the old kirk of Galashiels, decorates an advanced door, and looks very well. This little sly bit of sacrilege has given our spare rooms the name of *the chapel*. I earnestly invite you to a *pew* there, which you will find as commodious for the purpose of a nap as you have ever experienced when, under the guidance of old Mrs. Smollett, you were led to St. George's, Edinburgh.

I have been recommending to John Kemble (I dare say without any chance of success) to peruse a MS. Tragedy of Maturin's author of Montorio: it is one of those things which will either succeed greatly or be damned gloriously, for its merits are marked, deep, and striking, and its faults of a nature obnoxious to ridicule. He had our old friend Satan (none of your sneaking St. John Street devils, but the arch-fiend himself) brought on the stage bodily. I believe I have exorcised the foul fiend—for, though in reading he was a most terrible fellow, I feared for his reception in public. The last act is ill contrived. He piddles (so to speak) through a cullender, and divides the whole horrors of the catastrophe (though God wot there are enough of them) into a kind of drippity-droppity of four or five scenes, instead of inundating the audience with them at once in the finale, with a grand *"gardez l'eau."* With all this, which I should say had I written the thing myself, it is grand and powerful; the language most animated and poetical; and the characters sketched with a masterly enthusiasm. Many thanks for Captain Richard Falconer.[3] To your kindness I owe the two books in the world I most longed to see, not so much for their intrinsic merits, as because they bring back with vivid associations the sentiments of my childhood—I might almost say infancy. Nothing ever disturbed my feelings more than when, sitting by the old oak table, my aunt, Lady Raeburn, used to read the lamentable catastrophe of the ship's departing without Captain Falconer, in consequence of the whole party making free with lime-punch on the eve of its being launched. This and Captain Bingfield,[4] I much wished to read once more, and I owe the possession of both to your kindness. Everybody that I see talks highly of your steady interest with the public, wherewith, as I never doubted of it, I am pleased but not surprised. We are just now leaving this for the winter: the children went yesterday. Tom Purdie, Finella, and the greyhounds, all in excellent health; the latter have not been hunted this season!!! Can add nothing more to excite your admiration. Mrs. Scott sends her kind compliments.

W. SCOTT.

The following, dated a day after, refers to some lines which Mr. Morritt had sent him from Worthing.

TO J. B. S. MORRITT, ESQ., M. P., WORTHING.

ABBOTSFORD, November 11, 1814.

MY DEAR MORRITT,—I had your kind letter with the beautiful verses. May the Muse meet you often on the verge of the sea or among your own woods of Rokeby! May you have spirits to profit by her visits (and that implies all good wishes for the continuance of Mrs. M.'s convalescence), and may I often, by the fruits of your inspiration, have my share of pleasure! My Muse is a Tyranness, and not a Christian queen, and compels me to attend to longs and shorts, and I know not what, when, God wot, I had rather be planting evergreens

3

by my new old fountain. You must know that, like the complaint of a fine young boy who was complimented by a stranger on his being a smart fellow, "I am sair halded down by *the bubbly jock*." In other words, the turkey cock, at the head of a family of some forty or fifty infidels, lays waste all my shrubs. In vain I remonstrate with Charlotte upon these occasions; she is in league with the hen-wife, the natural protectress of these pirates; and I have only the inhuman consolation that I may one day, like a cannibal, eat up my enemies. This is but dull fun, but what else have I to tell you about? It would be worse if, like Justice Shallow's Davy, I should consult you upon sowing down the headland with wheat. My literary tormentor is a certain Lord of the Isles, famed for his tyranny of yore, and not unjustly. I am bothering some tale of him I have had long by me into a sort of romance. I think you will like it: it is Scottified up to the teeth, and somehow I feel myself like the liberated chiefs of the Rolliad, "who boast their native philabeg restored." I believe the frolics one can cut in this loose garb are all set down by you Sassenachs to the real agility of the wearer, and not the brave, free, and independent character of his clothing. It is, in a word, the real Highland fling, and no one is supposed able to dance it but a native. I always thought that epithet of Gallia *Braccata* implied subjugation, and was never surprised at Cæsar's easy conquests, considering that his Labienus and all his merry men wore, as we say, bottomless breeks.

      Ever yours,

W. S.

      Well might he describe himself as being hard at work with his Lord of the Isles. The date of Ballantyne's letter to Miss Edgeworth (November 11), in which he mentions the third Canto as completed; that of the communication from Mr. Train (November 18), on which so much of Canto Fifth was grounded; and that of a note from Scott to Ballantyne (December 16, 1814), announcing that he had sent the last stanza of the poem: these dates, taken together, afford conclusive evidence of the fiery rapidity with which the three last Cantos of The Lord of the Isles were composed.

      He writes, on the 25th December, to Constable that he "had corrected the last proofs, and was setting out for Abbotsford to refresh the machine." And in what did his refreshment of the machine consist? Besides having written within this year the greater part (almost, I believe, the whole) of the Life of Swift—Waverley—and The Lord of the Isles—he had given two essays to the Encyclopædia Supplement, and published, with an Introduction and notes, one of the most curious pieces of family history ever produced to the world, on which he labored with more than usual zeal and diligence, from his warm affection for the noble representative of its author. This inimitable Memorie of the Somervilles came out in October; and it was speedily followed by an annotated reprint of the strange old treatise, entitled "Rowland's letting off the humours of the blood in the head vein, 1611." He had also kept up his private correspondence on a scale which I believe never to have been exemplified in the case of any other person who wrote continually for the press—except, perhaps, Voltaire; and, to say nothing of strictly professional duties, he had, as a vast heap of documents now before me proves, superintended from day to day, except during his Hebridean voyage, the still perplexed concerns of the Ballantynes, with a watchful assiduity that might have done credit to the most diligent of tradesmen. The "machine" might truly require "refreshment."

      It was, as has been seen, on the 7th of November that Scott acknowledged the receipt of that communication from Mr. Train which included the story of the Galloway astrologer. There can be no doubt that this story recalled to his mind, if not the Durham ballad, the similar but more detailed corruption of it which he had heard told by his father's servant, John MacKinlay, in the days of George's Square and Green-breeks, and which he has preserved in the introduction to Guy Mannering, as the groundwork of that tale. It has been shown that the three last Cantos of The Lord of the Isles were written between the 11th of November and the 25th of December; and it is therefore scarcely to be supposed that any part of this novel had been penned before he thus talked of "refreshing the machine." It is quite certain that when James Ballantyne wrote to Miss Edgeworth on the 11th November, he could not have seen one page of Guy Mannering, since he in that letter announces that the new novel of his nameless friend would depict manners *more ancient* than those of 1745. And yet it is equally certain, that before The Lord of the Isles was *published*, which took place on the 18th of January, 1815, two volumes of Guy Mannering had been not only written and copied by an amanuensis, but printed.

Scott thus writes to Morritt, in sending him his copy of The Lord of the Isles:—

TO J. B. S. MORRITT, ESQ., M. P., WORTHING.

EDINBURGH, 19th January, 1815.

MY DEAR MORRITT,—I have been very foolishly putting off my writing until I should have time for a good long epistle; and it is astonishing what a number of trifles have interfered to prevent my commencing on a great scale. The last of these has been rather of an extraordinary kind, for your little friend Walter has chose to make himself the town talk, by taking what seemed to be the small-pox, despite of vaccination in infancy, and inoculation with the variolous matter thereafter, which last I resorted to by way of making assurance double sure. The medical gentleman who attended him is of opinion that he *has* had the real small-pox, but it shall never be averred by me—for the catastrophe of Tom Thumb is enough to deter any thinking person from entering into a feud with the cows. Walter is quite well again, which was the principal matter I was interested in. We had very nearly been in a bad scrape, for I had fixed the Monday on which he sickened, to take him with me for the Christmas vacation to Abbotsford. It is probable that he would not have pleaded headache when there was such a party in view, especially as we were to shoot wild ducks one day together at Cauldshiels Loch; and what the consequence of such a journey might have been, God alone knows.

I am clear of The Lord of the Isles, and I trust you have your copy. It closes my poetic labors upon an extended scale: but I dare say I shall always be dabbling in rhyme until the *solve senescentem*. I have directed the copy to be sent to Portland Place. I want to shake myself free of Waverley, and accordingly have made a considerable exertion to finish an odd little tale within such time as will mystify the public, I trust—unless they suppose me to be Briareus. Two volumes are already printed, and the only persons in my confidence, W. Erskine and Ballantyne, are of opinion that it is much more interesting than Waverley. It is a tale of private life, and only varied by the perilous exploits of smugglers and excisemen. The success of Waverley has given me a spare hundred or two, which I have resolved to spend in London this spring, bringing up Charlotte and Sophia with me. I do not forget my English friends—but I fear they will forget me, unless I show face now and then. My correspondence gradually drops, as must happen when people do not meet; and I long to see Ellis, Heber, Gifford, and one or two more. I do not include Mrs. Morritt and you, because we are much nearer neighbors, and within a whoop and a holla in comparison. I think we should come up by sea, if I were not a little afraid of Charlotte being startled by the March winds—for our vacation begins 12th March.

You will have heard of poor Caberfae's death? What a pity it is he should have outlived his promising young representative. His state was truly pitiable—all his fine faculties lost in paralytic imbecility, and yet not so entirely so but that he perceived his deprivation as in a glass darkly. Sometimes he was fretful and anxious because he did not see his son; sometimes he expostulated and complained that his boy had been allowed to die without his seeing him; and sometimes, in a less clouded state of intellect, he was sensible of, and lamented his loss in its full extent. These, indeed, are the "fears of the brave, and follies of the wise,"[5] which sadden and humiliate the lingering hours of prolonged existence. Our friend Lady Hood will now be Caberfae herself. She has the spirit of a chieftainess in every drop of her blood, but there are few situations in which the cleverest women are so apt to be imposed upon as in the management of landed property, more especially of an Highland estate. I do fear the accomplishment of the prophecy, that when there should be a deaf Caberfae, the house was to fall.[6]

I am delighted to find Mrs. Morritt is recovering health and strength—better walking on the beach at Worthing than on the *plainstanes* of Prince's Street, for the weather is very severe here indeed. I trust Mrs. M. will, in her milder climate, lay in such a stock of health and strength as may enable you to face the north in Autumn. I have got the nicest crib for you possible, just about twelve feet square, and in the harmonious vicinity of a piggery. You never saw so minute an establishment,—but it has all that we wish for, and all our friends will care about; and we long to see you there. Charlotte sends the kindest remembrances to Mrs. Morritt.

As for politics, I have thought little about them lately; the high and exciting interest is so completely subsided, that the wine is upon the lees. As for America, we have so managed as to give her the appearance of triumph, and what is worse, encouragement to resume the war upon a more favorable opportunity. It was our business to have given them a fearful memento that the babe unborn should have remembered; but, having missed this opportunity, I believe that this country would submit with great reluctance to continue a war, for which there is really no specific object. As for the Continental monarchs, there is no guessing what the folly of Kings and Ministers may do; but God knows! would any of them look at home, enough is to be done which might strengthen and improve their dominions in a different manner than by mere extension. I trust Ministers will go out rather than be engaged in war again, upon any account. If France is wise (I have no fear that any superfluous feeling of humanity will stand in the way), she will send 10,000 of her most refractory troops to fight with Christophe and the yellow fever in the Island of St. Domingo, and then I presume they may sit down in quiet at home.

But my sheet grows to an end, and so does the pleading of the learned counsel, who is thumping the poor bar as I write. He hems twice. Forward, sweet Orator Higgins!—at least till I sign myself, dear Morritt,

Yours most truly,

WALTER SCOTT.

Guy Mannering was published on the 24th of February—that is, exactly two months after The Lord of the Isles was dismissed from the author's desk; and—making but a narrow allowance for the operations of the transcriber, printer, bookseller, etc., I think the dates I have gathered together confirm the accuracy of what I have often heard Scott say, that his second novel "was the work of six weeks at a Christmas." Such was his recipe "for refreshing the machine."

I am sorry to have to add, that this severity of labor, like the repetition of it which had such deplorable effects at a later period of his life, was the result of his anxiety to acquit himself of obligations arising out of his connection with the commercial speculations of the Ballantynes. The approach of Christmas, 1814, brought with it the prospect of such a recurrence of difficulties about the discount of John's bills, as to render it absolutely necessary that Scott should either apply again for assistance to his private friends, or task his literary powers with some such extravagant effort as has now been recorded. The great object, which was still to get rid of the heavy stock that had been accumulated before the storm of May, 1813, at length determined the chief partner to break up, as soon as possible, the concern which his own sanguine rashness, and the gross irregularities of his mercurial lieutenant, had so lamentably perplexed; but Constable, having already enabled the firm to avoid public exposure more than once, was not now, any more than when he made his contract for The Lord of the Isles, disposed to burden himself with an additional load of Weber's Beaumont and Fletcher, and other almost as unsalable books. While they were still in hopes of overcoming his scruples, it happened that a worthy friend of Scott's, the late Mr. Charles Erskine, his sheriff-substitute in Selkirkshire, had immediate occasion for a sum of money which he had some time before advanced, at Scott's personal request, to the firm of John Ballantyne and Company; and on receiving his application, Scott wrote as follows:—

TO MR. JOHN BALLANTYNE, BOOKSELLER, EDINBURGH.

ABBOTSFORD, October 14, 1814.

DEAR JOHN,—Charles Erskine wishes his money, as he has made a purchase of land. This is a new perplexity—for paid he must be forthwith—as his advance was friendly and confidential. I do not at this moment see how it is to be raised, but believe I shall find means. In the mean while, it will be necessary to propitiate the Leviathans of Paternoster Row. My idea is, that you or James should write to them to the following effect: That a novel is offered you by the Author of Waverley; that the author is desirous it should be out before Mr. Scott's poem, or as soon thereafter as possible; and that having resolved, as they are aware, to relinquish publishing, you only wish to avail yourselves of this offer to the extent of helping off some of your stock. I leave it to you to consider whether you should condescend on any particular work to offer them as bread to their butter—or on any particular amount—as £500. One thing must be provided, that Constable shares to the extent of the Scottish sale—they, however, managing. My reason for letting them have this scent of roast meat is, in case it should be necessary for us to apply to them to renew bills in December. Yours,

W. S.

Upon receiving this letter, John Ballantyne suggested to Scott that he should be allowed to offer, not only the new novel, but the next edition of Waverley, to Longman, Murray, or Blackwood—in the hope that the prospect of being let in to the profits of the already established favorite, would overcome effectually the hesitation of one or other of these houses about venturing on the encumbrance which Constable seemed to shrink from with such pertinacity; but upon this ingenious proposition Scott at once set his *veto*. He writes (October 17, 1814):—

DEAR JOHN,—

Your expedients are all wretched, as far as regards me. I never will give Constable, or any one, room to say I have broken my word with him in the slightest degree. If I lose everything else, I will at least keep my honor unblemished; and I do hold myself bound in honor to offer him a Waverley, while he shall continue to comply with the conditions annexed. I intend the new novel to operate as something more permanent than a mere accommodation; and if I can but be permitted to do so, I will print it before it is sold to any one, and then propose, first to Constable and Longman—second, to Murray and Blackwood—to take the whole at such a rate as will give them one half of the fair profits; granting acceptances which, upon an edition of 3000, which we shall be quite authorized to print, will amount to an immediate command of £1500; and to this we may couple the condition, that they must take £500 or £600 of the old stock. I own I am not solicitous to deal with Constable alone, nor am I at all bound to offer him the new novel on any terms; but he, knowing of the intention, may expect to be treated with, at least, although it is possible we may not deal. However, if Murray and Blackwood were to come forward with any handsome proposal as to the stock, I should certainly have no objection to James's giving the pledge of the Author of W. for his next work. You are like the crane in the fable, when you boast of not having got anything from the business; you may thank God that it did not bite your head off. Would to God I were at let-a-be for let-a-be;—but you have done your best, and so must I.

Yours truly,

W. S.

Both Mr. Murray, and Longman's partner, Mr. Rees, were in Scotland about this time; and the former at least paid Scott a visit at Abbotsford. Of course, however, whatever propositions they may have made were received by one or other of the Ballantynes. The result was, that the house of Longman undertook Guy Mannering on the terms dictated by Scott—namely, granting bills for £1500, and relieving John Ballantyne and Company of stock to the extent of £500 more; and Constable's first information of the transaction was from Messrs. Longman themselves, when they, in compliance with Scott's wish, as signified in the letter last quoted, offered him a share in the edition which they had purchased. With one or two exceptions, originating in circumstances nearly similar, the house of Constable published all the subsequent series of the Waverley Novels.

I must not, however, forget that The Lord of the Isles was published a month before Guy Mannering. The poem was received with an interest much heightened by the recent and growing success of the mysterious Waverley. Its appearance, so rapidly following that novel, and accompanied with the announcement of another prose tale, just about to be published, by the same hand, puzzled and confounded the mob of dulness.[7] The more sagacious few said to themselves—Scott is making one serious effort more in his old line, and by this it will be determined whether he does or does not altogether renounce that for his new one.

The Edinburgh Review on The Lord of the Isles begins with,—

"Here is another genuine Lay of the Great Minstrel, with all his characteristic faults, beauties, and irregularities. The same glow of coloring—the same energy of narration—the same amplitude of description are conspicuous—with the same still more characteristic disdain of puny graces and small originalities—the true poetical hardihood, in the strength of which he urges on his Pegasus fearlessly through dense and rare, and aiming gallantly at the great ends of truth and effect, stoops but rarely to study the means by which they are to be attained; avails himself without scruple of common sentiments and common images wherever they seem fitted for his purpose; and is original by the very boldness of his borrowing, and impressive by his disregard of epigram and emphasis."

The conclusion of the contemporaneous article in the Quarterly Review is as follows:—

"The many beautiful passages which we have extracted from the poem, combined with the brief remarks subjoined to each canto, will sufficiently show, that although The Lord of the Isles is not likely to add very much to the reputation of Mr. Scott, yet this must be imputed rather to the greatness of his previous reputation, than to the absolute inferiority of the poem itself. Unfortunately, its merits are merely incidental, while its defects are mixed up with the very elements of the poem. But it is not in the power of Mr. Scott to write with tameness; be the subject what it will (and he could not easily have chosen one more impracticable), he impresses upon whatever scenes he describes so much movement and activity,—he infuses into his narrative such a flow of life, and, if we may so express ourselves, of animal spirits, that without satisfying the judgment, or moving the feelings, or elevating the mind, or even very greatly interesting the curiosity, he is able to seize upon, and, as it were, exhilarate the imagination of his readers, in a manner which is often truly unaccountable. This quality Mr. Scott possesses in an admirable degree; and supposing that he had no other object in view than to convince the world of the great poetical powers with which he is gifted, the poem before us would be quite sufficient for his purpose. But this is of very inferior importance to the public; what they want is a good poem, and, as experience has shown, this can only be constructed upon a solid foundation of taste, and judgment, and meditation."

These passages appear to me to condense the result of deliberate and candid reflection, and I have therefore quoted them. The most important remarks of either Essayist on the details of the plot and execution are annexed to the last edition of the poem; and show such an exact coincidence of judgment in two masters of their calling, as had not hitherto been exemplified in the professional criticism of his metrical romances. The defects which both point out are, I presume, but too completely explained by the preceding statement of the rapidity with which this, the last of those great performances, had been thrown off; nor do I see that either Reviewer has failed to do sufficient justice to the beauties which redeem the imperfections of The Lord of the Isles—except as regards the whole character of Bruce, its real hero, and the picture of the battle of Bannockburn, which, now that one can compare these works from something like the same point of view, does not appear to me in the slightest particular inferior to the Flodden of Marmion.

This poem is now, I believe, about as popular as Rokeby; but it has never reached the same station in general favor with the Lay, Marmion, or The Lady of the Lake. The first edition of 1800 copies in quarto was, however, rapidly disposed of, and the separate editions in 8vo, which ensued before his poetical works were collected, amounted together to 12,250 copies. This, in the case of almost any other author, would have been splendid success; but as compared with what he had previously experienced, even in his Rokeby, and still more so as compared with the enormous circulation at once attained by Lord Byron's early tales, which were then following each other in almost breathless succession, the falling off was decided. One evening, some days after the poem had been published, Scott requested James Ballantyne to call on him, and the printer found him alone in his library, working at the third volume of Guy Mannering. I give what follows from Ballantyne's Memoranda:—

"'Well, James,' he said, 'I have given you a week—what are people saying about The Lord of the Isles?' I hesitated a little, after the fashion of Gil Blas, but he speedily brought the matter to a point. 'Come,' he said, 'speak out, my good fellow; what has put it into your head to be on so much ceremony *with me* all of a sudden? But, I see how it is, the result is given in one word—*Disappointment*.' My silence admitted his inference to the fullest extent. His countenance certainly did look rather blank for a few seconds; in truth, he had been wholly unprepared for the event; for it is a singular fact, that before the public, or rather the booksellers, had given their decision, he no more knew whether he had written well or ill, than whether a die thrown out of a box was to turn up a size or an ace. However, he instantly resumed his spirits, and expressed his wonder rather that his poetical popularity should have lasted so long, than that it should have now at last given way. At length he said, with perfect cheerfulness, 'Well, well, James, so be it—but you know we must not droop, for we can't afford to give over. Since one line has failed, we must just stick to something else:'—and so he dismissed me and resumed his novel."

Ballantyne concludes the anecdote in these words:—

"He spoke thus, probably unaware of the undiscovered wonders then slumbering in his mind. Yet still he could not but have felt that the production of a few poems was nothing in comparison of what must be in reserve for him, for he was at this time scarcely more than forty.[8] An evening or two after, I called again on him, and found on the table a copy of The Giaour, which he seemed to have been reading. Having an enthusiastic young lady in my house, I asked him if I might carry the book home with me, but chancing to glance on the autograph blazon, 'To the Monarch of Parnassus from one of his subjects,' instantly retracted my request, and said I had not observed Lord Byron's inscription before. 'What inscription?' said he; 'oh yes, I had forgot, but inscription or no inscription, you are equally welcome.' I again took it up, and he continued, 'James, Byron hits the mark where I don't even pretend to fledge my arrow.' At this time he had never seen Byron, but I knew he meant soon to be in London, when, no doubt, the mighty consummation of the meeting of the two bards would be accomplished; and I ventured to say that he must be looking forward to it with some interest. His countenance became fixed, and he answered impressively, 'Oh, of course.' In a minute or two afterwards he rose from his chair, paced the room at a very rapid rate, which was his practice in certain moods of mind, then made a dead halt, and bursting into an extravaganza of laughter, 'James,' cried he, 'I'll tell you what Byron should say to me when we are about to accost each other,—

"Art thou the man whom men famed Grizzle call?"

And then how germane would be my answer,—

"Art thou the still more famed Tom Thumb the small?"'

"This," says the printer, "is a specimen of his peculiar humor; it kept him full of mirth for the rest of the evening."

The whole of the scene strikes me as equally and delightfully characteristic; I may add, hardly more so of Scott than of his printer; for Ballantyne, with all his profound worship of his friend and benefactor, was in truth, even more than he, an undoubting acquiescer in "the decision of the public, or rather of the booksellers;" and among the many absurdities into which his reverence for the popedom of Paternoster Row led him, I never could but consider with special astonishment, the facility with which he seemed to have adopted the notion that the Byron of 1814 was really entitled to supplant Scott as a popular poet. Appreciating, as a man of his talents could hardly fail to do, the splendidly original glow and depth of Childe Harold, he always appeared to me quite blind to the fact, that in The Giaour, in The Bride of Abydos, in Parisina, and indeed in all his early serious narratives, Byron owed at least half his success to clever, though perhaps unconscious imitation of Scott, and no trivial share of the rest to the lavish use of materials which Scott never employed, only because his genius was, from the beginning to the end of his career, under the guidance of high and chivalrous feelings of moral rectitude. All this Lord Byron himself seems to have felt most completely—as witness the whole sequence of his letters and diaries;[9] and I think I see many symptoms that both the decision of the million, and its index, "the decision of the booksellers," tend the same way at present; but my business is to record, as far as my means may permit, the growth and structure of one great mind, and the effect which it produced upon the actual witnesses of its manifestations, not to obtrude the conjectures of a partial individual as to what rank posterity may assign it amongst or above contemporary rivals.

The following letter was addressed to Lord Byron on the receipt of that copy of The Giaour to which Mr. Ballantyne's Memorandum refers: I believe the inscription to Scott first appeared on the ninth edition of the poem:

TO THE RIGHT HON. LORD BYRON, LONDON.

My Lord,—I have long owed you my best thanks for the uncommon pleasure I had in perusing your high-spirited Turkish fragment. But I should hardly have ventured to offer them, well knowing how you must be overwhelmed by volunteer intrusions of approbation (which always look as if the writer valued his opinion at fully more than it may be worth) unless I had to-day learned that I have an apology for entering upon the subject, from your having so kindly sent me a copy of the poem. I did not receive it sooner, owing to my absence from Edinburgh, where it had been lying quietly at my house in Castle Street; so that I must have seemed ungrateful, when, in truth, I was only modest. The last offence may be forgiven, as not common in a lawyer and poet; the first is said to be equal to the crime of witchcraft, but many an act of my life hath shown that I am no conjurer. If I were, however, ten times more modest than twenty years' attendance at the Bar renders probable, your flattering inscription would cure me of so unfashionable a malady. I might, indeed, lately have had a legal title to as much supremacy on Parnassus as can be conferred by a sign-manual, for I had a very flattering offer of the laurel; but as I felt obliged, for a great many reasons, to decline it, I am altogether unconscious of any other title to sit high upon the forked hill.

To return to The Giaour; I had lent my first edition, but the whole being imprinted in my memory, I had no difficulty in tracing the additions, which are great improvements, as I should have conjectured aforehand merely from their being additions. I hope your Lordship intends to proceed with this fascinating style of composition. You have access to a stream of sentiments, imagery, and manners, which are so little known to us as to convey all the interest of novelty, yet so endeared to us by the early perusal of Eastern tales, that we are not embarrassed with utter ignorance upon the subject. Vathek, bating some passages, would have made a charming subject for a tale. The conclusion is truly grand. I would give a great deal to know the originals from which it was drawn. Excuse this hasty scrawl, and believe me, my Lord, your Lordship's much obliged, very humble servant,

WALTER SCOTT.

If January brought the writer of this letter "disappointment," there was abundant consolation in store for February, 1815. Guy Mannering was received with eager curiosity, and pronounced by acclamation fully worthy to share the honors of Waverley. The easy transparent flow of its style; the beautiful simplicity, and here and there the wild solemn magnificence of its sketches of scenery; the rapid, ever heightening interest of the narrative; the unaffected kindliness of feeling, the manly purity of thought, everywhere mingled with a gentle humor and a homely sagacity; but, above all, the rich variety and skilful contrast of characters and manners, at once fresh in fiction, and stamped with the unforgeable seal of truth and nature: these were charms that spoke to every heart and mind; and the few murmurs of pedantic criticism were lost in the voice of general delight, which never fails to welcome the invention that introduces to the sympathy of imagination a new group of immortal realities.

The earlier chapters of the present narrative have anticipated much of what I might, perhaps with better judgment, have reserved for this page. Taken together with the author's Introduction and Notes, those anecdotes of his days of youthful wandering must, however, have enabled the reader to trace almost as minutely as he could wish, the sources from which the novelist drew his materials, both of scenery and character; and the Durham Garland, which I print in the Appendix to this volume, exhausts my information concerning the humble groundwork on which fancy reared this delicious romance.[10]

The first edition was, like that of Waverley, in three little volumes, with a humility of paper and printing which the meanest novelist would now disdain to imitate; the price a guinea. The 2000 copies of which it consisted were sold the day after the publication; and within three months came a second and a third impression, making together 5000 copies more. The sale, before those novels began to be collected, had reached nearly 10,000; and since then (to say nothing of foreign reprints of the text, and myriads of translations into every tongue of Europe) the domestic sale has amounted to 50,000.

On the rising of the Court of Session in March, Mr. and Mrs. Scott went by sea to London with their eldest girl, whom, being yet too young for general society, they again deposited with Joanna Baillie at Hampstead, while they themselves resumed, for two months, their usual quarters at kind Miss Dumergue's in Piccadilly. Six years had elapsed since Scott last appeared in the metropolis; and brilliant as his reception had then been, it was still more so on the present occasion. Scotland had been visited in the interim, chiefly from the interest excited by his writings, by crowds of the English nobility, most of whom had found introduction to his personal acquaintance—not a few had partaken of his hospitality at Ashestiel or Abbotsford. The generation among whom, I presume, a genius of this order feels his own influence with the proudest and sweetest confidence—on whose fresh minds and ears he has himself made the first indelible impressions—the generation with whose earliest romance of the heart and fancy his idea had been blended, was now grown to the full stature; the success of these recent novels, seen on every table, the subject of every conversation, had, with those who did not doubt their parentage, far more than counterweighed his declination, dubious after all, in the poetical balance; while the mystery that hung over them quickened the curiosity of the hesitating and conjecturing many—and the name on which ever and anon some new circumstance accumulated stronger suspicion, loomed larger through the haze in which he had thought fit to envelop it. Moreover, this was a period of high national pride and excitement.

"O who that shared them ever shall forget
The emotions of the spirit-rousing time,
When breathless in the mart the couriers met,
Early and late, at evening and at prime;
When the loud cannon and the merry chime
Hail'd news on news, as field on field was won,
When Hope, long doubtful, soared at length sublime,
And our glad eyes, awake as day begun,
Watch'd Joy's broad banner rise, to meet the rising sun?

"O these were hours, when thrilling joy repaid
A long, long course of darkness, doubts, and fears!
The heart-sick faintness of the hope delayed,
The waste, the woe, the bloodshed, and the tears
That tracked with terror twenty rolling years—
All was forgot in that blithe jubilee.
Her downcast eye even pale Affliction rears,
To sigh a thankful prayer amid the glee
That hailed the Despot's fall, and peace and liberty!"[11]

At such a time, Prince and people were well prepared to hail him who, more perhaps than any other master of the pen, had contributed to sustain the spirit of England throughout the struggle, which was as yet supposed to have been terminated on the field of Toulouse. "Thank Heaven you are coming at last!" Joanna Baillie had written a month or two before. "Make up your mind to be stared at only a little less than the Czar of Muscovy, or old Blücher."

And now took place James Ballantyne's "mighty consummation of the meeting of the two bards." Scott's own account of it, in a letter to Mr. Moore, must have been seen by most of my readers; yet I think it ought also to find a place here. He says:—

"It was in the spring of 1815, that, chancing to be in London, I had the advantage of a personal introduction to Lord Byron. Report had prepared me to meet a man of peculiar habits and a quick temper, and I had some doubts whether we were likely to suit each other in society. I was most agreeably disappointed in this respect. I found Lord Byron in the highest degree courteous, and even kind. We met for an hour or two almost daily, in Mr. Murray's drawing-room, and found a great deal to say to each other.[12] We also met frequently in parties and evening society, so that for about two months I had the advantage of a considerable intimacy with this distinguished individual. Our sentiments agreed a good deal, except upon the subjects of religion and politics, upon neither of which I was inclined to believe that Lord Byron entertained very fixed opinions. I remember saying to him, that I really thought that if he lived a few years he would alter his sentiments. He answered, rather sharply, 'I suppose you are one of those who prophesy I shall turn Methodist.' I replied: 'No, I don't expect your conversion to be of such an ordinary kind. I would rather look to see you retreat upon the Catholic faith, and distinguish yourself by the austerity of your penances. The species of religion to which you must, or may, one day attach yourself, must exercise a strong power on the imagination.' He smiled gravely, and seemed to allow I might be right.

"On politics, he used sometimes to express a high strain of what is now called Liberalism; but it appeared to me that the pleasure it afforded him, as a vehicle for displaying his wit and satire against individuals in office, was at the bottom of this habit of thinking, rather than any real conviction of the political principles on which he talked. He was certainly proud of his rank and ancient family, and, in that respect, as much an aristocrat as was consistent with good sense and good breeding. Some disgusts, how adopted I know not, seemed to me to have given this peculiar and (as it appeared to me) contradictory cast of mind; but, at heart, I would have termed Byron a patrician on principle.

"Lord Byron's reading did not seem to me to have been very extensive, either in poetry or history. Having the advantage of him in that respect, and possessing a good competent share of such reading as is little read, I was sometimes able to put under his eye objects which had for him the interest of novelty. I remember particularly repeating to him the fine poem of Hardyknute, an imitation of the old Scottish ballad, with which he was so much affected, that some one who was in the same apartment asked me what I could possibly have been telling Byron by which he was so much agitated.

"I saw Byron for the last time in 1815, after I returned from France. He dined, or lunched, with me at Long's, in Bond Street. I never saw him so full of gayety and good-humor, to which the presence of Mr. Mathews, the comedian, added not a little. Poor Terry was also present. After one of the gayest parties I ever was present at, my fellow-traveller, Mr. Scott of Gala, and I set off for Scotland, and I never saw Lord Byron again. Several letters passed between us—one perhaps every half-year. Like the old heroes in Homer, we exchanged gifts. I gave Byron a beautiful dagger mounted with gold, which had been the property of the redoubted Elfi Bey. But I was to play the part of Diomed in the Iliad, for Byron sent me, some time after, a large sepulchral vase of silver. It was full of dead men's bones, and had inscriptions on two sides of the base. One ran thus: 'The bones contained in this urn were found in certain ancient sepulchres within the long walls of Athens, in the month of February, 1811.' The other face bears the lines of Juvenal: '*Expende—quot libras in duce summo invenies?—Mors sola fatetur quantula sint hominum corpuscula.*'

"To these I have added a third inscription, in these words, 'The gift of Lord Byron to Walter Scott.'[13] There was a letter with this vase, more valuable to me than the gift itself, from the kindness with which the donor expressed himself towards me. I left it naturally in the urn with the bones; but it is now missing. As the theft was not of a nature to be practised by a mere domestic, I am compelled to suspect the inhospitality of some individual of higher station, most gratuitously exercised certainly, since, after what I have here said, no one will probably choose to boast of possessing this literary curiosity.

"We had a good deal of laughing, I remember, on what the public might be supposed to think, or say, concerning the gloomy and ominous nature of our mutual gifts.

"I think I can add little more to my recollections of Byron. He was often melancholy—almost gloomy. When I observed him in this humor, I used either to wait till it went off of its own accord, or till some natural and easy mode occurred of leading him into conversation, when the shadows almost always left his countenance, like the mist rising from a landscape. In conversation he was very animated.

"I met with him very frequently in society; our mutual acquaintances doing me the honor to think that he liked to meet with me. Some very agreeable parties I can recollect—particularly one at Sir George Beaumont's—where the amiable landlord had assembled some persons distinguished for talent. Of these I need only mention the late Sir Humphry Davy, whose talents for literature were as remarkable as his empire over science. Mr. Richard Sharpe and Mr. Rogers were also present.

"I think I also remarked in Byron's temper starts of suspicion, when he seemed to pause and consider whether there had not been a secret, and perhaps offensive, meaning in something casually said to him. In this case, I also judged it best to let his mind, like a troubled spring, work itself clear, which it did in a minute or two. I was considerably older, you will recollect, than my noble friend, and had no reason to fear his misconstruing my sentiments towards him, nor had I ever the slightest reason to doubt that they were kindly returned on his part. If I had occasion to be mortified by the display of genius which threw into the shade such pretensions as I was then supposed to possess, I might console myself that, in my own case, the materials of mental happiness had been mingled in a greater proportion.

"I rummage my brains in vain for what often rushes into my head unbidden—little traits and sayings which recall his looks, manner, tone, and gestures; and I have always continued to think that a crisis of life was arrived, in which a new career of fame was opened to him, and that had he been permitted to start upon it, he would have obliterated the memory of such parts of his life as friends would wish to forget."

I have nothing to add to this interesting passage, except that Joanna Baillie's tragedy of The Family Legend being performed at one of the theatres during Scott's stay in town, Lord Byron accompanied the authoress and Mr. and Mrs. Scott to witness the representation; and that the vase with the Attic bones appears to have been sent to Scott very soon after his arrival in London, not, as Mr. Moore had gathered from the hasty diction of his Reminiscences, at some "subsequent period of their acquaintance." This is sufficiently proved by the following note:—

TO THE RIGHT HONORABLE LORD BYRON, ETC., ETC.
PICCADILLY, MONDAY.

MY DEAR LORD,—I am not a little ashamed of the value of the shrine in which your Lordship has enclosed the Attic relics; but were it yet more costly, the circumstance could not add value to it in my estimation, when considered as a pledge of your Lordship's regard and friendship. The principal pleasure which I have derived from my connection with literature has been the access which it has given me to those who are distinguished by talents and accomplishments; and, standing so high as your Lordship justly does in that rank, my satisfaction in making your acquaintance has been proportionally great. It is one of those wishes which, after having been long and earnestly entertained, I have found completely gratified upon becoming personally known to you; and I trust you will permit me to profit by it frequently, during my stay in town. I am, my dear Lord, your truly obliged and faithful
WALTER SCOTT.

It was also in the spring of 1815 that Scott had, for the first time, the honor of being presented to the Prince Regent. His Royal Highness had (as has been seen from a letter to Joanna Baillie, already quoted) signified, more than a year before this time, his wish that the poet should revisit London—and, on reading his Edinburgh Address in particular, he said to Mr. Dundas, that "Walter Scott's charming behavior about the laureateship had made him doubly desirous of seeing him at Carlton House." More lately, on receiving a copy of The Lord of the Isles, his Royal Highness's librarian had been commanded to write to him in these terms:—

TO WALTER SCOTT, ESQ., EDINBURGH.
CARLTON HOUSE, January 19, 1815.

MY DEAR SIR,—You are deservedly so great a favorite with the Prince Regent, that his librarian is not only directed to return you the thanks of his Royal Highness for your valuable present, but to inform you that the Prince Regent particularly wishes to see you whenever you come to London; and desires you will always, when you are there, come into his library whenever you please. Believe me always, with sincerity, one of your warmest admirers, and most obliged friends,
J. S. CLARKE.

On hearing from Mr. Croker (then Secretary to the Admiralty) that Scott was to be in town by the middle of March, the Prince said, "Let me know when he comes, and I'll get up a snug little dinner that will suit him;" and, after he had been presented and graciously received at the levee, he was invited to dinner accordingly, through his excellent friend Mr. Adam (now Lord Chief Commissioner of the Jury Court in Scotland),[14] who at that time held a confidential office in the royal household. The Regent had consulted with Mr. Adam also as to the composition of the party. "Let us have," said he, "just a few friends of his own—and the more Scotch the better;" and both the Chief Commissioner and Mr. Croker assure me that the party was the most interesting and agreeable one in their recollection. It comprised, I believe, the Duke of York—the late Duke of Gordon (then Marquis of Huntly)—the Marquis of Hertford (then Lord Yarmouth)—the Earl of Fife—and Scott's early friend Lord Melville. "The Prince and Scott," says Mr. Croker, "were the two most brilliant story-tellers in their several ways, that I have ever happened to meet; they were both aware of their *forte*, and both exerted themselves that evening with delightful effect. On going home, I really could not decide which of them had shone the most. The Regent was enchanted with Scott, as Scott with him; and on all his subsequent visits to London, he was a frequent guest at the royal table." The Lord Chief Commissioner remembers that the Prince was particularly delighted with the poet's anecdotes of the old Scotch judges and lawyers, which his Royal Highness sometimes *capped* by ludicrous traits of certain ermined sages of his own acquaintance. Scott told, among others, a story, which he was fond of telling; and the commentary of his Royal Highness on hearing it amused Scott, who often mentioned it afterwards. The anecdote is this: A certain Judge, whenever he went on a particular circuit, was in the habit of visiting a gentleman of good fortune in the neighborhood of one of the assize towns, and staying at least one night, which, being both of them ardent chess-players, they usually concluded with their favorite game. One Spring circuit the battle was not decided at daybreak, so the Judge said, "Weel, Donald, I must e'en come back this gate in the harvest, and let the game lie ower for the present;" and back he came in October, but not to his old friend's hospitable house; for that gentleman had, in the interim, been apprehended on a capital charge (of forgery), and his name stood on the *Porteous Roll*, or list of those who were about to be tried under his former guest's auspices. The laird was indicted and tried accordingly, and the jury returned a verdict of *guilty*. The Judge forthwith put on his cocked hat (which answers to the black cap in England), and pronounced the sentence of the law in the usual terms: "To be hanged by the neck until you be dead; and may the Lord have mercy upon your unhappy soul!" Having concluded this awful formula in his most sonorous cadence, the Judge, dismounting his formidable beaver, gave a familiar nod to his unfortunate acquaintance, and said to him in a sort of chuckling whisper, "And now, Donald, my man, I think I've checkmated you for ance." The Regent laughed heartily at this specimen of judicial humor; and "I' faith, Walter," said he, "this old big-wig seems to have taken things as coolly as my tyrannical self. Don't you remember Tom Moore's description of me at breakfast,—

'The table spread with tea and toast,
Death-warrants and the Morning Post?'"

Towards midnight, the Prince called for "a bumper, with all the honors, to the Author of Waverley," and looked significantly, as he was charging his own glass, to Scott. Scott seemed somewhat puzzled for a moment, but instantly recovering himself, and filling his glass to the brim, said, "Your Royal Highness looks as if you thought I had some claim to the honors of this toast. I have no such pretensions, but shall take good care that the real Simon Pure hears of the high compliment that has now been paid him." He then drank off his claret, and joined in the cheering, which the Prince himself timed. But before the company could resume their seats, his Royal Highness exclaimed, "Another of the same, if you please, to the Author of Marmion—and now, Walter, my man, I have checkmated you for *ance*." The second bumper was followed by cheers still more prolonged: and Scott then rose and returned thanks in a short address, which struck the Lord Chief Commissioner as "alike grave and graceful." This story has been circulated in a very perverted shape. I now give it on the authority of my venerated friend. He adds, that having occasion, the day after, to call on the Duke of York, his Royal Highness said to him: "Upon my word, Adam, my brother went rather too near the wind about Waverley—but nobody could have turned the thing more prettily than Walter Scott did—and upon the whole I never had better fun."[15]

The Regent, as was his custom with those he most delighted to honor, uniformly addressed the poet, even at their first dinner, by his Christian name, "Walter."

Before he left town, he again dined at Carlton House, when the party was a still smaller one than before, and the merriment, if possible, still more free. That nothing might be wanting, the Prince sung several capital songs in the course of that evening—as witness the lines in Sultan Serendib:[16]—

"I love a Prince will bid the bottle pass,
Exchanging with his subjects glance and glass,
In fitting time can, gayest of the gay,
Keep up the jest and mingle in the lay.
Such Monarchs best our freeborn humor suit,
But despots must be stately, stern, and mute."[17]

Before he returned to Edinburgh, on the 22d of May, the Regent sent him a gold snuff-box, set in brilliants, with a medallion of his Royal Highness's head on the lid, "as a testimony" (writes Mr. Adam, in transmitting it) "of the high opinion his Royal Highness entertains of your genius and merit."

I transcribe what follows from James Ballantyne's *Memoranda*:—

"After Mr. Scott's first interview with his Sovereign, one or two intimate friends took the liberty of inquiring, what judgment he had formed of the Regent's talents? He declined giving any definite answer—but repeated that 'he was the first gentleman he had seen—certainly the first *English* gentleman of his day;—there was something about him which, independently of the *prestige*, the "divinity, which hedges a King," marked him as standing entirely by himself; but as to his abilities, spoken of as distinct from his charming manners, how could any one form a fair judgment of that man who introduced whatever subject he chose, discussed it just as long as he chose, and dismissed it when he chose?'"

Ballantyne adds:—

"What I have now to say is more important, not only in itself, but as it will enable you to give a final contradiction to an injurious report which has been in circulation; namely, that the Regent asked him as to the authorship of Waverley, and received a distinct and solemn denial. I took the bold freedom of requesting to know *from him* whether his Royal Highness had questioned him on that subject, and what had been his answer. He glanced at me with a look of mild surprise, and said, 'What answer I might have made to such a question, put to me by my Sovereign, perhaps I do not, or rather perhaps I do know; but I was never put to the test. He is far too well-bred a man ever to put so ill-bred a question.'"

The account I have already given of the convivial scene alluded to would probably have been sufficient; but it can do no harm to place Ballantyne's, or rather Scott's own testimony, also on record.

I ought not to have omitted, that during Scott's residence in London, in April, 1815, he lost one of the English friends, to a meeting with whom he had looked forward with the highest pleasure. Mr. George Ellis died on the 15th of that month, at his seat of Sunning Hill. This threw a cloud over what would otherwise have been a period of unmixed enjoyment. Mr. Canning penned the epitaph for that dearest of his friends, but he submitted it to Scott's consideration before it was engraved.[Back to Contents]

CHAPTER XXXV.

BATTLE OF WATERLOO. — LETTER OF SIR CHARLES BELL. — VISIT TO THE CONTINENT. — WATERLOO. — LETTERS FROM BRUSSELS AND PARIS. — ANECDOTES OF SCOTT AT PARIS. — THE DUKE OF WELLINGTON. — THE EMPEROR ALEXANDER. — BLÜCHER. — PLATOFF. — PARTY AT ERMENONVILLE, ETC. — LONDON. — PARTING WITH LORD BYRON. — SCOTT'S SHEFFIELD KNIFE. — RETURN TO ABBOTSFORD. — ANECDOTES BY MR. SKENE AND JAMES BALLANTYNE.

1815.

Goethe expressed, I fancy, a very general sentiment, when he said, that to him the great charm and value of my friend's Life of Buonaparte seemed quite independent of the question of its accuracy as to small details; that he turned eagerly to the book, not to find dates sifted, and countermarches analyzed, but to contemplate what could not but be a true record of the broad impressions made on the mind of Scott by the marvellous revolutions of his own time in their progress. Feeling how justly in the main that work has preserved those impressions, though gracefully softened and sobered in the retrospect of peaceful and more advanced years, I the less regret that I have it not in my power to quote any letters of his touching the reappearance of Napoleon on the soil of France—the immortal march from Cannes—the reign of the Hundred Days, and the preparations for another struggle, which fixed the gaze of Europe in May, 1815.

That he should have been among the first civilians who hurried over to see the field of Waterloo, and hear English bugles sound about the walls of Paris, could have surprised none who knew the lively concern he had always taken in the military efforts of his countrymen, and the career of the illustrious captain, who had taught them to reëstablish the renown of Agincourt and Blenheim,—

"Victor of Assaye's Eastern plain,
Victor of all the fields of Spain."

I had often heard him say, however, that his determination was, if not fixed, much quickened by a letter of an old acquaintance of his, who had, on the arrival of the news of the 18th of June, instantly repaired to Brussels, to tender his professional skill in aid of the overburdened medical staff of the conqueror's army. When, therefore, I found the letter in question preserved among Scott's papers, I perused it with a peculiar interest; and I now venture, with the writer's permission, to present it to the reader. It was addressed by Sir Charles Bell to his brother, an eminent barrister in Edinburgh, who transmitted it to Scott. "When I read it," said he, "it set me on fire." The marriage of Miss Maclean Clephane of Torloisk with the Earl Compton (now Marquis of Northampton), which took place on the 24th of July, was in fact the only cause why he did not leave Scotland instantly; for that dear young friend had chosen Scott for her guardian, and on him accordingly devolved the chief care of the arrangements on this occasion. The extract sent to him by Mr. George Joseph Bell is as follows:—

"BRUSSELS, 2d July, 1815.

"This country, the finest in the world, has been of late quite out of our minds. I did not, in any degree, anticipate the pleasure I should enjoy, the admiration forced from me, on coming into one of these antique towns, or in journeying through the rich garden. Can you recollect the time when there were gentlemen meeting at the Cross of Edinburgh, or those whom we thought such? They are all collected here. You see the very men, with their scraggy necks sticking out of the collars of their old-fashioned square-skirted coats—their canes—their cocked-hats; and, when they meet, the formal bow, the hat off to the ground, and the powder flying in the wind. I could divert you with the odd resemblances of the Scottish faces among the peasants, too—but I noted *them* at the time with my pencil, and I write to you only of things that you won't find in my pocket-book.

"I have just returned from seeing the French wounded received in their hospital; and could you see them laid out naked, or almost so—100 in a row of low beds on the ground—though wounded, exhausted, beaten, you would still conclude with me that these were men capable of marching unopposed from the west of Europe to the east of Asia. Strong, thickset, hardy veterans, brave spirits and unsubdued, as they cast their wild glance upon you,—their black eyes and brown cheeks finely contrasted with the fresh sheets,—you would much admire their capacity of adaptation. These fellows are brought from the field after lying many days on the ground; many dying—many in the agony—many miserably racked with pain and spasms; and the next mimics his fellow, and gives it a tune,—*Aha, vous chantez bien!* How they are wounded you will see in my notes. But I must not have you to lose the present impression on me of the formidable nature of these fellows as exemplars of the breed in France. It is a forced praise; for from all I have seen, and all I have heard of their fierceness, cruelty, and bloodthirstiness, I cannot convey to you my detestation of this race of trained banditti. By what means they are to be kept in subjection until other habits come upon them, I know not; but I am convinced that these men cannot be left to the bent of their propensities.

"This superb city is now ornamented with the finest groups of armed men that the most romantic fancy could dream of. I was struck with the words of a friend—E. 'I saw,' said he, '*that* man returning from the field on the 16th.' (This was a Brunswicker, of the Black or Death Hussars.) 'He was wounded, and had had his arm amputated on the field. He was among the first that came in. He rode straight and stark upon his horse—the bloody clouts about his stump—pale as death, but upright, with a stern, fixed expression of feature, as if loath to lose his revenge.' These troops are very remarkable in their fine military appearance; their dark and ominous dress sets off to advantage their strong, manly, northern features and

16

white mustachios; and there is something more than commonly impressive about the whole effect.

"This is the second Sunday after the battle, and many are not yet dressed. There are 20,000 wounded in this town, besides those in the hospitals, and the many in the other towns;—only 3000 prisoners; 80,000, they say, killed and wounded on both sides."

I think it not wonderful that this extract should have set Scott's imagination effectually on fire; that he should have grasped at the idea of seeing probably the last shadows of real warfare that his own age would afford; or that some parts of the great surgeon's simple phraseology are reproduced, almost verbatim, in the first of Paul's Letters to his Kinsfolk. No sooner was Scott's purpose known, than some of his young neighbors in the country proposed to join his excursion; and, in company with three of them, namely, his kinsman, John Scott of Gala, Alexander Pringle, the younger, of Whytbank (now M. P. for Selkirkshire), and Robert Bruce, advocate (now Sheriff of Argyle), he left Edinburgh for the south, at 5. A. M. on the 27th of July.

They travelled by the stage-coach, and took the route of Hull and Lincoln to Cambridge; for Gala and Whytbank, being both members of that university, were anxious to seize this opportunity of revisiting it themselves, and showing its beautiful architecture to their friend. After this wish had been gratified, they proceeded to Harwich, and thence, on the 3d of August, took ship for Helvoetsluys.

"The weather was beautiful," says Gala, "so we all went outside the coach from Cambridge to Harwich. At starting, there was a general complaint of thirst, the consequence of some experiments overnight on the celebrated *bishop* of my *Alma Mater*; our friend, however, was in great glee, and never was a merrier *basket* than he made it all the morning. He had cautioned us, on leaving Edinburgh, never to *name names* in such situations, and our adherence to this rule was rewarded by some amusing incidents. For example, as we entered the town where we were to dine, a heavy-looking man, who was to stop there, took occasion to thank Scott for the pleasure his anecdotes had afforded him: 'You have a good memory, sir,' said he; 'mayhap, now, you sometimes write down what you hear or be a-reading about?' He answered, very gravely, that he did occasionally put down a *few* notes, if anything struck him particularly. In the afternoon, it happened that he sat on the box, while the rest of us were behind him. Here, by degrees, he became quite absorbed in his own reflections. He frequently repeated to himself, or *composed* perhaps, for a good while, and often smiled or raised his hand, seeming completely occupied and amused. His neighbor, a vastly scientific and rather grave professor, in a smooth drab Benjamin and broad-brimmed beaver, cast many a curious sidelong glance at him, evidently suspecting that all was not right with the upper story, but preserved perfect politeness. The poet was, however, discovered by the captain of the vessel in which we crossed the Channel;—and a perilous passage it was, chiefly in consequence of the unceasing tumblers in which this worthy kept drinking his health."

Before leaving Edinburgh, Scott had settled in his mind the plan of Paul's Letters; for on that same day, his agent, John Ballantyne, addressed the following letter, from his marine villa near Newhaven:—

TO MESSRS. CONSTABLE & CO.

TRINITY, 27th July, 1815.

DEAR SIRS,—Mr. Scott left town to-day for the Continent. He proposes writing from thence a series of letters on a peculiar plan, varied in matter and style, and to different supposititious correspondents.

The work is to form a demy 8vo volume of twenty-two sheets, to sell at 12s. It is to be begun immediately on his arrival in France, and to be published, if possible, the second week of September, when he proposes to return.

We print 3000 of this, and I am empowered to offer you one third of the edition, Messrs. Longman & Co. and Mr. Murray having each the same share: the terms, twelve months' acceptance for paper and print, and half profits at six months, granted now as under. The over copies will pay the charge for advertising, I am, etc.,

JOHN BALLANTYNE.

Charge—

		sheets		£8
2	printing,	3 15 0	2 10 0	
		reams	1	21
45	demy,	10 0	7 10 0	

£3
00 00

	300	£1
0 at 8s.	200 0 0	
	Co	30
st,	0 0 0	

£9   profit—One half
00 0 0   is £450.

Before Scott reached Harwich, he knew that this offer had been accepted without hesitation; and thenceforth, accordingly, he threw his daily letters to his wife into the form of communications meant for an imaginary group, consisting of a spinster sister, a statistical laird, a rural clergyman of the Presbyterian Kirk, and a brother, a veteran officer on half-pay. The rank of this last personage corresponded, however, exactly with that of his own elder brother, John Scott, who also, like the Major of the book, had served in the Duke of York's unfortunate campaign of 1797; the sister is only a slender disguise for his aunt Christian Rutherford, already often mentioned; Lord Somerville, long President of the Board of Agriculture, was Paul's laird; and the shrewd and unbigoted Dr. Douglas of Galashiels was his "minister of the gospel." These epistles, after having been devoured by the little circle at Abbotsford, were transmitted to Major John Scott, his mother, and Miss Rutherford, in Edinburgh; from their hands they passed to those of James Ballantyne and Mr. Erskine, both of whom assured me that the copy ultimately sent to the press consisted, in great part, of the identical sheets that had successively reached Melrose through the post. The rest had of course been, as Ballantyne expresses it, "somewhat cobbled;" but, on the whole, Paul's Letters are to be considered as a true and faithful journal of this expedition; insomuch, that I might perhaps content myself, in this place, with a simple reference to that delightful volume. He found time, however, to write letters during his absence from Britain, to some others of his friends; and a specimen or two of these may interest the reader. I have also gathered, from the companions of the journey, a few more particulars, which Scott's modesty withheld him from recording; and some trivial circumstances which occur to me, from recollection of his own conversation, may also be acceptable.

But I hope that, if the reader has not perused Paul's Letters recently, he will refresh his memory, before he proceeds further, by bestowing an hour on that genuine fragment of the author's autobiography. He is now, unless he had the advantage of Scott's personal familiarity, much better acquainted with the man than he could have been before he took up this compilation of his private correspondence—and especially before he perused the full diary of the lighthouse yacht in 1814; and a thousand little turns and circumstances which may have, when he originally read the book, passed lightly before his eye, will now, I venture to say, possess a warm and vivid interest, as inimitably characteristic of a departed friend. The kindest of husbands and fathers never portrayed himself with more unaffected truth than in this vain effort, if such he really fancied he was making, to sustain the character of "a cross old bachelor." The whole man, just as he was, breathes in every line, with all his compassionate and benevolent sympathy of heart, all his sharpness of observation, and sober shrewdness of reflection; all his enthusiasm for nature, for country life, for simple manners and simple pleasures, mixed up with an equally glowing enthusiasm, at which many may smile, for the tiniest relics of feudal antiquity—and last, not least, a pulse of physical rapture for the "circumstance of war," which bears witness to the blood of *Boltfoot* and *Fire-the-Braes.*

At Brussels, Scott found the small English garrison left there in command of Major-General Sir Frederick Adam, the son of his highly valued friend, the Lord Chief Commissioner. Sir Frederick had been wounded at Waterloo, and could not as yet mount on horseback; but one of his aides-de-camp, Captain Campbell, escorted Scott and his party to the field of battle, on which occasion they were also accompanied by another old acquaintance of his, Major Pryse Gordon, who being then on half-pay, happened to be domesticated with his family at Brussels. Major Gordon has since published two lively volumes of Personal Memoirs; and Gala bears witness to the fidelity of certain reminiscences of Scott at Brussels and Waterloo, which occupy one of the chapters of this work. I shall, therefore, extract the passage:—

"Sir Walter Scott accepted my services to conduct him to Waterloo: the General's aide-de-camp was also of the party. He made no secret of his having undertaken to write something on the battle; and perhaps he took the greater interest on this account in everything that he saw. Besides, he had never seen the field of such a conflict; and never having been before on the Continent, it was all new to his comprehensive mind. The day was beautiful; and I had the precaution to send out a couple of saddle-horses, that he might not be fatigued in walking over the fields, which had been recently ploughed up. In our rounds we fell in with Monsieur de Costar, with whom he got into conversation. This man had attracted so much notice by his pretended story of being about the person of Napoleon, that he was of too much importance to be passed by: I did not, indeed, know as much of this fellow's charlatanism at that time as afterwards, when I saw him confronted with a blacksmith of La Belle Alliance, who had been his companion in a hiding-place ten miles from the field during the whole day; a fact which he could not deny. But he had got up a tale so plausible and so profitable, that he could afford to bestow hush-money on the companion of his flight, so that the imposition was but little known; and strangers continued to be gulled. He had picked up a good deal of information about the positions and details of the battle; and, being naturally a sagacious Walloon, and speaking French pretty fluently, he became the favorite cicerone, and every lie he told was taken for gospel. Year after year, until his death in 1824, he continued his popularity, and raised the price of his rounds from a couple of francs to five; besides as much for the hire of a horse, his own property; for he pretended that the fatigue of walking so many hours was beyond his powers. It has been said that in this way he realized every summer a couple of hundred Napoleons.

"When Sir Walter had examined every point of defence and attack, we adjourned to the 'Original Duke of Wellington' at Waterloo, to lunch after the fatigues of the ride. Here he had a crowded levee of peasants, and collected a great many trophies, from cuirasses down to buttons and bullets. He picked up himself many little relics, and was fortunate in purchasing a grand cross of the Legion of Honor. But the most precious memorial was presented to him by my wife—a French soldier's book, well stained with blood, and containing some songs popular in the French army, which he found so interesting that he introduced versions of them in his Paul's Letters; of which, he did me the honor to send me a copy, with a letter, saying, 'that he considered my wife's gift as the most valuable of all his Waterloo relics.'

"On our return from the field, he kindly passed the evening with us, and a few friends whom we invited to meet him. He charmed us with his delightful conversation, and was in great spirits from the agreeable day he had passed; and with great good-humor promised to write a stanza in my wife's album. On the following morning he fulfilled his promise by contributing some beautiful verses on Hougomont. I put him into my little library to prevent interruption, as a great many persons had paraded in the *Parc* opposite my window to get a peep of the celebrated man, many having dogged him from his hotel.

"Brussels affords but little worthy of the notice of such a traveller as the Author of Waverley; but he greatly admired the splendid tower of the Maison de Ville, and the ancient sculpture and style of architecture of the buildings which surround the Grand Place.

"He told us, with great humor, a laughable incident which had occurred to him at Antwerp. The morning after his arrival at that city from Holland, he started at an early hour to visit the tomb of Rubens in the church of St. Jacques, before his party were up. After wandering about for some time, without finding the object he had in view, he determined to make inquiry, and observing a person stalking about, he addressed him in his best French; but the stranger, pulling off his hat, very respectfully replied in the pure Highland accent, 'I'm vary sorry, sir, but I canna speak onything besides English.'—This is very unlucky indeed, Donald,' said Sir Walter, 'but we must help one another; for, to tell you the truth, I'm not good at any other tongue but the English, or rather, the Scotch.'—'Oh, sir, maybe,' replied the Highlander, 'you are a countryman, and ken my maister Captain Cameron of the 79th, and could tell me whare he lodges. I'm just cum in, sir, frae a place they ca' *Machlin*,[18] and ha' forgotten the name of the captain's quarters; it was something like the *Laaborer*.'—'I can, I think, help you with this, my friend,' rejoined Sir Walter. 'There is an inn just opposite to you' (pointing to the *Hôtel du Grand Laboureur*): 'I dare say that will be the captain's quarters;' and it was so. I cannot do justice to the humor with which Sir Walter recounted this dialogue."[19]

The following is the letter which Scott addressed to the Duke of Buccleuch immediately after seeing the field of Waterloo; and it may amuse the reader to compare it with Major Gordon's chapter, and with the writer's own fuller, and, of course, "cobbled" detail, in the pages of Paul:—

TO HIS GRACE THE DUKE OF BUCCLEUCH, ETC.

MY DEAR LORD DUKE,—I promised to let you hear of my wanderings, however unimportant; and have now the pleasure of informing your Grace that I am at this present time an inhabitant of the Premier Hôtel de Cambrai, after having been about a week upon the Continent. We landed at Helvoet, and proceeded to Brussels, by Bergen-op-Zoom and Antwerp, both of which are very strongly fortified. The ravages of war are little remarked in a country so rich by nature; but everything seems at present stationary, or rather retrograde, where capital is required. The châteaux are deserted, and going to decay; no new houses are built, and those of older date are passing rapidly into the possession of a class inferior to those for whom we must suppose them to have been built. Even the old gentlewoman of Babylon has lost much of her splendor, and her robes and pomp are of a description far subordinate to the costume of her more magnificent days. The dresses of the priests were worn and shabby, both at Antwerp and Brussels, and reminded me of the decayed wardrobe of a bankrupt theatre: yet, though the gentry and priesthood have suffered, the eternal bounty of nature has protected the lower ranks against much distress. The unexampled fertility of the soil gives them all, and more than they want; and could they but sell the grain which they raise in the Netherlands, nothing else would be wanting to render them the richest people (common people, that is to say) in the world.

On Wednesday last, I rode over the field of Waterloo, now forever consecrated to immortality. The more ghastly tokens of the carnage are now removed, the bodies both of men and horses being either burned or buried; but all the ground is still torn with the shot and shells, and covered with cartridges, old hats, and shoes, and various relics of the fray which the peasants have not thought worth removing. Besides, at Waterloo and all the hamlets in the vicinage, there is a mart established for cuirasses; for the eagles worn by the imperial guard on their caps; for casques, swords, carabines, and similar articles. I have bought two handsome cuirasses, and intend them, one for Bowhill, and one for Abbotsford, if I can get them safe over, which Major Pryse Gordon has promised to manage for me. I have also, for your Grace, one of the little memorandum-books, which I picked up on the field, in which every French soldier was obliged to enter his receipts and expenditure, his services, and even his punishments. The field was covered with fragments of these records. I also got a good MS. collection of French songs, probably the work of some young officer, and a croix of the Legion of Honor. I enclose, under another cover, a sketch of the battle, made at Brussels. It is not, I understand, strictly accurate; but sufficiently so to give a good notion of what took place. In fact, it would require twenty separate plans to give an idea of the battle at its various stages. The front, upon which the armies engaged, does not exceed a long mile. Our line, indeed, originally extended half a mile farther towards the village of Brain-la-Leude; but as the French indicated no disposition to attack in that direction, the troops which occupied this space were gradually concentrated by Lord Wellington, and made to advance till they had reached Hougomont—a sort of château, with a garden and wood attached to it, which was powerfully and effectually maintained by the Guards during the action. This place was particularly interesting. It was a quiet-looking gentleman's house, which had been burnt by the French shells. The defenders, burnt out of the house itself, betook themselves to the little garden, where, breaking loopholes through the brick walls, they kept up a most destructive fire on the assailants, who had possessed themselves of a little wood which surrounds the villa on one side. In this spot vast numbers had fallen; and, being hastily buried, the smell is most offensive at this moment. Indeed, I felt the same annoyance in many parts of the field; and, did I live near the spot, I should be anxious about the diseases which this steaming carnage might occasion. The rest of the ground, excepting this château, and a farmhouse called La Hay Sainte, early taken, and long held, by the French, because it was too close under the brow of the descent on which our artillery was placed to admit of the pieces being depressed so as to play into it,—the rest of the ground, I say, is quite open, and lies between two ridges, one of which (Mont St. Jean) was constantly occupied by the English; the other, upon which is the farm of La Belle Alliance, was the position of the French. The slopes between are gentle and varied; the ground everywhere practicable for cavalry, as was well experienced on that memorable day. The cuirassiers, despite their arms of proof, were quite inferior to our heavy dragoons. The meeting of the two bodies occasioned a noise, not unaptly compared to the tinkering and hammering of a smith's shop. Generally the cuirassiers came on stooping their heads very low, and giving point; the British frequently struck away their casques while they were in this position, and then laid at the bare head. Officers and soldiers all fought hand to hand without distinction; and many of the former owed their life to dexterity at their weapon, and personal strength of body. Shaw, the milling Life-Guardsman, whom your Grace may remember among the champions of The Fancy, maintained the honor of the fist, and killed or disabled upwards of twenty Frenchmen with his single arm, until he was killed by the assault of numbers.[20] At one place, where there is a precipitous sand or gravel pit, the heavy English cavalry drove many of the cuirassiers over pell-mell, and followed over themselves, like fox-hunters. The conduct of the infantry and artillery was equally, or, if possible, more distinguished, and it was all fully necessary; for, besides that our army was much outnumbered, a great part of the sum-total were foreigners. Of these, the Brunswickers and Hanoverians behaved very well; the Belgians but sorrily enough. On one occasion, when a Belgic regiment fairly ran off, Lord Wellington rode up to them, and said, "My lads, you must be a little blown; come, do take your breath for a moment, and then we'll go back, and try if we can do a little better;" and he actually carried them back to the charge. He was, indeed, upon that day, everywhere, and the soul of everything; nor could less than his personal endeavors have supported the spirits of the men through a contest so long, so desperate, and so unequal. At his last attack, Buonaparte brought up 15,000 of his Guard, who had never drawn trigger during the day. It was upon their failure that his hopes abandoned him.

I spoke long with a shrewd Flemish peasant, called John de Costar, whom he had seized upon as his guide, and who remained beside him the whole day, and afterwards accompanied him in his flight as far as Charleroi. Your Grace may be sure that I interrogated Mynheer very closely about what he heard and saw. He guided me to the spot where Buonaparte remained during the latter part of the action. It was in the highway from Brussels to Charleroi, where it runs between two high banks, on each of which was a French battery. He was pretty well sheltered from the English fire; and, though many bullets flew over his head, neither he nor any of his suite were touched. His other stations, during that day, were still more remote from all danger. The story of his having an observatory erected for him is a mistake. There is such a thing, and he repaired to it during the action; but it was built or erected some months before, for the purpose of a trigonometrical survey of the country, by the King of the Netherlands. Bony's last position was nearly fronting a tree where the Duke of Wellington was stationed; there was not more than a quarter of a mile between them; but Bony was well sheltered, and the Duke so much exposed, that the tree is barked in several places by the cannon-balls levelled at him. As for Bony, De Costar says he was very cool during the whole day, and even gay. As the cannon-balls flew over them, De Costar ducked; at which the Emperor laughed, and told him they would hit him all the same.

At length, about the time he made his grand and last effort, the fire of the Prussian artillery was heard upon his right, and the heads of their columns became visible pressing out of the woods. Aide-de-camp after aide-de-camp came with the tidings of their advance, to which Bony only replied, *Attendez, attendez un instant*, until he saw his troops, *fantassins et cavaliers*, return in disorder from the attack. He then observed hastily to a general beside him, *Je crois qu'ils sont mêlés.* The person to whom he spoke hastily raised the spyglass to his eye; but Bony, whom the first glance had satisfied of their total discomfiture, bent his face to the ground, and shook his head twice, his complexion being then as pale as death. The general then said something, to which Buonaparte answered, *C'est trop tard—sauvons nous.* Just at that moment, the allied troops, cavalry and infantry, appeared in full advance on all hands; and the Prussians, operating upon the right flank of the French, were rapidly gaining their rear. Bony, therefore, was compelled to abandon the high-road, which, besides, was choked with dead, with baggage, and with cannon; and, gaining the open country, kept at full gallop, until he gained, like Johnnie Cope, the van of the flying army. The marshals followed his example; and it was the most complete *sauve qui peut* that can well be imagined. Nevertheless, the prisoners who were brought into Brussels maintained their national impudence, and boldly avowed their intention of sacking the city with every sort of severity. At the same time they had friends there. One man of rank and wealth went over to Bony during the action, and I saw his hotel converted into an hospital for wounded soldiers. It occupied one half of one of the sides of the Place Royale, a noble square, which your Grace has probably seen. But, in general, the inhabitants of Brussels were very differently disposed; and their benevolence to our poor wounded fellows was unbounded. The difficulty was to prevent them from killing their guests with kindness, by giving them butcher's meat and wine during their fever. As I cannot put my letter into post until we get to Paris, I shall continue it as we get along.

12th August, Roye, in Picardy.—I imagine your Grace about this time to be tolerably well fagged with a hard day on the moors. If the weather has been as propitious as with us, it must be delightful. The country through which we have travelled is most uncommonly fertile, and skirted with beautiful woods; but its present political situation is so very uncommon, that I would give the world your Grace had come over for a fortnight. France may be considered as neither at peace nor war. Valenciennes, for example, is in a state of blockade; we passed through the posts of the allies, all in the utmost state of vigilance, with patrols of cavalry and vedettes of infantry, up to the very gates, and two or three batteries were manned and mounted. The French troops were equally vigilant at the gates, yet made no objections to our passing through the town. Most of them had the white cockade, but looked very sulky, and were in obvious disorder and confusion. They had not yet made their terms with the King, nor accepted a commander appointed by him; but as they obviously feel their party desperate, the soldiers are running from the officers, and the officers from the soldiers. In fact, the multiplied hosts which pour into this country, exhibiting all the various dresses and forms of war which can be imagined, must necessarily render resistance impracticable. Yet, like Satan, these fellows retain the unconquered propensity to defiance, even in the midst of defeat and despair. This morning we passed a great number of the disbanded garrison of Condé, and they were the most horrid-looking cut-throats I ever saw, extremely disposed to be very insolent, and only repressed by the consciousness that all the villages and towns around are occupied by the allies. They began by crying to us in an ironical tone, *Vive le Roi*; then followed, *sotto voce, Sacre B——, Mille diables*, and other graces of French eloquence. I felt very well pleased that we were armed, and four in number; and still more so that it was daylight, for they seemed most mischievous ruffians. As for the appearance of the country, it is, notwithstanding a fine harvest, most melancholy. The windows of all the detached houses on the road are uniformly shut up; and you see few people, excepting the peasants who are employed in driving the contributions to maintain the armies. The towns are little better, having for the most part been partially injured by shells or by storm, as was the case both of Cambrai and Peronne. The men look very sulky; and if you speak three words to a woman, she is sure to fall a-crying. In short, the *politesse* and good-humor of this people have fled with the annihilation of their self-conceit; and they look on you as if they thought you were laughing at them, or come to enjoy the triumph of our arms over theirs. Postmasters and landlords are all the same, and hardly to be propitiated even by English money, although they charge us about three times as much as they durst do to their countryfolks. As for the Prussians, a party of cavalry dined at our hotel at Mons, eat and drank of the best the poor devils had left to give, called for their horses, and laughed in the face of the landlord when he offered his bill, telling him they should pay as they came back. The English, they say, have always paid honorably, and upon these they indemnify themselves. It is impossible to *marchander*, for if you object, the poor landlady begins to cry, and tells you she will accept whatever *your lordship* pleases, but that she is almost ruined and bankrupt, etc., etc., etc.

This is a long stupid letter, but I will endeavor to send a better from Paris. Ever your Grace's truly obliged,

WALTER SCOTT.

The only letter which Scott addressed to Joanna Baillie, while in Paris, goes over partly the same ground: I transcribe the rest.

PARIS, 6th September, 1815.

MY DEAR FRIEND,—I owe you a long letter, but my late travels and the date of this epistle will be a tolerable plea for your indulgence. The truth is, I became very restless after the battle of Waterloo, and was only detained by the necessity of attending a friend's marriage, from setting off instantly for the Continent. At length, however, I got away to Brussels, and was on the memorable field of battle about five weeks after it had been fought....

If our army had been all British, the day would have been soon decided; but the Duke, or, as they call him here, from his detestation of all manner of foppery, the *Beau*, had not above 35,000 British. All this was to be supplied by treble exertion on the part of our troops. The Duke was everywhere during the battle; and it was the mercy of Heaven that protected him, when all his staff had been killed or wounded round him. I asked him, among many other questions, if he had seen Buonaparte; he said, "No; but at one time, from the repeated shouts of *Vive l'Empereur*, I thought he must be near." This was when John de Costar placed him in the hollow way. I think, so near as I can judge, there may at that time have been a quarter of a mile between these two great generals.

The fate of the French, after this day of decisive appeal, has been severe enough. There were never people more mortified, more subdued, and apparently more broken in spirit. They submit with sad civility to the extortions of the Prussians and the Russians, and avenge themselves at the expense of the English, whom they charge three prices for everything, because they are the only people who pay at all. They are in the right, however, to enforce discipline and good order, which not only maintains the national character in the mean time, but will prevent the army from suffering by habits of indulgence. I question if the Prussians will soon regain their discipline and habits of hardihood. At present their powers of eating and drinking, which are really something preternatural, are exerted to the very utmost. A thin Prussian boy, whom I sometimes see, eats in one day as much as three English ploughmen. At daybreak he roars for chocolate and eggs; about nine he breakfasts more solemnly, *à la fourchette*, when, besides all the usual apparatus of an English *déjeuner*, he eats a world of cutlets, oysters, fruit, etc., and drinks a glass of brandy and a bottle of champagne. His dinner might serve Gargantua, at which he gets himself about three parts drunk—a circumstance which does not prevent the charge upon cold meat, with tea and chocolate, about six o'clock; and concluding the whole with an immense supper. Positively the appetite of this lad reminds one of the Eastern tale of a man taken out of the sea by a ship's crew, who, in return, ate up all the provisions of the vessel. He was, I think, flown away with by a roc; but from what quarter of the heavens the French are to look for deliverance from these devourers, I cannot presume to guess.

The needless wreck and ruin which they make in the houses adds much to the inconvenience of their presence. Most of the châteaux, where the Prussians are quartered, are what is technically called *rumped*, that is to say, plundered out and out. In the fine château of Montmorency, for instance, the most splendid apartments, highly ornamented with gilding and carving, were converted into barracks for the dirtiest and most savage-looking hussars I have yet seen. Imagine the work these fellows make with velvet hangings and embroidery. I saw one hag boiling her camp-kettle with part of a picture frame; the picture

23

itself has probably gone to Prussia. With all this greediness and love of mischief, the Prussians are not bloodthirsty; and their utmost violence seldom exceeds a blow or two with the flat of the sabre. They are also very civil to the women, and in both respects behave much better than the French did in their country; but they follow the bad example quite close enough for the sake of humanity and of discipline. As for our people, they live in a most orderly and regular manner. All the young men pique themselves on imitating the Duke of Wellington in *nonchalance* and coolness of manner; so they wander about everywhere, with their hands in the pockets of their long waistcoats, or cantering upon Cossack ponies, staring and whistling, and trotting to and fro, as if all Paris was theirs. The French hate them sufficiently for the *hauteur* of their manner and pretensions, but the grounds of dislike against us are drowned in the actual detestation afforded by the other powers.

This morning I saw a grand military spectacle—about 20,000 Russians pass in review before all the Kings and Dominations who are now resident at Paris. The Emperor, King of Prussia, Duke of Wellington, with their numerous and brilliant attendance of generals, staff-officers, etc., were in the centre of what is called the Place Louis Quinze, almost on the very spot where Louis XVI. was beheaded. A very long avenue, which faces the station where they were placed, was like a glowing furnace, so fiercely were the sunbeams reflected from the arms of the host by which it was filled. A body of Cossacks kept the ground with their pikes, and, by their wild appearance, added to the singularity of the scene. On one hand was the extended line of the Tuileries, seen through the gardens and the rows of orange-trees; on the other, the long column of troops advancing to the music. Behind was a long colonnade, forming the front to the palace, where the Chamber of Representatives are to hold their sittings; and in front of the monarchs was a superb row of buildings, on which you distinguish the bronze pillar erected by Napoleon to commemorate his victories over Russia, Prussia, and Austria, whose princes were now reviewing their victorious armies in what was so lately his capital. Your fancy, my dear friend, will anticipate, better than I can express, the thousand sentiments which arose in my mind from witnessing such a splendid scene, in a spot connected with such various associations. It may give you some idea of the feelings of the French—once so fond of *spectacles*—to know that, I think, there were not a hundred of that nation looking on. Yet this country will soon recover the actual losses she has sustained, for never was there a soil so blessed by nature, or so rich in corn, wine, and oil, and in the animated industry of its inhabitants. France is at present the fabled giant, struggling, or rather lying supine, under the load of mountains which have been precipitated on her; but she is not, and cannot be crushed. Remove the incumbent weight of 600,000 or 700,000 foreigners, and she will soon stand upright—happy, if experience shall have taught her to be contented to exert her natural strength only for her own protection, and not for the annoyance of her neighbors. I am cut short in my lucubrations by an opportunity to send this letter with Lord Castlereagh's despatches, which is of less consequence, as I will endeavor to see you in passing through London. I leave this city for Dieppe on Saturday, but I intend to go round by Harfleur, if possible.

Ever your truly obliged and affectionate
WALTER SCOTT.

"Paul" modestly acknowledges, in his last letter, the personal attentions which he received, while in Paris, from Lords Cathcart, Aberdeen, and Castlereagh; and hints that, through their intervention, he had witnessed several of the splendid *fêtes* given by the Duke of Wellington, where he saw half the crowned heads of Europe grouped among the gallant soldiers who had cut a way for them to the guilty capital of France. Scott's reception, however, had been distinguished to a degree of which Paul's language gives no notion. The Noble Lords above named welcomed him with cordial satisfaction; and the Duke of Wellington, to whom he was first presented by Sir John Malcolm, treated him then, and ever afterwards, with a kindness and confidence, which, I have often heard him say, he considered as "the highest distinction of his life." He used to tell, with great effect, the circumstances of his introduction to the Emperor Alexander, at a dinner given by the Earl of Cathcart. Scott appeared, on that occasion, in the blue and red dress of the Selkirkshire Lieutenancy; and the Czar's first question, glancing at his lameness, was, "In what affair were you wounded?" Scott signified that he suffered from a natural infirmity; upon which the Emperor said, "I thought Lord Cathcart mentioned that you had served." Scott observed that the Earl looked a little embarrassed at this, and promptly answered, "Oh yes; in a certain sense I have served—that is, in the yeomanry cavalry; a home force resembling the Landwehr, or Landsturm."—"Under what commander?"—"Sous M. le Chevalier Rae."—"Were you ever engaged?"—"In some slight actions—such as the battle of the Cross Causeway and the affair of Moredun-Mill."—"This," says Mr. Pringle of Whytbank, "was, as he saw in Lord Cathcart's face, quite sufficient, so he managed to turn the conversation to some other subject." It was at the same dinner that he first met Platoff,[21]who seemed to take a great fancy to him, though, adds my friend, "I really don't think they had any common language to converse in." Next day, however, when Pringle and Scott were walking together in the Rue de la Paix, the Hetman happened to come up, cantering with some of his Cossacks; as soon as he saw Scott, he jumped off his horse, leaving it to the Pulk, and, running up to him, kissed him on each side of the cheek with extraordinary demonstrations of affection—and then made him understand, through an aide-de-camp, that he wished him to join his staff at the next great review, when he would take care to mount him on the gentlest of his Ukraine horses.

It will seem less surprising that Scott should have been honored with much attention by the leading soldiers and statesmen of Germany then in Paris. The fame of his poetry had already been established for some years in that country. Yet it may be doubted whether Blücher had heard of Marmion any more than Platoff; and old Blücher struck Scott's fellow-travellers as taking more interest in him than any foreign general, except only the Hetman.

A striking passage in Paul's 10th letter indicates the high notion which Scott had formed of the personal qualities of the Prince of Orange. After depicting, with almost prophetic accuracy, the dangers to which the then recent union of Holland and Belgium must be exposed, he concludes with expressing his hope that the firmness and sagacity of the King of the Netherlands, and the admiration which his heir's character and bearing had already excited among all, even Belgian observers, might ultimately prove effective in redeeming this difficult experiment from the usual failure of "*arrondissements*, indemnities, and all the other terms of modern date, under sanction of which cities and districts, and even kingdoms, have been passed from one government to another, as the property of lands or stock is transferred by a bargain between private parties."

It is not less curious to compare, with the subsequent course of affairs in France, the following brief hint in Paul's 16th letter: "The general rallying point of the *Libéralistes* is an avowed dislike to the present monarch and his immediate connections. They will sacrifice, they pretend, so much to the general inclinations of Europe, as to select a king from the Bourbon race; but he must be one of their own choosing, and the Duke of Orleans is most familiar in their mouths." Thus, in its very bud, had his eye detected the *conjuration de quinze ans!*

Among the gay parties of this festive period, Scott mentioned with special pleasure one fine day given to an excursion to Ermenonville, under the auspices of Lady Castlereagh. The company was a large one, including most of the distinguished personages whom I have been naming, and they dined *al fresco* among the scenes of Rousseau's retirement, but in a fashion less accordant with the spirit of his *rêveries d'un promeneur solitaire*, than with the song which commemorates some earlier tenants of that delicious valley,—
"La belle Gabrielle
Étoit dans ces lieux—
Et le souvenir d'elle
Nous rend heureux," etc.

At some stage of this merry day's proceedings, the ladies got tired of walking, and one of Lord Castlereagh's young diplomatists was despatched into a village in quest of donkeys for their accommodation. The *attaché* returned by and by with a face of disappointment, complaining that the charge the people made was so extravagant, he could not think of yielding to the extortion. "*Marshal Forwards*" said nothing, but nodded to an aide-de-camp. They had passed a Prussian picket a little while before;—three times the requisite number of donkeys appeared presently, driven before half-a-dozen hussars, who were followed by the screaming population of the refractory hamlet; and "an angry man was Blücher," said Scott, "when Lord Castlereagh condescended to go among them, all smiles, and sent them back with more Napoleons than perhaps the fee-simple of the whole stud was worth."

Another evening of more peaceful enjoyment has left a better record. But I need not quote here the lines on Saint Cloud.[22] They were sent, on the 16th of August, to the late Lady Alvanley, with whom and her daughters he spent much of his time while in Paris.

As yet, the literary reputation of Scott had made but little way among the French nation; but some few of their eminent men vied even with the enthusiastic Germans in their courteous and unwearied attentions to him. The venerable *Chevalier*, in particular, seemed anxious to embrace every opportunity of acting as his cicerone; and many mornings were spent in exploring, under his guidance, the most remarkable scenes and objects of historical and antiquarian interest both in Paris and its neighborhood. He several times also entertained Scott and his young companions at dinner; but the last of those dinners was thoroughly poisoned by a preliminary circumstance. The poet, on entering the saloon, was presented to a stranger, whose physiognomy struck him as the most hideous he had ever seen; nor was his disgust lessened, when he found, a few minutes afterwards, that he had undergone the *accolade* of David "of the blood-stained brush."

From Paris, Mr. Bruce and Mr. Pringle went on to Switzerland, leaving the poet and Gala to return home together, which they did by way of Dieppe, Brighton, and London. It was here, on the 14th of September, that Scott had that last meeting with Lord Byron, alluded to in his communication to Mr. Moore, already quoted. He carried his young friend in the morning to call on Lord Byron, who agreed to dine with them at their hotel, where he met also Charles Mathews and Daniel Terry. The only survivor of the party[23] has recorded it in his note-book as the most interesting day he ever spent. "How I did stare," he says, "at Byron's beautiful pale face, like a spirit's—good or evil. But he was *bitter*—what a contrast to Scott! Among other anecdotes of British prowess and spirit, Scott mentioned that a young gentleman —— —— —— had been awfully shot in the head while conveying an order from the Duke, and yet staggered on, and delivered his message when at the point of death. 'Ha!' said Byron, 'I dare say he could do as well as most people without his head—it was never of much use to him.' Waterloo did not delight him, probably—and Scott could talk or think of scarcely anything else."

Mathews accompanied them as far as Warwick and Kenilworth, both of which castles the poet had seen before, but now reëxamined with particular curiosity. They spent a night at Sheffield; and early next morning Scott sallied forth to provide himself with a planter's knife of the most complex contrivance and finished workmanship. Having secured one to his mind, and which for many years after was his constant pocket-companion, he wrote his name on a card, "Walter Scott, Abbotsford," and directed it to be engraved on the handle. On his mentioning this acquisition at breakfast, young Gala expressed his desire to equip himself in like fashion, and was directed to the shop accordingly. When he had purchased a similar knife, and produced his name in turn for the engraver, the master cutler eyed the signature for a moment, and exclaimed, "John Scott of Gala! Well, I hope your ticket may serve me in as good stead as another Mr. Scott's has just done. Upon my word, one of my best men, an honest fellow from the North, went out of his senses when he saw it—he offered me a week's work if I would let him keep it to himself—and I took *Saunders* at his word." Scott used to talk of this as one of the most gratifying compliments he ever received in his literary capacity.

Their next halt was at Rokeby; but since Scott had heard from thence, Mrs. Morritt's illness had made such alarming progress, that the travellers regretted having obtruded themselves on the scene of affliction, and resumed their journey early next morning.

Reaching Abbotsford, Scott found with his family his old friend Mr. Skene of Rubislaw, who had expected him to come home sooner, and James Ballantyne, who had arrived with a copious budget of bills, calendars, booksellers' letters, and proof sheets. From each of these visitors' *memoranda* I now extract an anecdote. Mr. Skene's is of a small enough matter, but still it places the man so completely before myself, that I am glad he thought it worth setting down.

"During Scott's absence," says his friend, "his wife had had the tiny drawing-room of the cottage fitted up with new chintz furniture,—everything had been set out in the best style,—and she and her girls had been looking forward to the pleasure which they supposed the little surprise of the arrangements would give him. He was received in the spruce fresh room, set himself comfortably down in the chair prepared for him, and remained in the full enjoyment of his own fireside, and a return to his family circle, without the least consciousness that any change had taken place—until, at length, Mrs. Scott's patience could hold out no longer, and his attention was expressly called to it. The vexation he showed at having caused such a disappointment, struck me as amiably characteristic—and in the course of the evening he every now and then threw out some word of admiration to reconsole *mamma*."

Ballantyne's note of their next morning's conference is in these terms:—

"He had just been reviewing a pageant of emperors and kings, which seemed, like another Field of the Cloth of Gold, to have been got up to realize before his eyes some of his own splendid descriptions. I begged him to tell me what was the general impression left on his mind. He answered, that he might now say he had seen and conversed with all classes of society, from the palace to the cottage, and including every conceivable shade of science and ignorance—but that he had never felt awed or abashed except in the presence of one man—the Duke of Wellington. I expressed some surprise. He said I ought not, for that the Duke of Wellington possessed every one mighty quality of the mind in a higher degree than any other man did, or had ever done. He said he beheld in him a great soldier and a great statesman—the greatest of each. When it was suggested that the Duke, on his part, saw before him a great poet and novelist, he smiled, and said, 'What would the Duke of Wellington think of a few *bits of novels*, which perhaps he had never read, and for which the strong probability is that he would not care a sixpence if he had?' You are not" (adds Ballantyne) "to suppose that he looked either sheepish or embarrassed in the presence of the Duke—indeed you well know that he did not, and could not do so; but the feeling, qualified and modified as I have described it, unquestionably did exist to a certain extent. Its origin forms a curious moral problem; and may probably be traced to a secret consciousness, which he might not himself advert to, that the Duke, however great as a soldier and statesman, was so defective in imagination as to be incapable of appreciating that which had formed the charm of his own life, as well as of his works."

It is proper to add to Mr. Ballantyne's solution of his "curious moral problem," that he was in his latter days a strenuous opponent of the Duke of Wellington's politics; to which circumstance he ascribes, in these same *memoranda*, the only coolness that ever occurred between him and Scott. I need hardly repeat, what has been already distinctly stated more than once, that Scott never considered any amount of literary distinction as entitled to be spoken of in the same breath with mastery in the higher departments of practical life—least of all, with the glory of a first-rate captain. To have done things worthy to be written was in his eyes a dignity to which no man made any approach, who had only written things worthy to be read. He on two occasions, which I can never forget, betrayed painful uneasiness when his works were alluded to as reflecting honor on the age that had produced Watt's improvement of the steam-engine, and the safety-lamp of Sir Humphry Davy. Such was his modest creed—but from all I ever saw or heard of his intercourse with the Duke of Wellington, I am not disposed to believe that he partook it with the only man in whose presence he ever felt awe and abashment.[24]

A charming page in Mr. Washington Irving's Abbotsford and Newstead affords us another anecdote connected with this return from Paris. Two years after this time, when the amiable American visited Scott, he walked with him to a quarry, where his people were at work.

"The face of the humblest dependent," he says, "brightened at his approach—all paused from their labor to have a pleasant 'crack wi' the laird.' Among the rest was a tall straight old fellow, with a healthful complexion and silver hairs, and a small round-crowned white hat. He had been about to shoulder a hod, but paused, and stood looking at Scott with a slight sparkling of his blue eye as if waiting his turn; for the old fellow knew he was a favorite. Scott accosted him in an affable tone, and asked for a pinch of snuff. The old man drew forth a horn snuff-box. 'Hoot man,' said Scott, 'not that old mull. Where's the bonnie French one that I brought you from Paris?'—'Troth, your honor,' replied the old fellow, 'sic a mull as that is nae for week-days.' On leaving the quarry, Scott informed me, that, when absent at Paris, he had purchased several trifling articles as presents for his dependents, and, among others, the gay snuff-box in question, which was so carefully reserved for Sundays by the veteran. 'It was not so much the value of the gifts,' said he, 'that pleased them, as the idea that the laird should think of them when so far away.'"

One more incident of this return—it was told to me by himself, some years afterwards, with gravity, and even sadness. "The last of my chargers," he said, "was a high-spirited and very handsome one, by name Daisy, all over white, without a speck, and with such a mane as Rubens delighted to paint. He had, among other good qualities, one always particularly valuable in my case, that of standing like a rock to be mounted. When he was brought to the door, after I came home from the Continent, instead of signifying, by the usual tokens, that he was pleased to see his master, he looked askant at me like a devil; and when I put my foot in the stirrup, he reared bolt upright, and I fell to the ground rather awkwardly. The experiment was repeated twice or thrice, always with the same result. It occurred to me that he might have taken some capricious dislike to my dress; and Tom Purdie, who always falls heir to the white hat and green jacket, and so forth, when Mrs. Scott has made me discard a set of garments, was sent for, to try whether these habiliments would produce him a similar reception from his old friend Daisy: but Daisy allowed Tom to back him with all manner of gentleness. The thing was inexplicable—but he had certainly taken some part of my conduct in high dudgeon and disgust; and after trying him again, at the interval of a week, I was obliged to part with Daisy—and wars and rumors of wars being over, I resolved thenceforth to have done with such dainty blood. I now stick to a good sober cob." Somebody suggested that Daisy might have considered himself as ill-used, by being left at home when *the laird* went on his journey. "Ay," said he, "these creatures have many thoughts of their own, no doubt, that we can never penetrate." Then, laughing, "Troth," said he, "maybe some bird had whispered Daisy that I had been to see the grand reviews at Paris on a little scrag of a Cossack, while my own gallant trooper was left behind bearing Peter and the post-bag to Melrose."

A few letters, written shortly after this return to Abbotsford, will, among other things, show with what zeal he at once resumed his literary industry, if indeed that can be said to have been at all interrupted by a journey, in the course of which a great part of Paul's narrative, and also of the poem of The Field of Waterloo, must have been composed.

TO J. B. S. MORRITT, ESQ., M. P., ROKEBY PARK.

ABBOTSFORD, 2d October, 1815.

MY DEAR MORRITT,—Few things could have given me more real pain, than to see Mrs. Morritt under such severe suffering, and the misery you sustain in witnessing it. Yet let us trust in the goodness of Providence, which restored the health so deservedly dear to you, from as great a state of depression upon a former occasion. Our visit was indeed a melancholy one, and, I fear, added to your distress, when, God knows, it required no addition.—The contrast of this quiet bird's-nest of a place, with the late scene of confusion and military splendor which I have witnessed, is something of a stunning nature—and, for the first five or six days, I have been content to fold my hands, and saunter up and down in a sort of indolent and stupefied tranquillity, my only attempt at occupation having gone no farther than pruning a young tree now and then. Yesterday, however, and to-day, I began, from necessity, to prune verses, and have been correcting proofs of my little attempt at a poem on Waterloo. It will be out this week, and you shall have a copy by the Carlisle coach, which pray judge favorably, and remember it is not always the grandest actions which are best adapted for the arts of poetry and painting. I believe I shall give offence to my old friends the Whigs, by not condoling with Buonaparte. Since his sentence of transportation, he has begun to look wonderfully comely in their eyes. I would they had hanged him, that he might have died a perfect Adonis. Every reasonable creature must think the Ministers would have deserved the cord themselves, if they had left him in a condition again to cost us the loss of 10,000 of our best and bravest, besides thirty millions of good money. The very threats and frights which he has given the well-meaning people of this realm (myself included), deserved no less a punishment than banishment, since the "putting in bodily fear" makes so material a part of every criminal indictment. But, no doubt, we shall see Ministers attacked for their want of generosity to a fallen enemy, by the same party who last year, with better grounds, assailed them for having left him in a situation again to disturb the tranquillity of Europe.—My young friend Gala has left me, after a short visit to Abbotsford. He is my nearest (conversible) neighbor, and I promise myself much comfort in him, as he has a turn both for the sciences and for the arts, rather uncommon among our young Scotch lairds. He was delighted with Rokeby and its lord, though he saw both at so melancholy a period, and endured, not only with good-humor but with sympathy, the stupidity of his fellow-traveller, who was not by any means *dans son brillant* for some time after leaving you.

We visited Corby Castle on our return to Scotland, which remains, in point of situation, as beautiful as when its walks were celebrated by David Hume, in the only rhymes he was ever known to be guilty of. Here they are, from a pane of glass in an inn at Carlisle:—
"Here chicks in eggs for breakfast sprawl,
Here godless boys God's glories squall,
Here Scotchmen's heads do guard the wall,
But Corby's walks atone for all."

Would it not be a good quiz to advertise *The Poetical Works of David Hume*, with notes, critical, historical, and so forth—with an historical inquiry into the use of eggs for breakfast, a physical discussion on the causes of their being addled; a history of the English Church music, and of the choir of Carlisle in particular; a full account of the affair of 1745, with the trials, last speeches, and so forth, of the poor *plaids* who were strapped up at Carlisle; and, lastly, a full and particular description of Corby, with the genealogy of every family who ever possessed it? I think, even without more than the usual waste of margin, the Poems of David would make a decent twelve-shilling touch. I shall think about it when I have exhausted mine own *century of inventions*.

I do not know whether it is perverseness of state, or old associations, but an excellent and very handsome modern house, which Mr. Howard has lately built at Corby, does not, in my mind, assimilate so well with the scenery as the old irregular monastic hall, with its weather-beaten and antique appearance, which I remember there some years ago.

Out of my Field of Waterloo has sprung an odd wild sort of thing, which I intend to finish separately, and call it The Dance of Death.[25] These matters take up my time so much, that I must bid you adieu for the present. Besides, I am summoned to attend a grand *chasse*, and I see the children are all mounted upon the ponies. By the way, Walter promises to be a gallant horseman. Ever most truly yours,
WALTER SCOTT.

I shall close this chapter with a transcript of some *Notes* on the proof sheets of The Field of Waterloo. John Ballantyne being at Abbotsford on the 3d of October, his brother the printer addressed the packet containing the sheets to him. John appears to have considered James's observations on the margin before Scott saw them; and the record of the style in which the Poet repelled, or yielded to, his critics, will at all events illustrate his habitual good-nature.

John Ballantyne writes on the fly-leaf of the proofs, to his confidential clerk: "Mr. Hodgson, I beg these sheets and all the MS. may be carefully preserved just as they stand, and put in my father's desk. J. B."

James prefaces his animadversions with this quotation:—
"Cut deep and spare not.—*Penruddock*."
The *Notes* are these:—
STANZA I.—"Fair Brussels, thou art far behind."
James Ballantyne.—I do not like this line. It is tame, and the phrase "far behind," has, to my feeling, some associated vulgarity.
Scott.—Stet.
STANZA II.—"Let not *the* stranger with disdain
The architecture view."
James.—These two words are cacophonous. Would not *its* do?
Scott.—Th. is a bad sound. Ts. a much worse. Read *their*.

29

STANZA IV.—"A stranger might reply."

James.—My objection to this is probably fantastical, and I state it only because, from the first moment to the last, it has always made me boggle. I don't like a *stranger*—Query, "The questioned"—The "spectator"—"gazer," etc.

Scott.—*Stranger* is appropriate—it means stranger to the circumstances.

STANZA VI.—*James.*—You had changed "garner-house profound," which I think quite admirable, to "garner under ground," which I think quite otherways. I have presumed not to make the change—must I?

Scott.—I acquiesce, but with doubts; *profound* sounds affected.

STANZA VIII.—"The deadly tug of war at length
Must limits find in human strength,
And *cease* when these are passed.
Vain hope!" etc.

James.—I must needs repeat, that the deadly tug *did* cease in the case supposed. It lasted long—very long; but, when the limits of resistance, of human strength, were past—that is, after they had fought for ten hours, then the deadly tug *did* cease. Therefore the "hope" was not "vain."

Scott.—I answer, it did *not*,—because the observation relates to the strength of those actually engaged, and when *their* strength was exhausted, other squadrons were brought up. Suppose you saw two lawyers scolding at the bar, you might say this must have an end—human lungs cannot hold out—but, if the debate were continued by the senior counsel, your well-grounded expectations would be disappointed—"Cousin, thou wert not wont to be so dull!"—

IBID.—"Nor ceased the *intermitted* shot."

James.—Mr. Erskine contends that "intermitted" is redundant.

Scott.—"Nor ceased the *storm of shell and shot.*"

STANZA X.—"——— Never shall our country say
We gave one inch of ground away,
When battling for her right."

James.—In conflict?

John B.—*Warring?* I am afraid *battling* must stand.

Scott.—All worse than the text.

STANZA XI.—"Peal'd wildly the imperial name."

James.—I submit with diffidence whether this be not a somewhat tame conclusion to so very animated a stanza? And, at any rate, you will observe, that as it stands, you have no rhyme whatever to "The Cohort eagles *fly.*"—You have no rhyme to *fly.* Flew and *fly*, also, are perhaps too near, considering that each word closes a line of the same sort. I don't well like "*Thus* in a torrent," either. If it were, "In one broad torrent," etc., it strikes me that it would be more spirited.

Scott.—Granted as to most of these observations—Read, "in one *dark* torrent broad and strong," etc.—The "imperial name" is *true*, therefore must stand.

STANZA XII.—"Nor was one forward footstep *stopped.*"

James.—This staggering word was intended, I presume, but I don't like it.

Scott.—Granted. Read *staid*, etc.

IBID.—"Down were the eagle banners sent,
Down, down the horse and horsemen went."

James.—This is very spirited and very fine; but it is unquestionably liable to the charge of being very nearly a direct repetition of yourself. See *Lord of the Isles*, Canto vi. Stanza 24:—

"*Down! down!* in headlong overthrow,
Horseman and horse, the foremost go," etc.

This passage is at once so striking and so recent, that its close similarity to the present, if not indeed its identity, must strike every reader; and really, to borrow from one's self is hardly much better than to borrow from one's neighbors. And yet again, a few lines lower—

"As hammers on the *anvils* reel,
Against the cuirass *clangs* the steel."

30

See *Lady of the Lake*, Canto vi. Stanza 18:—

"I heard the broadswords' deadly *clang*,
As if an hundred *anvils* rang."

Here is precisely the same image, in very nearly the same words.

Scott.—I have altered the expression, but made a note, which, I think, will vindicate my retaining the simile.

STANZA XIII.—"As their own Ocean-rocks hold *stance*."

John.—I do not know such an English word as *stance*.

Scott.—Then we'll make it one for the *nance*.

IBID.—"And *newer* standards fly."

James.—I don't like *newer*.

Scott.—"And *other* standards fly."

IBID.—"Or can thy memory fail to *quote*,
Heard to thy cost the vengeful note."

James.—Would to God you would alter this *quote*!

John.—Would to God *I* could!—I certainly should.—

Scott.—"Or can thy memory fail to know,
Heard oft before in hour of woe."

Or—

"Or dwells not in thy memory still,
Heard frequent in thine hour of ill."

STANZA XV.—"Wrung forth by pride, *regret*, and shame."

James.—I have ventured to submit to your choice—
"Wrung forth by pride, *and rage*, and shame."

Regret appearing a faint epithet amidst such a combination of bitter feelings.

Scott.—Granted.

IBID.—"So mingle banner, wain, and gun,
Where in one tide of horror run
The warriors," etc.

James.—In the first place, warriors *running* in a tide is a clashing metaphor; in the second, the warriors *running* at all is a little homely. It is true, no doubt; but really running is little better than scampering. For these causes, one or both, I think the lines should be altered.

Scott.—You are wrong in one respect. A tide is always said to *run*,—but I thought of the tide without attending to the equivoque, which must be altered. Read,—
"Where the tumultuous flight rolls on."

STANZA XVI.—"—— found *gallant* grave."

James.—This is surely a singular epithet to a grave. I think the whole of this stanza eminently fine; and, in particular, the conclusion.

Scott.—"—— found *soldier's* grave." ——

STANZA XXI.—"*Redoubted* Picton's soul of fire."

James.—From long association, this epithet strikes me as conveying a semi-ludicrous idea.

Scott.—It is here appropriate, and your objection seems merely personal to your own association.

IBID.—"Through his friends' heart to *wound* his own."

James.—Quære—*Pierce*, or rather *stab*—*wound* is faint.

Scott.—"Pierce."

STANZA XXII.—"Forgive, *brave fallen*, the imperfect lay."

James.—Don't like "brave fallen" at all; nor "appropriate praise," three lines after. The latter in particular is prosaic.

Scott.—"Forgive, *brave dead*," —— "*The dear-earned praise.*"[Back to Contents]

CHAPTER XXXVI.

FIELD OF WATERLOO PUBLISHED. — REVISION OF PAUL'S LETTERS, ETC. — QUARREL AND RECONCILIATION WITH HOGG. — FOOTBALL MATCH AT CARTERHAUGH. — SONGS ON THE BANNER OF BUCCLEUCH. — DINNER AT BOWHILL. — DESIGN FOR A PIECE

1815.

The poem of The Field of Waterloo was published before the end of October; the profits of the first edition being the author's contribution to the fund raised for the relief of the widows and children of the soldiers slain in the battle. This piece appears to have disappointed those most disposed to sympathize with the author's views and feelings. The descent is indeed heavy from his Bannockburn to his Waterloo: the presence, or all but visible reality of what his dreams cherished, seems to have overawed his imagination, and tamed it into a weak pomposity of movement. The burst of pure native enthusiasm upon the *Scottish* heroes that fell around the Duke of Wellington's person bears, however, the broadest marks of the "Mighty Minstrel:"—

"Saw gallant Miller's fading eye
Still bent where Albyn's standards fly,
And Cameron, in the shock of steel,
Die like the offspring of Lochiel," etc.;—

and this is far from being the only redeeming passage. There is one, indeed, in which he illustrates what he then thought Buonaparte's poorness of spirit in adversity, which always struck me as preëminently characteristic of Scott's manner of interweaving, both in prose and verse, the moral energies with analogous natural description, and combining thought with imagery,—

"Or is thy soul like mountain tide,
That, swelled by winter storm and shower,
Rolls down in turbulence of power,
A torrent fierce and wide;
Reft of these aids, a rill obscure,
Shrinking unnoticed, mean and poor,
Whose channel shows displayed
The wrecks of its impetuous course,
But not one symptom of the force
By which these wrecks were made!"

The poem was the first upon a subject likely to be sufficiently hackneyed; and, having the advantage of coming out in a small cheap form—(prudently imitated from Murray's innovation with the tales of Byron, which was the death-blow to the system of verse in quarto)—it attained rapidly a measure of circulation above what had been reached either by Rokeby or The Lord of the Isles.

Meanwhile the revision of Paul's Letters was proceeding; and Scott had almost immediately on his return to Abbotsford concluded his bargain for the first edition of a third novel—The Antiquary—to be published also in the approaching winter. Harold the Dauntless, too, was from time to time taken up as the amusement of *horæ subsecivæ*. As for Scott's out-of-doors occupations of that autumn, sufficient light will be thrown on them by the following letter; from which it is seen that he had now completed a rather tedious negotiation with another bonnet-laird, and definitively added the lands of *Kaeside* to the original estate of Abbotsford.

TO MISS JOANNA BAILLIE, HAMPSTEAD.

ABBOTSFORD, November 12, 1815.

I have been long in acknowledging your letter, my dear friend, and yet you have not only been frequent in my thoughts, as must always be the case, but your name has been of late familiar in my mouth as a household word. You must know that the pinasters you had the goodness to send me some time since, which are now fit to be set out of the nursery, have occupied my mind as to the mode of disposing of them. Now, mark the event: there is in the middle of what will soon be a bank of fine young wood, a certain old gravel-pit, which is the present scene of my operations. I have caused it to be covered with better earth, and gently altered with the spade, so as, if possible, to give it the air of one of those accidental hollows which the surface of a hill frequently presents. Having arranged my ground, I intend to plant it all round with the pinasters, and other varieties of the pine species, and in the interior I will have a rustic seat, surrounded by all kinds of evergreen shrubs (laurels in particular), and all varieties of the holly and cedar, and so forth, and this is to be called and entitled *Joanna's Bower*. We are determined in the choice of our ornaments by necessity, for our ground fronts (in poetic phrase) the rising sun, or, in common language, looks to the east; and being also on the north side of the hill—(don't you shiver at the thought?)—why, to say truth, George Wynnos and I are both of opinion that nothing but evergreens will flourish there; but I trust I shall convert a present deformity into a very pretty little hobby-horsical sort of thing. It will not bear looking at for years, and that is a pity; but it will so far resemble the person from whom it takes name, that it is planted, as she has written, for the benefit as well of posterity as for the passing generation. Time and I, says the Spaniard, against any two; and fully confiding in the proverb, I have just undertaken another grand task. You must know, I have purchased a large lump of wild land, lying adjoining to this little property, which greatly more than doubles my domains. The land is said to be reasonably bought, and I am almost certain I can turn it to advantage by a little judicious expenditure; for this place is already allowed to be worth twice what it cost me; and our people here think so little of planting, and do it so carelessly, that they stare with astonishment at the alteration which well-planted woods make on the face of a country. There is, besides, a very great temptation, from the land running to within a quarter of a mile of a very sweet wild sheet of water, of which (that is, one side of it) I have every chance to become proprietor: this is a poetical circumstance not to be lost sight of, and accordingly I keep it full in my view. Amid these various avocations, past, present, and to come, I have not thought much about Waterloo, only that I am truly glad you like it. I might, no doubt, have added many curious anecdotes, but I think the pamphlet long enough as it stands, and never had any design of writing copious notes.

I do most devoutly hope Lord Byron will succeed in his proposal of bringing out one of your dramas; that he is your sincere admirer is only synonymous with his being a man of genius; and he has, I am convinced, both the power and inclination to serve the public, by availing himself of the treasures you have laid before them. Yet I long for "some yet untasted spring," and heartily wish you would take Lord B. into your counsels, and adjust, from your yet unpublished materials, some drama for the public. In such a case, I would, in your place, conceal my name till the issue of the adventure. It is a sickening thing to think how many angry and evil passions the mere name of admitted excellence brings into full activity. I wish you would consider this hint, and I am sure the result would be great gratification to the public, and to yourself that sort of satisfaction which arises from receiving proofs of having attained the mark at which you aimed. Of this last, indeed, you cannot doubt, if you consult only the voices of the intelligent and the accomplished; but the object of the dramatist is professedly to delight the public at large, and therefore I think you should make the experiment fairly.

Little Sophia is much obliged by your kind and continued recollection: she is an excellent good child, sufficiently sensible, very affectionate, not without perception of character; but the gods have not made her poetical, and I hope she will never attempt to act a part which nature has not called her to. I am myself a poet, writing to a poetess, and therefore cannot be suspected of a wish to degrade a talent, to which, in whatever degree I may have possessed it, I am indebted for much happiness: but this depends only on the rare coincidence of some talent falling in with a novelty in style and diction and conduct of story, which suited the popular taste; and were my children to be better poets than me, they would not be such in general estimation, simply because the second cannot be the first, and the first (I mean in point of date) is everything, while others are nothing, even with more intrinsic merit. I am therefore particularly anxious to store the heads of my young damsels with something better than the tags of rhymes; and I hope Sophia is old enough (young though she be) to view her little incidents of celebrity, such as they are, in the right point of view. Mrs. Scott and she are at present in Edinburgh; the rest of the children are with me in this place; my eldest boy is already a bold horseman and a fine shot, though only about fourteen years old. I assure you I was prouder of the first blackcock he killed, than I have been of anything whatever since I first killed one myself, and that is twenty years ago. This is all stupid gossip; but, as Master Corporal Nym says, "things must be as they may:" you cannot expect grapes from thorns, or much amusement from a brain bewildered with thorn hedges at Kaeside, for such is the sonorous title of my new possession, in virtue of which I subscribe myself,

ABBOTSFORD & KAESIDE.

There is now to be mentioned a little pageant of December, 1815, which perhaps interested *Abbotsford and Kaeside* not very much less than the "Field of the Cloth of Gold," as James Ballantyne calls it, of the preceding autumn. This was no other than a football match, got up under the auspices of the Duke of Buccleuch, between the men of the Vale of Yarrow and the Burghers of Selkirk, the particulars of which will be sufficiently explained by an extract from Ballantyne's newspaper, written, I can have no doubt, by the Sheriff of the Forest. But the part taken in this solemnity by the Ettrick Shepherd reminds me of an extraordinary epistle which Scott had received from him some months before this time, and of the account given by Hogg himself, in one of his autobiographies, of the manner in which Scott's kindness terminated the alienation it refers to.

The Shepherd, being as usual in pecuniary straits, had projected a work, to be called The Poetic Mirror, in which should appear some piece by each popular poet of the time, the whole to be edited by himself, and published for his benefit; and he addressed, accordingly, to his brother bards a circular petition for their best assistance. Scott—like Byron and most of the other persons thus applied to—declined the proposition. The letter in which he signified his refusal has not been preserved;—indeed it is sufficiently remarkable, that of all the many letters which Hogg must have received from his distinguished contemporaries, he appears to have kept not one; but Scott's decided aversion to joint-stock adventures in authorship must have been well known ere now to Hogg—and, at all events, nobody can suspect that his note of refusal was meant to be an unfriendly communication. The Shepherd, however, took some phrase in high dudgeon, and penned an answer virulently insolent in spirit and in language, accusing him of base jealousy of his own superior natural genius. I am not sure whether it was on this or another occasion of the like sort, that James varied the usual formulas of epistolary composition, by beginning with "Damned Sir," and ending, "Believe me, Sir, yours with disgust, etc.;" but certainly the performance was such that no intercourse took place between the parties for some weeks, or perhaps months, afterwards. The letter in which Hogg at length solicits a renewal of kindliness says nothing, it may be observed, of the circumstance which, according to his autobiography, confirmed by the recollection of two friends, whom he names in the letter itself (Mr. John Grieve and Mr. William Laidlaw), had really caused him to repent of his suspicions, and their outrageous expression. The fact was, that hearing, shortly after the receipt of the offensive epistle, that Hogg was confined to his lodgings, in an obscure alley of Edinburgh, called Gabriel's Road, by a dangerous illness, Scott called on Mr. Grieve to make inquiries about him, and to offer to take on himself the expenses of the best medical attendance. He had, however, cautioned the worthy hatter that no hint of this offer must reach Hogg; and, in consequence, it might perhaps be the Shepherd's feeling at the time that he should not, in addressing his lifelong benefactor, betray any acquaintance with this recent interference on his behalf. There can be no doubt, however, that he obeyed the genuine dictates of his better nature when he penned this apologetic effusion:—

TO WALTER SCOTT, ESQ., CASTLE STREET.

GABRIEL'S ROAD, February 28, 1815.

MR. SCOTT,—I think it is great nonsense for two men who are friends at heart, and who ever must be so,—indeed it is not in the nature of things that they can be otherwise,—should be professed enemies.

Mr. Grieve and Mr. Laidlaw, who were very severe on me, and to whom I was obliged to show your letter, have long ago convinced me that I mistook part of it, and that it was not me you held in such contempt, but the opinion of the public. The idea that you might mean that (though I still think the reading will bear either construction) has given me much pain; for I know I answered yours intemperately, and in a mortal rage. I meant to have enclosed yours, and begged of you to return mine, but I cannot find it, and am sure that some one to whom I have been induced to show it, has taken it away. However, as my troubles on that subject were never like to wear to an end, I could no longer resist telling you that I am extremely vexed about it. I desire not a renewal of our former intimacy, for haply, after what I have written, your family would not suffer it; but I wish it to be understood that, when we meet *by chance*, we might shake hands, and speak to one another as old acquaintances, and likewise that we may exchange a letter occasionally, for I find there are many things which I yearn to communicate to you, and the tears rush to my eyes when I consider that I may not.

If you allow of this, pray let me know, and if you do not, let me know. Indeed, I am anxious to hear from you, for "as the day of trouble is with me, so shall my strength be." To be friends *from the teeth forwards* is common enough; but it strikes me that there is something still more ludicrous in the reverse of the picture, and so to be enemies—and why should I be, *from the teeth forwards*, yours sincerely,

JAMES HOGG?

Scott's reply was, as Hogg says, "a brief note, telling him to think no more of the business, and come to breakfast next morning." The misunderstanding being thus closed, they appear to have counselled and coöperated together in the most cordial fashion, in disciplining their rural allies for the muster of Carterhaugh—the Duke of Buccleuch's brother-in-law, the Earl of Home, having appointed the Shepherd his Lieutenant over the Yarrow Band, while the Sheriff took under his special cognizance the *Sutors*, i.e., *shoemakers*, of Selkirk—for so the burgesses of that town have for ages styled themselves, and under that denomination their warlike prowess in days of yore has been celebrated in many an old ballad, besides the well-known one which begins with

"'Tis up wi' the Sutors o' Selkirk,
And 'tis down wi' the Earl of Home!"

In order to understand all the allusions in the newspaper record of this important day, one must be familiar with the notes to the Minstrelsy of the Scottish Border; but I shall not burden it with further comment here.

FOOTBALL MATCH.

"On Monday, 4th December, there was played, upon the extensive plain of Carterhaugh, near the junction of the Ettrick and Yarrow, the greatest match at the ball which has taken place for many years. It was held by the people of the Dale of Yarrow, against those of the parish of Selkirk; the former being brought to the field by the Right Hon. the Earl of Home, and the Gallant Sutors by their Chief Magistrate, Ebenezer Clarkson, Esq. Both sides were joined by many volunteers from other parishes; and the appearance of the various parties marching from their different glens to the place of rendezvous, with pipes playing and loud acclamations, carried back the coldest imagination to the old times when the Foresters assembled with the less peaceable purpose of invading the English territory, or defending their own. The romantic character of the scenery aided the illusion, as well as the performance of a feudal ceremony previous to commencing the games.

"His Grace the Duke of Buccleuch and Queensberry came upon the ground about eleven o'clock, attended by his sons, the young Earl of Dalkeith and Lord John Scott; the Countess of Home; the Ladies Anne, Charlotte, and Isabella Scott; Lord and Lady Montagu and family; the Hon. General Sir Edward Stopford, K. B.; Sir John Riddell of Riddell; Sir Alexander Don of Newton; Mr. Elliot Lockhart, member for the county; Mr. Pringle of Whytbank, younger; Mr. Pringle of Torwoodlee; Captain Pringle, Royal Navy; Mr. Boyd of Broadmeadows and family; Mr. Chisholm of Chisholm; Major Pott of Todrig; Mr. Walter Scott, Sheriff of Selkirkshire, and family,—and many other gentlemen and ladies.—The ancient banner of the Buccleuch family, a curious and venerable relique, emblazoned with armorial bearings, and with the word '*Bellendaine*,' the ancient war-cry of the clan of Scott, was then displayed, as on former occasions when the Chief took the field in person, whether for the purpose of war or sport. The banner was delivered by Lady Anne Scott to Master Walter Scott, younger of Abbotsford, who attended suitably mounted and armed, and riding over the field displayed it to the sound of the war-pipes, and amid the acclamations of the assembled spectators, who could not be fewer than 2000 in number. That this singular renewal of an ancient military custom might not want poetical celebrity, verses were distributed among the spectators, composed for the occasion by Mr. Walter Scott and the

Ettrick Shepherd.—Mr. James Hogg acted as aide-de-camp to the Earl of Home in the command of the Yarrow men, and Mr. Robert Henderson of Selkirk to Mr. Clarkson, both of whom contributed not a little to the good order of the day.

"The ball was thrown up between the parties by the Duke of Buccleuch, and the first game was gained, after a severe conflict of an hour and a half duration, by the Selkirk men. The second game was still more severely contested, and after a close and stubborn struggle of more than three hours, with various fortune, and much display of strength and agility on both sides, was at length carried by the Yarrow men. The ball should then have been thrown up a third time, but considerable difficulty occurred in arranging the voluntary auxiliaries from other parishes, so as to make the match equal; and, as the day began to close, it was found impossible to bring the strife to an issue, by playing a decisive game.

"Both parties, therefore, parted with equal honors, but, before they left the ground, the Sheriff threw up his hat, and in Lord Dalkeith's name and his own, challenged the Yarrow men, on the part of the Sutors, to a match to be played upon the first convenient opportunity, with 100 picked men only on each side. The challenge was mutually accepted by Lord Home, on his own part, and for Lord John Scott, and was received with acclamation by the players on both sides. The principal gentlemen present took part with one side or other, except the Duke of Buccleuch, who remains neutral. Great play is expected, and all bets are to be paid by the losers to the poor of the winning parish. We cannot dismiss the subject without giving our highest commendation to the Earl of Home, and to Mr. Clarkson, for the attention which they showed in promoting the spirit and good order of the day. For the players themselves, it was impossible to see a finer set of active and athletic young fellows than appeared on the field. But what we chiefly admired in their conduct was, that though several hundreds in number, exceedingly keen for their respective parties, and engaged in so rough and animated a contest, they maintained the most perfect good-humor, and showed how unnecessary it is to discourage manly and athletic exercises among the common people, under pretext of maintaining subordination and good order. We have only to regret that the great concourse of spectators rendered it difficult to mention the names of the several players who distinguished themselves by feats of strength or agility; but we must not omit to record that the first ball was *hailed* by Robert Hall, mason in *Selkirk*, and the second by George Brodie, from *Greatlaws*, upon *Aillwater*.

"The Selkirk party wore slips of fir as their mark of distinction—the Yarrow men, sprigs of heath.

"Refreshments were distributed to the players by the Duke of Buccleuch's domestics, in a booth erected for the purpose; and no persons were allowed to sell ale or spirits on the field.

"In the evening there was a dance at the Duke's hunting-seat at Bowhill, attended by the nobility and gentry who had witnessed the sport of the day; and the fascination of Gow's violin and band detained them in the dancing-room till the dawn of the winter morning."

The newspaper then gives the songs above alluded to—namely, Scott's Lifting of the Banner:—

"From the brown crest of Newark its summons extending,
Our signal is waving in smoke and in flame,
And each Forester blithe, from his mountain descending,
Bounds light o'er the heather to join in the game;
Then up with the Banner! let forest winds fan her!
She has blazed over Ettrick eight ages and more;
In sport we'll attend her, in battle defend her,
With heart and with hand, like our Fathers before," etc.[26]

—and that excellent ditty by Hogg, entitled The Ettrick Garland, to the Ancient Banner of the House of Buccleuch:—

"And hast thou here, like hermit gray,
Thy mystic characters unroll'd,
O'er peaceful revellers to play,
Thou emblem of the days of old?
All hail! memorial of the brave,

36

The liegeman's pride, the Border's awe!
May thy gray pennon never wave
On sterner field than Carterhaugh!" etc.

I have no doubt the Sheriff of the Forest was a prouder man, when he saw his boy ride about Carterhaugh with the pennon of Bellenden, than when Platoff mounted himself for the imperial review of the *Champ de Mars*. It is a pity that I should have occasion to allude, before I quit a scene so characteristic of Scott, to another outbreak of Hogg's jealous humor. His Autobiography informs us, that when the more distinguished part of the company assembled on the conclusion of the sport to dine at Bowhill, he was proceeding to place himself at a particular table—but the Sheriff seized his arm, told him *that* was reserved for the nobility, and seated him at an inferior board—"between himself and the Laird of Harden"—the first gentleman of the clan Scott. "The fact is," says Hogg, "I am convinced he was sore afraid of my getting to be too great a favorite among the young ladies of Buccleuch!" Who can read this, and not be reminded of Sancho Panza and the Duchess? And, after all, he quite mistook what Scott had said to him; for certainly there was, neither on this, nor on any similar occasion at Bowhill, any *high table for the nobility*, though there was a *side-table for the children*, at which, when the Shepherd of Ettrick was about to seat himself, his friend probably whispered that it was reserved for the "*little* lords and ladies, and their playmates." This blunder may seem undeserving of any explanation; but it is often in small matters that the strongest feelings are most strikingly betrayed—and this story is, in exact proportion to its silliness, indicative of the jealous feeling which mars and distorts so many of Hogg's representations of Scott's conduct and demeanor.

It appears from the account of this football match in the Edinburgh Journal, that Scott took a lead in proposing a renewal of the contest. This, however, never occurred; and that it ought not to do so had probably occurred from the first to the Duke of Buccleuch, who is mentioned as having alone abstained from laying any bets on the final issue.

When Mr. Washington Irving visited Scott two years afterwards at Abbotsford, he told his American friend that "the old feuds and local interests, and rivalries and animosities of the Scotch, still slept in their ashes, and might easily be roused; their hereditary feeling for names was still great; it was not always safe to have even the game of football between villages;—the old clannish spirit was too apt to break out."[27]

The good Duke of Buccleuch's solitary exemption from these heats of Carterhaugh might read a significant lesson to minor politicians of all parties on more important scenes. In pursuance of the same peace-making spirit, he appears to have been desirous of doing something gratifying to the men of the town of Selkirk, who had on this occasion taken the field against his Yarrow tenantry. His Grace consulted Scott about the design of a piece of plate to be presented to their community; and his letter on this weighty subject must not be omitted in the memoirs of a Sheriff of Selkirk:—

TO HIS GRACE THE DUKE OF BUCCLEUCH, ETC., BOWHILL.

EDINBURGH, Thursday.

MY DEAR LORD,—I have proceeded in my commission about the cup. It will be a very handsome one. But I am still puzzled to dispose of the birse[28] in a becoming manner. It is a most unmanageable decoration. I tried it upright on the top of the cup; it looked like a shaving-brush, and the goblet might be intended to make the lather. Then I thought I had a brilliant idea. The arms of Selkirk are a female seated on a sarcophagus, decorated with the arms of Scotland, which will make a beautiful top to the cup. So I thought of putting the birse into the lady's other hand; but, alas, it looked so precisely like the rod of chastisement uplifted over the poor child, that I laughed at the drawing for half an hour. Next I tried to take off the castigatory appearance, by inserting the bristles in a kind of handle; but then it looked as if the poor woman had been engaged in the capacities of housemaid and child-keeper at once, and, fatigued with her double duty, had sat down on the wine-cooler, with the broom in one hand, and the bairn in the other. At length, after some conference with Charles Sharpe, I have hit on a plan, which, I think, will look very well, if tolerably executed,—namely, to have the lady seated in due form on the top of the lid (which will look handsome, and will be well taken), and to have a thistle wreathed around the sarcophagus and rising above her head, and from the top of the thistle shall proceed the birse. I will bring a drawing with me, and they shall get the cup ready in the mean time. I hope to be at Abbotsford on Monday night, to stay for a week. My cat has eat two or three birds, while regaling on the crumbs that were thrown for them. This was a breach of hospitality; but *oportet vivere*—and *micat inter omnes*—with which stolen pun, and my respectful compliments to Lord Montagu and the ladies, I am, very truly, your Grace's most faithful and obliged servant,

WALTER SCOTT.

P. S.—Under another cover, which I have just received, I send the two drawings of the front and reverse of the lid of the proposed cup. Your Grace will be so good as understand that the thistle—the top of which is garnished with the bristle—is entirely detached, in working, from the figure, and slips into a socket. The following lines are humbly suggested for a motto, being taken from an ancient Scottish canzonetta,—unless the Yarrow committee can find any better:—

"The sutor ga'e the sow a kiss:
Grumph! quo' the sow, it's a' for my birss."

Some weeks before the year 1815 closed, Mr. Morritt sustained the heaviest of domestic afflictions; and several letters on that sad subject had passed between Rokeby and Abbotsford,[29] before the date of the following:—

TO J. B. S. MORRITT, ESQ., M. P., ROKEBY PARK.

EDINBURGH, 22d December, 1815.

MY DEAR MORRITT,—While you know what satisfaction it would have given me to have seen you here, I am very sensible of the more weighty reasons which you urge for preferring to stay at Rokeby for some time. I only hope you will remember that Scotland has claims on you, whenever you shall find your own mind so far at ease as to permit you to look abroad for consolation; and if it should happen that you thought of being here about our time of vacation, I have my time then entirely at my own command, and I need not say, that as much of it as could in any manner of way contribute to your amusement, is most heartily at yours. I have myself at present the melancholy task of watching the declining health of my elder brother, Major Scott, whom, I think, you have seen.

My literary occupation is getting through the press the Letters of Paul, of whose lucubrations I trust soon to send you a copy. As the observations of a bystander, perhaps you will find some amusement in them, especially as I had some channels of information not accessible to every one. The recess of our courts, which takes place to-morrow, for three weeks, will give me ample time to complete this job, and also the second volume of Triermain, which is nearly finished,—a strange rude story, founded partly on the ancient northern traditions respecting the Berserkers, whose peculiar habits and fits of martial frenzy make such a figure in the Sagas. I shall then set myself seriously to The Antiquary, of which I have only a very general sketch at present; but when once I get my pen to the paper it will walk fast enough. I am sometimes tempted to leave it alone, and try whether it will not write as well without the assistance of my head as with it. A hopeful prospect for the reader. In the mean while, the snow, which is now falling so fast as to make it dubious when this letter may reach Rokeby, is likely to forward these important avocations, by keeping me a constant resident in Edinburgh, in lieu of my plan of going to Abbotsford, where I had a number of schemes in hand, in the way of planting and improving. I believe I told you I have made a considerable addition to my little farm, and extended my domains towards a wild lake, which I have a good prospect of acquiring also. It has a sort of legendary fame; for the persuasion of the solitary shepherds who approach its banks is, that it is tenanted by a very large amphibious animal called by them a water-bull, and which several of them pretend to have seen. As his dimensions greatly exceed those of an otter, I am tempted to think with Trinculo, "This is the devil, and no monster." But, after all, is it not strange, that as to almost all the lakes in Scotland, both Lowland and Highland, such a belief should prevail? and that the description popularly given uniformly corresponds with that of the hippopotamus? Is it possible, that at some remote period, that remarkable animal, like some others which have now disappeared, may have been an inhabitant of our large lakes? Certainly the vanishing of the mammoth and other animals from the face of the creation renders such a conjecture less wild than I would otherwise esteem it. It is certain we have lost the beaver, whose bones have been more than once found in our Selkirkshire bogs and marlmosses. The remains of the wild bull are very frequently found; and I have more than one skull with horns of most formidable dimensions.

About a fortnight ago we had a great football match in Selkirkshire, when the Duke of Buccleuch raised his banner (a very curious and ancient pennon) in great form. Your friend Walter was banner-bearer, dressed, like a forester of old, in green, with a green bonnet, and an eagle feather in it; and, as he was well mounted, and rode handsomely over the field, he was much admired by all his clansmen.

I have thrown these trifles together, without much hope that they will afford you amusement; but I know you will wish to know what I am about, and I have but trifles to send to those friends who interest themselves about a trifler. My present employment is watching, from time to time, the progress of a stupid cause, in order to be ready to reduce the sentence into writing, when the Court shall have decided whether Gordon of Kenmore or MacMichan of Meikleforthhead be the superior of the lands of Tarschrechan and Dalbrattie, and entitled to the feudal casualties payable forth thereof, which may amount to twopence sterling, once in half a dozen of years. Marry, sir, they make part of a freehold qualification, and the decision may wing a voter. I did not send the book you received by the Selkirk coach. I wish I could have had sense enough to send anything which could afford you consolation. I think our friendLady Louisa was likely to have had this attention; she has, God knows, been herself tried with affliction, and is well acquainted with the sources from which comfort can be drawn. My wife joins in kindest remembrances, as do Sophia and Walter. Ever yours affectionately,

WALTER SCOTT.

This letter is dated the 22d of December. On the 26th, John Ballantyne, being then at Abbotsford, writes to Messrs. Constable: "Paul is *all* in hand;" and an envelope, addressed to James Ballantyne on the 29th, has preserved another little fragment of Scott's playful doggerel:—

"Dear James—I'm done, thank God, with the long yarns
Of the most prosy of Apostles—Paul;
And now advance, sweet Heathen of Monkbarns,
Step out, old quizz, as fast as I can scrawl."[Back to Contents]

CHAPTER XXXVII.

PUBLICATION OF PAUL'S LETTERS TO HIS KINSFOLK. — GUY MANNERING "TERRY-FIED." — DEATH OF MAJOR JOHN SCOTT. — LETTERS TO THOMAS SCOTT. — PUBLICATION OF THE ANTIQUARY. — HISTORY OF 1814 FOR THE EDINBURGH ANNUAL REGISTER. — LETTERS ON THE HISTORY OF SCOTLAND PROJECTED. — PUBLICATION OF THE FIRST TALES OF MY LANDLORD BY MURRAY AND BLACKWOOD. — ANECDOTES BY MR. TRAIN. — QUARTERLY REVIEW ON THE TALES. — BUILDING AT ABBOTSFORD BEGUN. — LETTERS TO MORRITT, TERRY, MURRAY, AND THE BALLANTYNES.

1816.

The year 1815 may be considered as, for Scott's peaceful tenor of life, an eventful one. That which followed has left almost its only traces in the successive appearance of nine volumes, which attest the prodigal genius, and hardly less astonishing industry of the man. Early in January were published Paul's Letters to his Kinsfolk, of which I need not now say more than that they were received with lively curiosity, and general, though not vociferous applause. The first edition was an octavo, of 6000 copies; and it was followed, in the course of the next two or three years, by a second and a third, amounting together to 3000 more. The popularity of the novelist was at its height; and this admitted, if not avowed, specimen of Scott's prose must have been perceived, by all who had any share of discrimination, to flow from the same pen.

MAIDA
After Landseer's painting.

Mr. Terry produced, in the spring of 1816, a dramatic piece, entitled Guy Mannering, which met with great success on the London boards, and still continues to be a favorite with the theatrical public. What share the novelist himself had in this first specimen of what he used to call "the art of *Terryfying*," I cannot exactly say; but his correspondence shows that the pretty song of the Lullaby[30] was not his only contribution to it; and I infer that he had taken the trouble to modify the plot, and rearrange, for stage purposes, a considerable part of the original dialogue. The casual risk of discovery, through the introduction of the song which had, in the mean time, been communicated to one of his humble friends, the late Mr. Alexander Campbell,[31] editor of Albyn's Anthology—(commonly known at Abbotsford as, by way of excellence, *The Dunniewassal*,)—and Scott's suggestions on that difficulty will amuse the reader of the following letter:—

TO D. TERRY, ESQ., ALFRED PLACE, BLOOMSBURY, LONDON.

ABBOTSFORD, 18th April, 1816.

MY DEAR TERRY,—I give you joy of your promotion to the dignity of an householder, and heartily wish you all the success you so well deserve, to answer the approaching enlargement of your domestic establishment. You will find a house a very devouring monster, and that the purveying for it requires a little exertion, and a great deal of self-denial and arrangement. But when there is domestic peace and contentment, all that would otherwise be disagreeable, as restraining our taste and occupying our time, becomes easy. I trust Mrs. Terry will get her business easily over, and that you will soon "dandle Dickie on your knee."—I have been at the spring circuit, which made me late in receiving your letter, and there I was introduced to a man whom I never saw in my life before, namely, the proprietor of all the Pepper and Mustard family,—in other words, the genuine Dandie Dinmont. Dandie is himself modest, and says, "he b'lives it's only the dougs that is in the buik, and no himsel'." As the surveyor of taxes was going his ominous rounds past Hyndlea, which is the abode of Dandie, his whole pack rushed out upon the man of execution, and Dandie followed them (conscious that their number greatly exceeded his return), exclaiming, "The tae hauf o' them is but whalps, man." In truth, I knew nothing of the man, except his odd humor of having only two names for twenty dogs. But there are lines of general resemblance among all these hill-men, which there is no missing; and Jamie Davidson of Hyndlea certainly looks Dandie Dinmont remarkably well. He is much flattered with the compliment, and goes uniformly by the name among his comrades, but has never read the book. Ailie used to read it to him, but it set him to sleep. All this you will think funny enough. I am afraid I am in a scrape about the song, and that of my own making; for as it never occurred to me that there was anything odd in my writing two or three verses for you, which have no connection with the novel, I was at no pains to disown them; and Campbell is just that sort of crazy creature, with whom there is no confidence, not from want of honor and disposition to oblige, but from his flighty temper. The music of *Cadil gŭ lo* is already printed in his publication, and nothing can be done with him, for fear of setting his tongue a-going. Erskine and you may consider whether you should barely acknowledge an obligation to an unknown friend, or pass the matter altogether in silence. In my opinion, my *first* idea was preferable to both, because I cannot see what earthly connection there is between the song and the novel, or how acknowledging the one is fathering the other. On the contrary, it seems to me that acknowledgment tends to exclude the idea of farther obligation than to the extent specified. I forgot also that I had given a copy of the lines to Mrs. Macleod of Macleod, from whom I had the air. But I remit the matter entirely to you and Erskine, for there must be many points in it which I cannot be supposed a good judge of. At any rate, don't let it delay your publication, and believe I shall be quite satisfied with what you think proper.

I have got from my friend Glengarry the noblest dog ever seen on the Border since Johnnie Armstrong's time. He is between the wolf and deer greyhound, about six feet long from the tip of the nose to the tail, and high and strong in proportion: he is quite gentle, and a great favorite: tell Will Erskine he will eat off his plate without being at the trouble to put a paw on the table or chair.[32] I showed him to Mathews, who dined one day in Castle Street before I came here, where, except for Mrs. S., I am like unto

"The spirit who bideth by himself,
In the land of mist and snow"—[33]

for it is snowing and hailing eternally, and will kill all the lambs to a certainty, unless it changes in a few hours. At any rate, it will cure us of the embarrassments arising from plenty and low markets. Much good luck to your dramatic exertions: when I can be of use, command me. Mrs. Scott joins me in regards to Mrs. Terry, and considers the house as the greatest possible bargain: the situation is all you can wish. Adieu! yours truly,

WALTER SCOTT.

P. S.—On consideration, and comparing difficulties, I think I will settle with Campbell to take my name from the verses, as they stand in his collection. The verses themselves I cannot take away without imprudent explanations; and as they go to other music, and stand without any name, they will probably not be noticed, so you need give yourself no farther trouble on the score. I should like to see my copy: pray send it to the post-office, under cover to Mr. Freeling, whose unlimited privilege is at my service on all occasions.

Early in May appeared the novel of The Antiquary, which seems to have been begun a little before the close of 1815. It came out at a moment of domestic distress.

Throughout the year 1815, Major John Scott had been drooping. He died on the 8th of May, 1816; and I extract the letter in which this event was announced to Mr. Thomas Scott by his only surviving brother.

TO THOMAS SCOTT, ESQ., PAYMASTER OF THE 70TH REGIMENT, CANADA.

EDINBURGH, 15th May, 1816.

MY DEAR TOM,—This brings you the melancholy news of our brother John's concluding his long and lingering illness by death, upon Thursday last. We had thought it impossible he should survive the winter, but, as the weather became milder, he gathered strength, and went out several times. In the beginning of the week he became worse, and on Wednesday kept his bed. On Thursday, about two o'clock, they sent me an express to Abbotsford—the man reached me at nine. I immediately set out, and travelled all night—but had not the satisfaction to see my brother alive. He had died about four o'clock, without much pain, being completely exhausted. You will naturally feel most anxious about my mother's state of health and spirits. I am happy to say she has borne this severe shock with great firmness and resignation, is perfectly well in her health, and as strong in her mind as ever you knew her. She feels her loss, but is also sensible that protracted existence, with a constitution so irretrievably broken up, could have been no blessing. Indeed I must say, that, in many respects, her situation will be more comfortable on account of this removal, when the first shock is over; for to watch an invalid, and to undergo all the changes of a temper fretted by suffering, suited ill with her age and habits. The funeral, which took place yesterday, was decent and private, becoming our father's eldest son, and the head of a quiet family. After it, I asked Hay Donaldson and Mr. Macculloch[34] to look over his papers, in case there should be any testamentary provision, but none such was found; nor do I think he had any intention of altering the destination which divides his effects between his surviving brothers.—Your affectionate

W. S.

A few days afterwards, he hands to Mr. Thomas Scott a formal statement of pecuniary affairs; the result of which was, that the Major had left something not much under £6000. Major Scott, from all I have heard, was a sober, sedate bachelor, of dull mind and frugal tastes, who, after his retirement from the army, divided his time between his mother's primitive fireside, and the society of a few whist-playing brother officers, that met for an evening rubber at Fortune's tavern. But, making every allowance for his retired and thrifty habits, I infer that the payments made to each of the three brothers out of their father's estate must have, prior to 1816, amounted to £5000. From the letter conveying this statement (29th May), I extract a few sentences:—

DEAR TOM,—... Should the possession of this sum, and the certainty that you must, according to the course of nature, in a short space of years succeed to a similar sum of £3000 belonging to our mother, induce you to turn your thoughts to Scotland, I shall be most happy to forward your views with any influence I may possess; and I have little doubt that, sooner or later, something may be done. But, unfortunately, every avenue is now choked with applicants, whose claims are very strong; for the number of disbanded officers, and public servants dismissed in consequence of Parliament turning restive and refusing the income-tax, is great and increasing. Economy is the order of the day, and I assure you they are shaving properly close. It would, no doubt, be comparatively easy to get you a better situation where you are, but then it is bidding farewell to your country, at least for a long time, and separating your children from all knowledge of those with whom they are naturally connected. I shall anxiously expect to hear from you on your views and wishes. I think, at all events, you ought to get rid of the drudgery of the paymastership—but not without trying to exchange it for something else. I do not know how it is with you—but I do not feel myself quite so *young* as I was when we met last, and I should like well to see my only brother return to his own country and settle, without thoughts of leaving it, till it is exchanged for one that is dark and distant.... I left all Jack's personal trifles at my mother's disposal. There was nothing of the slightest value, excepting his gold watch, which was my sister's, and a good one. My mother says he had wished my son Walter should have it, as his male representative—which I can only accept on condition *your* little Walter will accept a similar token of regard from his remaining uncle.—Yours affectionately,

W. S.

The letter in which Scott communicated his brother's death to Mr. Morritt gives us his own original opinion of The Antiquary. It has also some remarks on the separation of Lord and Lady Byron—and the "domestic verses" of the noble poet.

TO J. B. S. MORRITT, ESQ., M. P., LONDON.

EDINBURGH, May 16, 1816.

MY DEAR MORRITT,—I have been occupied of late with scenes of domestic distress, my poor brother, Major John Scott, having last week closed a life which wasting disease had long rendered burthensome. His death, under all the circumstances, cannot be termed a subject of deep affliction; and though we were always on fraternal terms of mutual kindness and good-will, yet our habits of life, our taste for society and circles of friends, were so totally different, that there was less frequent intercourse between us than our connection and real liking to each other might have occasioned. Yet it is a heavy consideration to have lost the last but one who was interested in our early domestic life, our habits of boyhood, and our first friends and connections. It makes one look about and see how the scene has changed around him, and how he himself has been changed with it. My only remaining brother is in Canada, and seems to have an intention of remaining there; so that my mother, now upwards of eighty, has now only one child left to her out of thirteen whom she has borne. She is a most excellent woman, possessed, even at her advanced age, of all the force of mind and sense of duty which have carried her through so many domestic griefs, as the successive deaths of eleven children, some of them come to men and women's estate, naturally infers. She is the principal subject of my attention at present, and is, I am glad to say, perfectly well in body and composed in mind.

Nothing can give me more pleasure than the prospect of seeing you in September, which will suit our motions perfectly well. I trust I shall have an opportunity to introduce you to some of our glens which you have not yet seen. But I hope we shall have some mild weather before that time, for we are now in the seventh month of winter, which almost leads me to suppose that we shall see no summer this season. As for spring, that is past praying for. In the month of November last, people were skating in the neighborhood of Edinburgh; and now, in the middle of May, the snow is lying white on Arthur's Seat, and on the range of the Pentlands. It is really fearful, and the sheep are perishing by scores. *Jam satis terræ nivis*, etc., may well be taken up as the song of eighteen hundred and sixteen.

So Lord Byron's romance seems to be concluded for one while—and it is surely time, after he has announced, or rather they themselves have announced, half-a-dozen blackguard newspaper editors, to have been his confidants on the occasion. Surely it is a strange thirst of public fame that seeks such a road to it. But Lord Byron, with high genius and many points of a noble and generous feeling, has Childe Harolded himself, and outlawed himself, into too great a resemblance with the pictures of his imagination. He has one excuse, however, and it is a sad one. I have been reckoned to make a good hit enough at a pirate, or an outlaw, or a smuggling bandit; but I cannot say I was ever so much enchanted with my work as to think of carrying off a *drift* of my neighbor's sheep, or half a dozen of his milk cows. Only I remember, in the rough times, having a scheme with the Duke of Buccleuch, that when the worst came to the worst, we should repair Hermitage Castle, and live, like Robin Hood and his merry men, at the expense of all round us. But this presupposed a grand *bouleversement* of society. In the mean while, I think my noble friend is something like my old peacock, who chooses to bivouac apart from his lady, and sit below my bedroom window, to keep me awake with his screeching lamentation. Only I own he is not equal in melody to Lord Byron, for *Fare-thee-well—and if for ever*, etc., is a very sweet dirge indeed. After all, *C'est génie mal logé*, and that's all that can be said about it.

I am quite reconciled to your opinions on the income-tax, and am not at all in despair at the prospect of keeping £200 a year in my pocket, since the ministers can fadge without it. But their throwing the helve after the hatchet, and giving up the malt-duty because they had lost the other, was droll enough. After all, our fat friend[35] must learn to live within compass, and fire off no more crackers in the Park, for John Bull is getting dreadfully sore on all sides when money is concerned.

I sent you, some time since, The Antiquary. It is not so interesting as its predecessors—the period did not admit of so much romantic situation. But it has been more fortunate than any of them in the sale, for 6000 went off in the first six days, and it is now at press again; which is very flattering to the unknown author. Another incognito proposes immediately to resume the second volume of Triermain, which is at present in the state of the Bear and Fiddle.[36] Adieu, dear Morritt.

Ever yours,
WALTER SCOTT.

Speaking of his third novel in a letter of the same date to Terry, Scott says: "It wants the romance of Waverley and the adventure of Guy Mannering; and yet there is some salvation about it, for if a man will paint from nature, he will be likely to amuse those who are daily looking at it."

After a little pause of hesitation, The Antiquary attained popularity not inferior to Guy Mannering; and though the author appears for a moment to have shared the doubts which he read in the countenance of James Ballantyne, it certainly was, in the sequel, his chief favorite among all his novels. Nor is it difficult to account for this preference, without laying any stress on the fact, that, during a few short weeks, it was pretty commonly talked of as a falling off from its immediate predecessors—and that some minor critics reëchoed this stupid whisper in print. In that view, there were many of its successors that had much stronger claims on the parental instinct of protection. But the truth is, that although Scott's Introduction of 1830 represents him as pleased with fancying that, in the principal personage, he had embalmed a worthy friend of his boyish days, his own antiquarian propensities, originating perhaps in the kind attentions of George Constable of Wallace-Craigie, and fostered not a little, at about as ductile a period, by those of old Clerk of Eldin, and John Ramsay of Ochtertyre, had by degrees so developed themselves, that he could hardly, even when The Antiquary was published, have scrupled about recognizing a quaint caricature of the founder of Abbotsford Museum, in the inimitable portraiture of the Laird of Monkbarns. The Descriptive Catalogue of that collection, which he began towards the close of his life, but, alas, never finished, is entitled "Reliquiæ Trottcosianæ—or the Gabions of the late Jonathan Oldbuck, Esq."

But laying this, which might have been little more than a good-humored pleasantry, out of the question, there is assuredly no one of all his works on which more of his own early associations have left their image. Of those early associations, as his full-grown tastes were all the progeny, so his genius, in all its happiest efforts, was the "Recording Angel;" and when George Constable first expounded his "Gabions" to the child that was to immortalize his name, they were either wandering hand in hand over the field where the grass still grew rank upon the grave of *Balmawhapple*, or sauntering on the beach where the *Mucklebackets* of Prestonpans dried their nets, singing,—

"Weel may the boatie row, and better may she speed,
O weel may the boatie row that wins the bairns' bread"—

or telling wild stories about cliff-escapes and the funerals of shipwrecked fishermen.

Considered by itself, without reference to these sources of personal interest, this novel seems to me to possess, almost throughout, in common with its two predecessors, a kind of simple unsought charm, which the subsequent works of the series hardly reached, save in occasional snatches: like them it is, in all its humbler and softer scenes, the transcript of actual Scottish life, as observed by the man himself. And I think it must also be allowed that he has nowhere displayed his highest art, that of skilful contrast, in greater perfection. Even the tragic romance of Waverley does not set off its Macwheebles and Callum Begs better than the oddities of Jonathan Oldbuck and his circle are relieved, on the one hand, by the stately gloom of the Glenallans, on the other, by the stern affliction of the poor fisherman, who, when discovered repairing the "auld black bitch o' a boat" in which his boy had been lost, and congratulated by his visitor on being capable of the exertion, makes answer,—"And what would you have me to do, unless I wanted to see four children starve, because one is drowned? *It's weel wi' you gentles, that can sit in the house wi' handkerchers at your een, when ye lose a friend; but the like o' us maun to our wark again, if our hearts were beating as hard as my hammer.*"

It may be worth noting, that it was in correcting the proof sheets of this novel that Scott first took to equipping his chapters with mottoes of his own fabrication. On one occasion he happened to ask John Ballantyne, who was sitting by him, to hunt for a particular passage in Beaumont and Fletcher. John did as he was bid, but did not succeed in discovering the lines. "Hang it, Johnnie," cried Scott, "I believe I can make a motto sooner than you will find one." He did so accordingly; and from that hour, whenever memory failed to suggest an appropriate epigraph, he had recourse to the inexhaustible mines of "*old play*" or "*old ballad*," to which we owe some of the most exquisite verses that ever flowed from his pen.

Unlike, I believe, most men, whenever Scott neared the end of one composition, his spirits seem to have caught a new spring of buoyancy, and before the last sheet was sent from his desk, he had crowded his brain with the imagination of another fiction. The Antiquary was published, as we have seen, in May, but by the beginning of April he had already opened to the Ballantynes the plan of the first Tales of my Landlord; and—to say nothing of Harold the Dauntless, which he began shortly after The Bridal of Triermain was finished, and which he seems to have kept before him for two years as a congenial plaything, to be taken up whenever the coach brought no proof sheets to jog him as to serious matters—he had also, before this time, undertaken to write the historical department of the Register for 1814. Mr. Southey had, for reasons upon which I do not enter, discontinued his services to that work: and it was now doubly necessary, after trying for one year a less eminent hand, that if the work were not to be dropped altogether, some strenuous exertion should be made to sustain its character. Scott had not yet collected the materials requisite for his historical sketch of a year distinguished for the importance and complexity of its events; but these, he doubted not, would soon reach him, and he felt no hesitation about pledging himself to complete, not only that sketch, but four new volumes of prose romances—and his Harold the Dauntless also, if Ballantyne could make any suitable arrangement on that score—between the April and the Christmas of 1816.

The Antiquary had been published by Constable, but I presume that, in addition to the usual stipulations, he had been again, on that occasion, solicited to relieve John Ballantyne and Co.'s stock to an extent which he did not find quite convenient; and at all events he had of late shown a considerable reluctance to employ James Ballantyne and Co. as printers. One or other of these impediments is alluded to in a note of Scott's, which, though undated, has been pasted into John Ballantyne's private letter-book among the documents of the period in question. It is in these words:—

DEAR JOHN,—I have seen the great swab, who is supple as a glove, and will do ALL, which some interpret NOTHING. However, we shall do well enough.

W. S.

Constable had been admitted, almost from the beginning, into the *secret* of the Novels—and for that, among other reasons, it would have been desirable for the Novelist to have him continue the publisher without interruption; but Scott was led to suspect, that if he were called upon to conclude a bargain for a fourth novel before the third had made its appearance, his scruples as to the matter of *printing* might at least protract the treaty; and why Scott should have been urgently desirous of seeing the transaction settled before the expiration of the half-yearly term of Whitsunday is sufficiently explained by the fact, that though so much of the old unfortunate stock of John Ballantyne and Co. still remained on hand—and with it some occasional recurrence of commercial difficulty as to floating bills was to be expected—while James Ballantyne's management of the pecuniary affairs of the printing-house had continued to be highly negligent and irregular[37]—nevertheless, the sanguine author had gone on purchasing one patch of land after another, until his estate at Abbotsford had already grown from 150 to nearly 1000 acres. The property all about his original farm had been in the hands of various small holders (Scotticè *cock-lairds*;) these persons were sharp enough to understand, erelong, that their neighbor could with difficulty resist any temptation that might present itself in the shape of an offer of more acres; and thus he proceeded buying up lot after lot of unimproved ground, at extravagant prices,—his "appetite increasing by what it fed on," while the ejected yeomen set themselves down elsewhere, to fatten at their leisure upon the profits—most commonly the anticipated profits—of "The Scotch Novels."

He was ever and anon pulled up with a momentary misgiving,—and resolved that the latest acquisition should be the last, until he could get rid entirely of "John Ballantyne and Co." But John Ballantyne was, from the utter lightness of his mind, his incapacity to look a day before him, and his eager impatience to enjoy the passing hour, the very last man in the world who could, under such circumstances, have been a serviceable agent. Moreover, John, too, had his professional ambition: he was naturally proud of his connection, however secondary, with the publication of these works—and this connection, though subordinate, was still very profitable; he must have suspected, that should his name disappear altogether from the list of booksellers, it would be a very difficult matter for him to retain any concern in them; and I cannot, on the whole, but consider it as certain that, the first and more serious embarrassments being overcome, he was far from continuing to hold by his patron's anxiety for the total abolition of their unhappy copartnership. He, at all events, unless when some sudden emergency arose, flattered Scott's own gay imagination, by uniformly representing everything in the most smiling colors; and though Scott, in his replies, seldom failed to introduce some passing hint of caution—such as "*Nullum numen abest si sit prudentia*"—he more and more took home to himself the agreeable cast of his *Rigdum's* anticipations, and wrote to him in a vein as merry as his own;—*e. g.*—"As for our stock,

"'T will be wearing awa', John,
Like snaw-wreaths when it's thaw, John," etc., etc., etc.

I am very sorry, in a word, to confess my conviction that John Ballantyne, however volatile and light-headed, acted at this period with cunning selfishness, both by Scott and by Constable. He well knew that it was to Constable alone that his firm had more than once owed its escape from utter ruin and dishonor; and he must also have known, that had a fair straightforward effort been made for that purpose, after the triumphant career of the Waverley series had once commenced, nothing could have been more easy than to bring all the affairs of his "back-stock," etc., to a complete close, by entering into a distinct and candid treaty on that subject, in connection with the future works of the great Novelist, either with Constable or with any other first-rate house in the trade. But John, foreseeing that, were that unhappy concern quite out of the field, he must himself subside into a mere clerk of the printing company, seems to have parried the blow by the only arts of any consequence in which he ever was an adept. He appears to have systematically disguised from Scott the extent to which the whole Ballantyne concern had been sustained by Constable—especially during his Hebridean tour of 1814, and his Continental one of 1815— and prompted and enforced the idea of trying other booksellers from time to time, instead of adhering to Constable, merely for the selfish purposes,—first, of facilitating the immediate discount of bills;—secondly, of further perplexing Scott's affairs, the entire disentanglement of which would have been, as he fancied, prejudicial to his own personal importance.

It was resolved, accordingly, to offer the risk and half profits of the first edition of another new novel—or rather collection of novels—not to Messrs. Constable, but to Mr.

Murray of Albemarle Street, and Mr. Blackwood, who was then Murray's agent in Scotland; but it was at the same time resolved, partly because Scott wished to try another experiment on the public sagacity, but partly also, no question, from the wish to spare Constable's feelings, that the title-page of the Tales of my Landlord should not bear the magical words "By the Author of Waverley." The facility with which both Murray and Blackwood embraced such a proposal, as no untried novelist, being sane, could have dreamt of hazarding, shows that neither of them had any doubt as to the identity of the author. They both considered the withholding of the avowal on the forthcoming title-page as likely to check very much the first success of the book; but they were both eager to prevent Constable's acquiring a sort of prescriptive right to publish for the unrivalled novelist, and willing to disturb his tenure at this additional, and, as they thought it, wholly unnecessary risk.

How sharply the unseen parent watched this first negotiation of his *Jedediah Cleishbotham* will appear from one of his letters:—

TO MR. JOHN BALLANTYNE, HANOVER STREET, EDINBURGH.

ABBOTSFORD, April 29, 1816.

DEAR JOHN,—James has made one or two important mistakes in the bargain with Murray and Blackwood. Briefly as follows:—

1stly, Having only authority from me to promise 6000 copies, he proposes they shall have the copyright *forever*. I will see their noses cheese first.

2dly, He proposes I shall have twelve months' bills—I have always got six. However, I would not stand on that.

3dly, He talks of volumes being put into the publisher's hands to consider and decide on. No such thing; a bare perusal at St. John Street[38] only.

Then for omissions—It is NOT stipulated that we supply the paper and print of successive editions. This must be nailed, and not left to understanding.—Secondly, I will have London bills as well as Blackwood's.

If they agree to these conditions, good and well. If they demur, Constable must be instantly tried; giving half to the Longmans, and *we* drawing on *them* for that moiety, or Constable lodging their bill in our hands. You will understand it is a four-volume touch—a work totally different in style and structure from the others; a new cast, in short, of the net which has hitherto made miraculous draughts. I do not limit you to terms, because I think you will make them better than I can do. But he must do more than others, since he will not or cannot print with us. For every point but that, I would rather deal with Constable than any one; he has always shown himself spirited, judicious, and liberal. Blackwood must be brought to the point*instantly*; and *whenever* he demurs, Constable must be treated with; for there is no use in suffering the thing to be blown on. At the same time, you need not conceal from him that there were some proposals elsewhere, but you may add, with truth, I would rather close with him. Yours truly,

W. S.

P. S.—I think Constable should jump at this affair; for I believe the work will be very popular.

Messrs. Murray and Blackwood agreed to all the author's conditions here expressed. They also relieved John Ballantyne and Co. of stock to the value of £500; and at least Mr. Murray must, moreover, have subsequently consented to anticipate the period of his payments. At all events, I find, in a letter of Scott's, dated in the subsequent August, this new echo of the old advice:—

TO MR. JOHN BALLANTYNE.

DEAR JOHN,—I have the pleasure to enclose Murray's acceptances. I earnestly recommend to you to push, realizing as much as you can.

"Consider weel, gude man,
We hae but borrowed gear;
The horse that I ride on,br> It is John Murray's mear."

Yours truly,

W. SCOTT.

I know not how much of the tale of The Black Dwarf had been seen by Blackwood, in St. John Street, before he concluded this bargain for himself and his friend Murray; but when the closing sheets of that novel reached him, he considered them as by no means sustaining the delightful promise of the opening ones. He was a man of strong talents, and, though without anything that could be called learning, of very respectable information—greatly superior to what has, in this age, been common in his profession; acute, earnest, eminently zealous in whatever he put his hand to; upright, honest, sincere, and courageous. But as Constable owed his first introduction to the upper world of literature and of society in general to his Edinburgh Review, so did Blackwood his to the Magazine, which has now made his name familiar to the world—and at the period of which I write, that miscellany was unborn; he was known only as a diligent antiquarian bookseller of the old town of Edinburgh, and the Scotch agent of the great London publisher, Murray. The abilities, in short, which he lived to develop, were as yet unsuspected—unless, perhaps, among a small circle; and the knowledge of the world, which so few men gather from anything but painful collision with various conflicting orders of their fellow-men, was not his. He was to the last plain and blunt; at this time I can easily believe him to have been so to a degree which Scott might look upon as "ungracious"—I take the epithet from one of his letters to James Ballantyne. Mr. Blackwood, therefore, upon reading what seemed to him the lame and impotent conclusion of a well-begun story, did not search about for any glossy periphrase, but at once requested James Ballantyne to inform the unknown author that such was his opinion. This might possibly have been endured; but Blackwood, feeling, I have no doubt, a genuine enthusiasm for the author's fame, as well as a just tradesman's anxiety as to his own adventure, proceeded to suggest the outline of what would, in his judgment, be a better upwinding of the plot of The Black Dwarf, and concluded with announcing his willingness, in case the proposed alteration were agreed to, that the whole expense of cancelling and reprinting a certain number of sheets should be charged to his own account. He appears to have further indicated that he had taken counsel with some literary person, on whose taste he placed great reliance, and who, if he had not originated, at least approved of the proposed process of recasting. Had Scott never possessed any such system of inter-agency as the Ballantynes supplied, he would, among other and perhaps greater inconveniences, have escaped that of the want of personal familiarity with several persons, with whose confidence,—and why should I not add?—with the innocent gratification of whose little vanities—his own pecuniary interests were often deeply connected. A very little personal contact would have introduced such a character as Blackwood's to the respect, nay, to the affectionate respect, of Scott, who, above all others, was ready to sympathize cordially with honest and able men, in whatever condition of life he discovered them. He did both know and appreciate Blackwood better in after-times; but in 1816, when this communication reached him, the name was little more than a name, and his answer to the most solemn of go-betweens was in these terms, which I sincerely wish I could tell how Signior Aldiborontiphoscophornio translated into any dialect submissible to Blackwood's apprehension:—

DEAR JAMES,—

I have received Blackwood's impudent proposal. G— d— his soul! Tell him and his coadjutor that I belong to the Black Hussars of Literature, who neither give nor receive criticism. I'll be cursed but this is the most impudent proposal that ever was made.

W. S.[39]

While these volumes were in progress, Scott found time to make an excursion into Perthshire and Dumbartonshire, for the sake of showing the scenery, made famous in The Lady of the Lake and Waverley, to his wife's old friends, Miss Dumergue and Mrs. Sarah Nicolson,[40] who had never before been in Scotland. The account which he gives of these ladies' visit at Abbotsford, and this little tour, in a letter to Mr. Morritt, shows the "Black Hussar of Literature" in his gentler and more habitual mood.

TO J. B. S. MORRITT, ESQ., M. P., ROKEBY PARK.

ABBOTSFORD, 21st August, 1816.

MY DEAR MORRITT,—I have not had a moment's kindly leisure to answer your kind letter, and to tell how delighted I shall be to see you in this least of all possible dwellings, but

47

where we, nevertheless, can contrive a pilgrim's quarters and the warmest welcome for you and any friend of your journey;—if young Stanley, so much the better. Now, as to the important business with the which I have been occupied: You are to know we have had our kind hostesses of Piccadilly upon a two months' visit to us. We owed them so much hospitality, that we were particularly anxious to make Scotland agreeable to the good girls. But, alas, the wind has blown, and the rain has fallen, in a style which beats all that ever I remembered. We accomplished, with some difficulty, a visit to Loch Katrine and Loch Lomond, and, by dint of the hospitality of Cambusmore and the Ross, we defied bad weather, wet roads, and long walks. But the weather settled into regular tempest, when we settled at Abbotsford; and, though the natives, accustomed to bad weather (though not at such a time of year), contrived to brave the extremities of the season, it only served to increase the dismay of our unlucky visitors, who, accustomed only to Paris and London, expected *fiacres* at the Milestone Cross, and a pair of oars at the Deadman's Haugh. Add to this a strong disposition to *commérage*, when there was no possibility of gratifying it, and a total indisposition to scenery or rural amusements, which were all we had to offer—and you will pity both hosts and guests. I have the gratification to think I fully supported the hospitality of my country. I walked them to death, I talked them to death, I showed them landscapes which the driving rain hardly permitted them to see, and told them of feuds about which they cared as little as I do about their next-door news in Piccadilly. Yea, I even played at cards, and as I had Charlotte for a partner, so ran no risk of being scolded, I got on pretty well. Still the weather was so execrable, that, as the old drunken landlord used to say at Arroquhar, "I was perfectly ashamed of it;" and, to this moment, I wonder how my two friends fought it out so patiently as they did. But the young people and the cottages formed considerable resources. Yesterday they left us, deeply impressed with the conviction, which I can hardly blame, that the sun never shone in Scotland,—which that noble luminary seems disposed to confirm, by making this the first fair day we have seen this month—so that his beams will greet them at Longtown, as if he were determined to put Scotland to utter shame.

In you I expect a guest of a different calibre; and I think (barring downright rain) I can promise you some sport of one kind or other. We have a good deal of game about us; and Walter, to whom I have resigned my gun and license, will be an excellent attendant. He brought in six brace of moor-fowl on the 12th, which had (*si fas est dicere*) its own effect in softening the minds of our guests towards this unhappy climate. In other respects things look melancholy enough here. Corn is, however, rising, and the poor have plenty of work, and wages which, though greatly inferior to what they had when hands were scarce, assort perfectly well with the present state of the markets. Most folks try to live as much on their own produce as they can, by way of fighting off distress; and though speculating farmers and landlords must suffer, I think the temporary ague-fit will, on the whole, be advantageous to the country. It will check that inordinate and unbecoming spirit of expense, or rather extravagance, which was poisoning all classes, and bring us back to the sober virtues of our ancestors. It will also have the effect of teaching the landed interest, that their connection with their farmers should be of a nature more intimate than that of mere payment and receipt of rent, and that the largest offerer for a lease is often the person least entitled to be preferred as a tenant. Above all, it will complete the destruction of those execrable quacks, terming themselves land-doctors, who professed, from a two days' scamper over your estate, to tell you its constitution,—in other words its value,—acre by acre. These men, paid according to the golden hopes they held out, afforded by their reports one principal means of deceiving both landlord and tenant, by setting an ideal and extravagant value upon land, which seemed to entitle the one to expect, and the other to offer, rent far beyond what any expectation formed by either, upon their own acquaintance with the property, could rationally have warranted. More than one landed gentleman has cursed, in my presence, the day he ever consulted one of those empirics, whose prognostications induced him to reject the offers of substantial men, practically acquainted with the *locale*.

Ever, my dear Morritt, most truly yours,
WALTER SCOTT.

In October, 1816, appeared the Edinburgh Annual Register, containing Scott's historical sketch of the year 1814—a composition which would occupy at least four such volumes as the reader has now in his hand.[41] Though executed with extraordinary rapidity, the sketch is as clear as spirited; but I need say no more of it here, as the author travels mostly over the same ground again in his Life of Napoleon.

Scott's correspondence proves, that during this autumn he had received many English guests besides the good spinsters of Piccadilly and Mr. Morritt. I regret to add, it also proves that he had continued all the while to be annoyed with calls for money from John Ballantyne; yet before the 12th of November called him to Edinburgh, he appears to have nearly finished the first Tales of my Landlord. He had, moreover, concluded a negotiation with Constable and Longman for a series of Letters on the History of Scotland: of which, however, if he ever wrote any part, the MS. has not been discovered. It is probable that he may have worked some detached fragments into his long-subsequent Tales of a Grandfather.[42] The following letter shows likewise that he was now busy with plans of building at Abbotsford, and deep in consultation on that subject with an artist eminent for his skill in Gothic architecture,—Mr. Edward Blore:—

TO DANIEL TERRY, ESQ.

November 12, 1816.

MY DEAR TERRY,—I have been shockingly negligent in acknowledging your repeated favors; but it so happened, that I have had very little to *say*, with a great deal to *do*; so that I trusted to your kindness to forgive my apparent want of kindness, and indisputable lack of punctuality. You will readily suppose that I have heard with great satisfaction of the prosperity of your household, particularly of the good health of my little namesake and his mother. Godmothers of yore used to be fairies; and though only a godfather, I think of sending you, one day, a *fairy*gift—a little drama, namely, which, if the audience be indulgent, may be of use to him. Of course, you will stand godfather to it yourself: it is yet only in embryo—a sort of poetical Hans in Kelder—nor am I sure when I can bring him forth; not for this season, at any rate. You will receive, in the course of a few days, my late *whereabouts* in four volumes: there are two tales—the last of which I really prefer to any fictitious narrative I have yet been able to produce—the first is wish-washy enough. The subject of the second tale lies among the old Scottish Cameronians—nay, I'll tickle ye off a Covenanter as readily as old Jack could do a young Prince; and a rare fellow he is, when brought forth in his true colors. Were it not for the necessity of using Scriptural language, which is essential to the character, but improper for the stage, it would be very dramatic. But of all this you will judge by and by. To give the go-by to the public, I have doubled and leaped into my form, like a hare in snow: that is, I have changed my publisher, and come forth like a maiden knight's white shield (there is a conceit!) without any adhesion to fame gained in former adventures (another!) or, in other words, with a virgin title-page (another!)—I should not be so light-hearted about all this, but that it is very nearly finished and out, which is always a blithe moment for Mr. Author. And now to other matters. The books came safe, and were unpacked two days since, on our coming to town—most ingeniously were they stowed in the legs of the very handsome stand for Lord Byron's vase, with which our friend George Bullock has equipped me. I was made very happy to receive him at Abbotsford, though only for a start; and no less so to see Mr. Blore, from whom I received your last letter. He is a very fine young man, modest, simple, and unaffected in his manners, as well as a most capital artist. I have had the assistance of both these gentlemen in arranging an addition to the cottage at Abbotsford, intended to connect the present farmhouse with the line of low buildings to the right of it. Mr. Bullock will show you the plan, which I think is very ingenious. He has promised to give it his consideration with respect to the interior; and Mr. Blore has drawn me a very handsome elevation, both to the road and to the river. I expect to get some decorations from the old Tolbooth of Edinburgh, particularly the cope-stones of the doorway, or lintels, as we call them, and a *niche* or two—one very handsome indeed! Better get a niche *from* the Tolbooth than a niche *in* it, to which such building operations are apt to bring the projectors. This addition will give me: first, a handsome boudoir, in which I intend to place Mr. Bullock's Shakespeare,[43] with his superb cabinet, which serves as a pedestal. This opens into the little drawing-room, to which it serves as a chapel of ease; and on the other side, to a handsome dining-parlor of 27 feet by 18, with three windows to the north, and one to the south,—the last to be Gothic, and filled with stained glass. Besides these commodities, there is a small conservatory or greenhouse; and a study for myself, which we design to fit up with ornaments from Melrose Abbey. Bullock made several casts with his own hands—masks, and so forth, delightful for cornices, etc.

Do not let Mrs. Terry think of the windows till little Wat is duly cared after.[44] I am informed by Mr. Blore that he is a fine thriving fellow, very like papa. About my armorial bearings: I will send you a correct drawing as I can get hold of Blore; namely—of the scutcheons of my grandsires on each side, and my own. I could detail them in the jargon of heraldry, but it is better to speak to your eyes by translating them into colored drawings, as the sublime science of armory has fallen into some neglect of late years, with all its mascles, buckles, crescents, and boars of the first, second, third, and fourth.

I was very sorry I had no opportunity of showing attention to your friend Mr. Abbot, not being in town at the time. I grieve to say that neither the genius of Kean nor the charms of Miss O'Neill could bring me from the hillside and the sweet society of Tom Purdie. All our family are very well—Walter as tall nearly as I am, fishing salmon and shooting moor-fowl and blackcock, in good style; the girls growing up, and, as yet, not losing their simplicity of character; little Charles excellent at play, and not deficient at learning, when the young dog will take pains. Abbotsford is looking pretty at last, and the planting is making some show. I have now several hundred acres thereof, running out as far as beyond the lake. We observe with great pleasure the steady rise which you make in public opinion, and expect, one day, to hail you stage-manager. Believe me, my dear Terry, always very much yours,

W. SCOTT.

P. S.—The Counsellor and both the Ballantynes are well and hearty.

JOHN MURRAY
From the painting by Pickersgill.

On the first of December, the first series of the Tales of my Landlord appeared, and notwithstanding the silence of the title-page, and the change of publishers, and the attempt which had certainly been made to vary the style both of delineation and of language, all doubts whether they were or were not from the same hand with Waverley had worn themselves out before the lapse of a week.—The enthusiasm of their reception among the highest literary circles of London may be gathered from the following letter:—

TO WALTER SCOTT, ESQ., EDINBURGH.

ALBEMARLE STREET, 14th December, 1816.

DEAR SIR,—Although I dare not address you as the author of certain "Tales" (which, however, must be written either by Walter Scott or the Devil), yet nothing can restrain me from thinking it is to your influence with the author that I am indebted for the essential honor of being one of their publishers, and I must intrude upon you to offer my most hearty thanks—not divided, but doubled—alike for my worldly gain therein, and for the great acquisition of professional reputation which their publication has already procured me. I believe I might, under any oath that could be proposed, swear that I never experienced such unmixed pleasure as the reading of this exquisite work has afforded me; and if you could see me, as the author's literary chamberlain, receiving the unanimous and vehement praises of every one who has read it, and the curses of those whose needs my scanty supply could not satisfy, you might judge of the sincerity with which I now entreat you to assure him of the most complete success. Lord Holland said, when I asked his opinion—"Opinion! We did not one of us go to bed last night—nothing slept but my gout." Frere, Hallam, Boswell,[45] Lord Glenbervie, William Lamb,[46] all agree that it surpasses all the other novels. Gifford's estimate is increased at every reperusal. Heber says there are only two men in the world—Walter Scott and Lord Byron. Between you, you have given existence to a third—Ever your faithful servant,

JOHN MURRAY.

To this cordial effusion Scott returned the following answer. It was necessary, since he had fairly resolved against compromising his incognito, that he should be prepared not only to repel the impertinent curiosity of strangers, but to evade the proffered congratulations of overflowing kindness. He contrived, however, to do so, on this and all similar occasions, in a style of equivoque which could never be seriously misunderstood:[47]—

TO JOHN MURRAY, ESQ., ALBEMARLE STREET, LONDON.
EDINBURGH, 18th December, 1816.

MY DEAR SIR,—I give you heartily joy of the success of the Tales, although I do not claim that paternal interest in them which my friends do me the credit to assign me. I assure you I have never read a volume of them until they were printed, and can only join with the rest of the world in applauding the true and striking portraits which they present of old Scottish manners. I do not expect implicit reliance to be placed on my disavowal, because I know very well that he who is disposed not to own a work must necessarily deny it, and that otherwise his secret would be at the mercy of all who choose to ask the question, since silence in such a case must always pass for consent, or rather assent. But I have a mode of convincing you that I am perfectly serious in my denial—pretty similar to that by which Solomon distinguished the fictitious from the real mother—and that is, by reviewing the work, which I take to be an operation equal to that of quartering the child. But this is only on condition I can have Mr. Erskine's assistance, who admires the work greatly more than I do, though I think the painting of the second Tale both true and powerful. I knew Old Mortality very well; his name was Paterson, but few knew him otherwise than by his nickname. The first Tale is not very original in its concoction, and lame and impotent in its conclusion. My love to Gifford. I have been over head and ears in work this summer, or I would have sent the Gypsies; indeed I was partly stopped by finding it impossible to procure a few words of their language.

Constable wrote to me about two months since, desirous of having a new edition of Paul; but not hearing from you, I conclude you are still on hand. Longman's people had then only sixty copies.

Kind compliments to Heber, whom I expected at Abbotsford this summer; also to Mr. Croker and all your four o'clock visitors. I am just going to Abbotsford to make a small addition to my premises there. I have now about 700 acres, thanks to the booksellers and the discerning public. Yours truly,

WALTER SCOTT.

P. S.—I have much to ask about Lord Byron if I had time. The third canto of the Childe is inimitable. Of the last poems, there are one or two which indicate rather an irregular play of imagination.[48] What a pity that a man of such exquisite genius will not be contented to be happy on the ordinary terms![49] I declare my heart bleeds when I think of him, self-banished from the country to which he is an honor.[50]

Mr. Murray, gladly embracing this offer of an article for his journal on the Tales of my Landlord, begged Scott to take a wider scope, and dropping all respect for the idea of a divided parentage, to place together any materials he might have for the illustration of the Waverley Novels in general; he suggested in particular, that, instead of drawing up a long-promised disquisition on the Gypsies in a separate shape, whatever he had to say concerning that picturesque generation might be introduced by way of comment on the character of Meg Merrilies. What Scott's original conception had been I know not; he certainly gave his review all the breadth which Murray could have wished, and, *inter alia*, diversified it with a few anecdotes of the Scottish Gypsies. But the late excellent biographer of John Knox, Dr. Thomas M'Crie, had, in the mean time, considered the representation of the Covenanters, in the story of Old Mortality, as so unfair as to demand at his hands a very serious rebuke. The Doctor forthwith published, in a magazine called the Edinburgh Christian Instructor, a set of papers, in which the historical foundations of that tale were attacked with indignant warmth; and though Scott, when he first heard of these invectives, expressed his resolution never even to read them, he found the impression they were producing so strong, that he soon changed his purpose, and finally devoted a very large part of his article for the Quarterly Review to an elaborate defence of his own picture of the Covenanters.[51]

Before the first Tales of my Landlord were six weeks old, two editions of 2000 copies disappeared, and a third of 2000 was put to press; but notwithstanding this rapid success, which was still further continued, and the friendly relations which always subsisted between the author and Mr. Murray, circumstances erelong occurred which carried the publication of the work into the hands of Messrs. Constable.

The author's answer to Dr. M'Crie, and his Introduction of 1830, have exhausted the historical materials on which he constructed his Old Mortality; and the origin of The Black Dwarf—as to the conclusion of which story he appears on reflection to have completely adopted the opinion of honest Blackwood—has already been sufficiently illustrated by an anecdote of his early wanderings in Tweeddale. The latter tale, however imperfect, and unworthy as a work of art to be placed high in the catalogue of his productions, derives a singular interest from its delineation of the dark feelings so often connected with physical deformity; feelings which appear to have diffused their shadow over the whole genius of Byron—and which, but for this single picture, we should hardly have conceived ever to have passed through Scott's happier mind.[52] All the bitter blasphemy of spirit which, from infancy to the tomb, swelled up in Byron against the unkindness of nature; which sometimes perverted even his filial love into a sentiment of diabolical malignity; all this black and desolate train of reflections must have been encountered and deliberately subdued by the manly parent of The Black Dwarf. Old Mortality, on the other hand, is remarkable as the *novelist's* first attempt to repeople the past by the power of imagination working on materials furnished by books. In Waverley he revived the fervid dreams of his boyhood, and drew, not from printed records, but from the artless oral narratives of his *Invernahyles*. In Guy Mannering and The Antiquary he embodied characters and manners familiar to his own wandering youth. But whenever his letters mention Old Mortality in its progress, they represent him as strong in the confidence that the industry with which he had pored over a library of forgotten tracts would enable him to identify himself with the time in which they had birth, as completely as if he had listened with his own ears to the dismal sermons of Peden, ridden with Claverhouse and Dalzell in the rout of Bothwell, and been an advocate at the bar of the Privy Council, when Lauderdale catechised and tortured the assassins of Archbishop Sharp. To reproduce a departed age with such minute and lifelike accuracy as this tale exhibits, demanded a far more energetic sympathy of imagination than had been called for in any effort of his serious verse. It is indeed most curiously instructive for any student of art to compare the Roundheads of Rokeby with the Bluebonnets of Old Mortality. For the rest—the story is framed with a deeper skill than any of the preceding novels: the canvas is a broader one; the characters are contrasted and projected with a power and felicity which neither he nor any other master ever surpassed; and, notwithstanding all that has been urged against him as a disparager of the Covenanters, it is to me very doubtful whether the inspiration of romantic chivalry ever prompted him to nobler emotions than he has lavished on the re-animation of their stern and solemn enthusiasm. This work has always appeared to me the Marmion of his novels.[53]

I have disclaimed the power of farther illustrating its historical groundworks, but I am enabled by Mr. Train's kindness to give some interesting additions to Scott's own account of this novel as a composition. The generous Supervisor visited him in Edinburgh in May, 1816, a few days after the publication of The Antiquary, carrying with him several relics which he wished to present to his collection; among others a purse that had belonged to Rob Roy, and also a fresh heap of traditionary gleanings, which he had gathered among the tale-tellers of his district. One of these last was in the shape of a letter to Mr. Train from a Mr. Broadfoot, "schoolmaster at the clachan of Penningham, and author of the *celebrated song* of the Hills of Galloway"—with which I confess myself unacquainted. Broadfoot had facetiously signed his communication *Clashbottom*,—"a professional appellation derived," says Mr. Train, "from the use of the birch, and by which he was usually addressed among his companions,—who assembled, not at the Wallace Inn of Gandercleuch, but at the sign of the Shoulder of Mutton in Newton-Stewart." Scott received these gifts with benignity, and invited the friendly donor to breakfast next morning. He found him at work in his library, and surveyed with enthusiastic curiosity the furniture of the room, especially its only picture, a portrait of Graham of Claverhouse. Train expressed the surprise with which every one, who had known Dundee only in the pages of the Presbyterian Annalists, must see for the first time that beautiful and melancholy visage, worthy of the most pathetic dreams of romance. Scott replied, "that no character had been so foully traduced as the Viscount of

Dundee; that, thanks to Wodrow, Cruickshanks, and such chroniclers, he, who was every inch a soldier and a gentleman, still passed among the Scottish vulgar for a ruffian desperado, who rode a goblin horse, was proof against shot, and in league with the Devil." "Might he not," said Mr. Train, "be made, in good hands, the hero of a national romance as interesting as any about either Wallace or Prince Charlie?" "He might," said Scott, "but your western zealots would require to be faithfully portrayed in order to bring him out with the right effect."[54] "And what," resumed Train, "if the story were to be delivered as if from the mouth of *Old Mortality*? Would *he* not do as well as *the Minstrel* did in the Lay?" "Old Mortality!" said Scott—"who was he?" Mr. Train then told what he could remember of old Paterson, and seeing how much his story interested the hearer, offered to inquire farther about that enthusiast on his return to Galloway. "Do so by all means," said Scott; "I assure you I shall look with anxiety for your communication." He said nothing at this time of his own meeting with Old Mortality in the churchyard of Dunnottar—and I think there can be no doubt that that meeting was thus recalled to his recollection; or that to this intercourse with Mr. Train we owe the whole machinery of the Tales of my Landlord, as well as the adoption of Claverhouse's period for the scene of one of its first fictions. I think it highly probable that we owe a further obligation to the worthy Supervisor's presentation of Rob Roy's *spleuchan*.

The original design for the First Series of Jedediah Cleishbotham was, as Scott told me, to include four separate tales illustrative of four districts of the country, in the like number of volumes; but, his imagination once kindled upon any theme, he could not but pour himself out freely—so that notion was soon abandoned.[Back to Contents]

CHAPTER XXXVIII.

HAROLD THE DAUNTLESS PUBLISHED. — SCOTT ASPIRES TO BE A BARON OF THE EXCHEQUER. — LETTER TO THE DUKE OF BUCCLEUCH CONCERNING POACHERS, ETC. — FIRST ATTACK OF CRAMP IN THE STOMACH. — LETTERS TO MORRITT, TERRY, AND MRS. MACLEAN CLEPHANE. — STORY OF THE DOOM OF DEVORGOIL. — JOHN KEMBLE'S RETIREMENT FROM THE STAGE. — WILLIAM LAIDLAW ESTABLISHED AT KAESIDE. — NOVEL OF ROB ROY PROJECTED. — LETTER TO SOUTHEY ON THE RELIEF OF THE POOR, ETC. — LETTER TO LORD MONTAGU ON HOGG'S QUEEN'S WAKE, AND ON THE DEATH OF FRANCES, LADY DOUGLAS.

1817.

Within less than a month, The Black Dwarf and Old Mortality were followed by "Harold the Dauntless, by the author of The Bridal of Triermain." This poem had been, it appears, begun several years back; nay, part of it had been actually printed before the appearance of Childe Harold, though that circumstance had escaped the author's remembrance when he penned, in 1830, his Introduction to The Lord of the Isles; for he there says, "I am still astonished at my having committed the gross error of selecting the very name which Lord Byron had made so famous." The volume was published by Messrs. Constable, and had, in those booksellers' phrase, "considerable success." It has never, however, been placed on a level with Triermain; and though it contains many vigorous pictures, and splendid verses, and here and there some happy humor, the confusion and harsh transitions of the fable, and the dim rudeness of character and manners, seem sufficient to account for this inferiority in public favor. It is not surprising that the author should have redoubled his aversion to the notion of any more serious performances in verse. He had seized on an instrument of wider compass, and which, handled with whatever rapidity, seemed to reveal at every touch treasures that had hitherto slept unconsciously within him. He had thrown off his fetters, and might well go forth rejoicing in the native elasticity of his strength.

It is at least a curious coincidence in literary history, that, as Cervantes, driven from the stage of Madrid by the success of Lope de Vega, threw himself into prose romance, and produced, at the moment when the world considered him as silenced forever, the Don Quixote which has outlived Lope's two thousand triumphant dramas—so Scott, abandoning verse to Byron, should have rebounded from his fall by the only prose romances, which seem to be classed with the masterpiece of Spanish genius, by the general judgment of Europe.

I shall insert two letters, in which he announces the publication of Harold the Dauntless. In the first of them he also mentions the light and humorous little piece entitled The Sultan of Serendib, or the Search after Happiness, originally published in a weekly paper, after the fashion of the old Essayists, which about this time issued from John Ballantyne's premises, under the appropriate name of "The SALE-ROOM." The paper had slender success; and though Scott wrote several things for it, none of them, except this metrical essay, attracted any notice. The Sale-Room was, in fact, a dull and hopeless concern; and I should scarcely have thought it worth mentioning, but for the confirmation it lends to my suspicion that Mr. John Ballantyne was very unwilling, after all his warnings, to retire completely from the field of publishing.

TO J. B. S. MORRITT, ESQ., M. P., ROKEBY PARK.
EDINBURGH, January 30, 1817.

MY DEAR MORRITT,—I hope to send you in a couple of days Harold the Dauntless, which has not turned out so good as I thought it would have done. I begin to get too old and stupid, I think, for poetry, and will certainly never again adventure on a grand scale. For amusement, and to help a little publication that is going on here, I have spun a doggerel tale called The Search after Happiness, of which I shall send you a copy by post, if it is of a frankable size; if not, I can put it up with the Dauntless. Among other misfortunes of Harold is his name, but the thing was partly printed before Childe Harold was in question.

My great and good news at present is, that the bog (that perpetual hobby-horse) has produced a commodity of most excellent marle, and promises to be of the very last consequence to my wild ground in the neighborhood; for nothing can equal the effect of marle as a top-dressing. Methinks (in my mind's eye, Horatio) I see all the blue-bank, the hinny-lee, and the other provinces of my poor kingdom, waving with deep rye-grass and clover, like the meadows at Rokeby. In honest truth, it will do me yeoman's service.

My next good tidings are, that Jedediah carries the world before him. Six thousand have been disposed of, and three thousand more are pressing onward, which will be worth £2500 to the worthy pedagogue of Gandercleuch. Some of the Scotch Whigs, of the right old fanatical leaven, have waxed wroth with Jedediah,—

"But shall we go mourn for that, my dear?
The cold moon shines by night,
And when we wander here and there,
We then do go most right."[55]

After all, these honest gentlemen are like Queen Elizabeth in their ideas of portrait-painting. They require the pictures of their predecessors to be likenesses, and at the same time demand that they shall be painted without shade, being probably of opinion, with the virgin majesty of England, that there is no such thing in nature.

I presume you will be going almost immediately to London—at least all our Scotch members are requested to be at their posts, the meaning of which I cannot pretend to guess. The finances are the only ticklish matter, but there is, after all, plenty of money in the country, now that our fever-fit is a little over. In Britain, when there is the least damp upon the spirits of the public, they are exactly like people in a crowd, who take the alarm, and shoulder each other to and fro till some dozen or two of the weakest are borne down and trodden to death; whereas, if they would but have patience and remain quiet, there would be a safe and speedy end to their embarrassment. How we want Billie Pitt now to get up and give the tone to our feelings and opinions!

As I take up this letter to finish the same, I hear the Prince Regent has been attacked and fired at. Since he was not hurt (for I should be sincerely sorry for my fat friend), I see nothing but good luck to result from this assault. It will make him a good manageable boy, and, I think, secure you a quiet session of Parliament.—Adieu, my dear Morritt, God bless you. Let me know if the gimcracks come safe—I mean the book, etc.

Ever yours,
WALTER SCOTT.

TO THE LADY LOUISA STUART, GLOUCESTER PLACE, LONDON.
EDINBURGH, January 31, 1817.

MY DEAR LADY LOUISA,—This accompanies Harold the Dauntless. I thought once I should have made it something clever, but it turned vapid upon my imagination; and I finished it at last with hurry and impatience. Nobody knows, that has not tried the feverish trade of poetry, how much it depends upon mood and whim. I don't wonder, that, in dismissing all the other deities of Paganism, the Muse should have been retained by common consent; for, in sober reality, writing good verses seems to depend upon something separate from the volition of the author. I sometimes think my fingers set up for themselves, independent of my head; for twenty times I have begun a thing on a certain plan, and never in my life adhered to it (in a work of imagination, that is) for half an hour together. I would hardly write this sort of egotistical trash to any one but yourself, yet it is very true for all that. What my kind correspondent had anticipated on account of Jedediah's effusions has actually taken place; and the author of a very good Life of Knox has, I understand, made a most energetic attack, upon the score that the old Covenanters are not treated with decorum. I have not read it, and certainly never shall. I really think there is nothing in the book that is not very fair and legitimate subject of raillery; and I own I have my suspicions of that very susceptible devotion which so readily takes offence: such men should not read books of amusement; but do they suppose, because they are virtuous, and choose to be thought outrageously so, "there shall be no cakes and ale"?—"Ay, by our lady, and ginger shall be hot in the mouth too."[56] As for the consequences to the author, they can only affect his fortune or his temper—the former, such as it is, has been long fixed beyond shot of these sort of fowlers; and for my temper, I considered always, that by subjecting myself to the irritability which much greater authors have felt on occasions of literary dispute, I should be laying in a plentiful stock of unhappiness for the rest of my life. I therefore make it a rule never to read the attacks made upon me. I remember being capable of something like this sort of self-denial at a very early period of life, for I could not be six years old. I had been put into my bed in the nursery, and two servant girls sat down by the embers of the fire, to have their own quiet chat, and the one began to tell a most dismal ghost story, of which I remember the commencement distinctly at this moment; but perceiving which way the tale was tending, and though necessarily curious, being at the same time conscious that, if I listened on, I should be frightened out of my wits for the rest of the night, I had the force to cover up my head in the bed-clothes, so that I could not hear another word that was said. The only inconvenience attending a similar prudential line of conduct in the present case is, that it may seem like a deficiency of spirit; but I am not much afraid of that being laid to my charge—my fault in early life (I hope long since corrected) having lain rather the other way. And so I say, with mine honest Prior,—

"Sleep, Philo, untouch'd, on my peaceable shelf,
Nor take it amiss that so little I heed thee;
I've no malice at thee, and some love for myself—
Then why should I answer, since first I must read thee?"

So you are getting finely on in London. I own I am very glad of it. I am glad the banditti act like banditti, because it will make men of property look round them in time. This country is very like the toys which folks buy for children, and which, tumble them about in any way the urchins will, are always brought to their feet again, by the lead deposited in their extremities. The mass of property has the same effect on our Constitution, and is a sort of ballast which will always *right* the vessel, to use a sailor's phrase, and bring it to its due equipoise.

Ministers have acted most sillily in breaking up the burgher volunteers in large towns. On the contrary, the service should have been made coercive. Such men have a moral effect upon the minds of the populace, besides their actual force, and are so much interested in keeping good order, that you may always rely on them, especially as a corps in which there is necessarily a common spirit of union and confidence. But all this is nonsense again, quoth my Uncle Toby to himself. Adieu, my dear Lady Louisa; my sincere good wishes always attend you.

W. S.

Not to disturb the narrative of his literary proceedings, I have deferred until now the mention of an attempt which Scott made during the winter of 1816-1817, to exchange his seat at the Clerk's table for one on the Bench of the Scotch Court of Exchequer. It had often occurred to me, in the most prosperous years of his life, that such a situation would have suited him better in every respect than that which he held, and that his never attaining a promotion, which the Scottish public would have considered so naturally due to his character and services, reflected little honor on his political allies. But at the period when I was entitled to hint this to him, he appeared to have made up his mind that the rank of Clerk of Session was more compatible than that of a Supreme Judge with the habits of a literary man, who was perpetually publishing, and whose writings were generally of the imaginative order. I had also witnessed the zeal with which he seconded the views of more than one of his own friends, when their ambition was directed to the Exchequer Bench. I remained, in short, ignorant that he ever had seriously thought of it for himself, until the ruin of his worldly fortunes in 1826; nor had I any information that his wish to obtain it had ever been distinctly stated, until certain letters, one of which I shall introduce, were placed in my hands after his death, by the present Duke of Buccleuch. The late Duke's answers to these letters are also before me; but of them it is sufficient to say, that while they show the warmest anxiety to serve Scott, they refer to private matters, which rendered it inconsistent with his Grace's feelings to interfere at the time in question with the distribution of Crown patronage. I incline to think, on the whole, that the death of this nobleman, which soon after left the influence of his house in abeyance, must have, far more than any other circumstance, determined Scott to renounce all notions of altering his professional position.

    TO THE DUKE OF BUCCLEUCH, ETC., ETC.

    EDINBURGH, 11th December, 1816.

    MY DEAR LORD DUKE,—Your Grace has been so much my constant and kind friend and patron through the course of my life, that I trust I need no apology for thrusting upon your consideration some ulterior views, which have been suggested to me by my friends, and which I will either endeavor to prosecute, time and place serving, or lay aside all thoughts of, as they appear to your Grace feasible, and likely to be forwarded by your patronage. It has been suggested to me, in a word, that there would be no impropriety in my being put in nomination as a candidate for the situation of a Baron of Exchequer, when a vacancy shall take place. The difference of the emolument between that situation and those which I now hold, is just £400 a year, so that, in that point of view, it is not a very great object. But there is a difference in the rank, and also in the leisure afforded by a Baron's situation; and a man may, without condemnation, endeavor, at my period of life, to obtain as much honor and ease as he can handsomely come by. My pretensions to such an honor (next to your Grace's countenancing my wishes) would rest very much on the circumstance that my nomination would vacate two good offices (Clerk of Session and Sheriff of Selkirkshire) to the amount of £1000 and £300 a year; and, besides, would extinguish a pension of £300 which I have for life, over and above my salary as Clerk of Session, as having been in office at the time when the Judicature Act deprived us of a part of our vested fees and emoluments. The extinction of this pension would be just so much saved to the public. I am pretty confident also that I should be personally acceptable to our friend the Chief Baron.[57] But whether all or any of these circumstances will weigh much in my favor, must solely and entirely rest with your Grace, without whose countenance it would be folly in me to give the matter a second thought. *With* your patronage, both my situation and habits of society may place my hopes as far as any who are likely to apply; and your interest would be strengthened by the opportunity of placing some good friend in Selkirkshire, besides converting the Minstrel of the Clan into a Baron,—a transmutation worthy of so powerful and kind a chief. But if your Grace thinks I ought to drop thoughts of this preferment, I am bound to say, that I think myself as well provided for by my friends and the public as I have the least title to expect, and that I am perfectly contented and grateful for what I have received. Ever your Grace's faithful and truly obliged servant,

    WALTER SCOTT.

    The following letter, to the same noble friend, contains a slight allusion to this affair of the Barony; but I insert it for a better reason. The Duke had, it seems, been much annoyed by some depredations on his game in the district of Ettrick Water; and more so by the ill use which some boys from Selkirk made of his liberality in allowing the people of that town free access to his beautiful walks on the banks of the Yarrow, adjoining Newark and Bowhill. The Duke's forester, by name Thomas Hudson, had recommended rigorous measures with reference to both these classes of offenders, and the Sheriff was of course called into council:—

TO HIS GRACE THE DUKE OF BUCCLEUCH, ETC., ETC., ETC.

ABBOTSFORD, January 11, 1817.

MY DEAR LORD DUKE,—I have been thinking anxiously about the disagreeable affair of Tom Hudson, and the impudent ingratitude of the Selkirk rising generation, and I will take the usual liberty your friendship permits me, of saying what occurs to me on each subject. Respecting the shooting, the crime is highly punishable, and we will omit no inquiries to discover the individuals guilty. Charles Erskine, who is a good police-officer, will be sufficiently active. I know my friend and kinsman, Mr. Scott of Harden, feels very anxious to oblige your Grace, and I have little doubt that if you will have the goodness to mention to him this unpleasant circumstance, he would be anxious to put his game under such regulations as should be agreeable to you. But I believe the pride and pleasure he would feel in obliging your Grace, as heading one of the most ancient and most respectable branches of your name (if I may be pardoned for saying so much in our favor), would be certainly much more gratified by a compliance with your personal request, than if it came through any other channel. Your Grace knows there are many instances in life in which the most effectual way of conferring a favor is condescending to accept one. I have known Harden long and most intimately—a more respectable man, either for feeling, or talent, or knowledge of human life, is rarely to be met with. But he is rather indecisive—requiring some instant stimulus in order to make him resolve to do, not only what he knows to be right, but what he really wishes to do, and means to do one time or other. He is exactly Prior's Earl of Oxford:—

"Let that be done which Mat doth say."
"Yea," quoth the Earl, "*but not to-day.*"

And so exit Harden, and enter Selkirk.

I know hardly anything more exasperating than the conduct of the little blackguards, and it will be easy to discover and make an example of the biggest and most insolent. In the mean while, my dear Lord, pardon my requesting you will take no general or sweeping resolution as to the Selkirk folks. Your Grace lives near them—your residence, both from your direct beneficence, and the indirect advantages which they derive from that residence, is of the utmost consequence; and they must be made sensible that all these advantages are endangered by the very violent and brutal conduct of their children. But I think your Grace will be inclined to follow this up only for the purpose of correction, not for that of requital. They are so much beneath you, and so much in your power, that this would be unworthy of you—especially as all the inhabitants of the little country town must necessarily be included in the punishment. Were your Grace really angry with them, and acting accordingly, you might ultimately feel the regret of my old schoolmaster, who, when he had knocked me down, apologized by saying he did not know his own strength. After all, those who look for anything better than ingratitude from the uneducated and unreflecting mass of a corrupted population, must always be deceived; and the better the heart is that has been expanded towards them, their wants and their wishes, the deeper is the natural feeling of disappointment. But it is our duty to fight on, doing what good we can (and surely the disposition and the means were never more happily united than in your Grace), and trusting to God Almighty, whose grace ripens the seeds we commit to the earth, that our benefactions shall bear fruit. And now, my Lord, asking your pardon for this discharge of my conscience, and assuring your Grace I have no wish to exchange my worsted gown, or the remote *Pisgah* exchange of a silk one, for the cloak of a Presbyterian parson, even with the certainty of succeeding to the first of your numerous Kirk-presentations, I take the liberty to add my own opinion. The elder boys must be looked out and punished, and the parents severely reprimanded, and the whole respectable part of the town made sensible of the loss they must necessarily sustain by the discontinuance of your patronage. And at, or about the same time, I should think it proper if your Grace were to distinguish by any little notice such Selkirk people working with you as have their families under good order.

I am taking leave of Abbotsford *multum gemens*, and have been just giving directions for planting upon *Turn-again*. When shall we eat a cold luncheon there, and look at the view, and root up the monster in his abyss? I assure you none of your numerous vassals can show a finer succession of *distant* prospects. For the home-view—ahem!—We must wait till the trees grow.

Ever your Grace's truly faithful

W. SCOTT.

While the abortive negotiation as to the exchequer was still pending, Scott was visited, for the first time since his childish years, with a painful illness, which proved the harbinger of a series of attacks, all nearly of the same kind, continued at short intervals during more than two years. Various letters, already introduced, have indicated how widely his habits of life when in Edinburgh differed from those of Abbotsford. They at all times did so to a great extent; but he had pushed his liberties with a most robust constitution to a perilous extreme while the affairs of the Ballantynes were laboring, and he was now to pay the penalty.

This first serious alarm occurred towards the close of a merry dinner-party in Castle Street (on the 5th of March), when Scott suddenly sustained such exquisite torture from cramp in the stomach, that his masculine powers of endurance gave way, and he retired from the room with a scream of agony which electrified his guests. This scene was often repeated, as we shall see presently. His friends in Edinburgh continued all that spring in great anxiety on his account. Scarcely, however, had the first symptoms yielded to severe medical treatment, than he is found to have beguiled the intervals of his suffering by planning a dramatic piece on a story supplied to him by one of Train's communications, which he desired to present to Terry, on behalf of the actor's first-born son who had been christened by the name of Walter Scott.[58] Such was the origin of the Fortunes of Devorgoil—a piece which, though completed soon afterwards, and submitted by Terry to many manipulations with a view to the stage, was never received by any manager, and was first published, towards the close of the author's life, under the title, slightly altered for an obvious reason, of The Doom of Devorgoil. The sketch of the story which he gives in the following letter will probably be considered by many besides myself as well worth the drama. It appears that the actor had mentioned to Scott his intention of *Terryfying* The Black Dwarf.

TO DANIEL TERRY, ESQ., LONDON.

EDINBURGH, 12th March, 1817.

DEAR TERRY,—I am now able to write to you on your own affairs, though still as weak as water from the operations of the medical faculty, who, I think, treated me as a recusant to their authority, and having me once at advantage, were determined I should not have strength to rebel again in a hurry. After all, I believe it was touch and go; and considering how much I have to do for my own family and others, my elegy might have been that of the Auld Man's Mare,—

"The peats and turf are all to lead,
What ail'd the beast to die?"

You don't mention the nature of your undertaking in your last, and in your former you spoke both of the Black Dwarf and of Triermain. I have some doubts whether the town will endure a second time the following up a well-known tale with a dramatic representation—and there is no *vis comica* to redeem the Black Dwarf, as in the case of Dominie Sampson. I have thought of two subjects for you, if, like the Archbishop's homilies, they do not smell of the apoplexy. The first is a noble and very dramatic tradition preserved in Galloway, which runs briefly thus: The Barons of Plenton (the family name, I think, was —— by Jupiter, forgot!) boasted of great antiquity, and formerly of extensive power and wealth, to which the ruins of their huge castle, situated on an inland loch, still bear witness. In the middle of the seventeenth century, it is said, these ruins were still inhabited by the lineal descendant of this powerful family. But the ruinous halls and towers of his ancestors were all that had descended to him, and he cultivated the garden of the castle, and sold its fruits for a subsistence. He married in a line suitable rather to his present situation than the dignity of his descent, and was quite sunk into the rank of peasantry, excepting that he was still called—more in mockery, or at least in familiarity, than in respect—the Baron of Plenton. A causeway connected the castle with the mainland; it was

58

cut in the middle, and the moat only passable by a drawbridge which yet subsisted, and which the poor old couple contrived to raise every night by their joint efforts, the country being very unsettled at the time. It must be observed that the old man and his wife occupied only one apartment in the extensive ruins, a small one adjoining to the drawbridge; the rest was waste and dilapidated.

As they were about to retire one night to rest, they were deterred by a sudden storm which, rising in the wildest manner possible, threatened to bury them under the ruins of the castle. While they listened in terror to the complicated sounds of thunder, wind, and rain, they were astonished to hear the clang of hoofs on the causeway, and the voices of people clamoring for admittance. This was a request not rashly to be granted. The couple looked out, and dimly discerned through the storm that the causeway was crowded with riders. "How many of you are there?" demanded John.—"Not more than the hall will hold," was the answer; "but open the gate, lower the bridge, and do not keep the *ladies* in the rain."— John's heart was melted for the *ladies*, and, against his wife's advice, he undid the bolts, sunk the drawbridge, and bade them enter in the name of God. Having done so, he instantly retired into his *sanctum sanctorum* to await the event, for there was something in the voices and language of his guests that sounded mysterious and awful. They rushed into the castle, and appeared to know their way through all its recesses. Grooms were heard hurrying their horses to the stables—sentinels were heard mounting guard—a thousand lights gleamed from place to place through the ruins, till at length they seemed all concentrated in the baronial hall, whose range of broad windows threw a resplendent illumination on the moss-grown court below.

After a short time, a domestic, clad in a rich but very antique dress, appeared before the old couple, and commanded them to attend his lord and lady in the great hall. They went with tottering steps, and to their great terror found themselves in the midst of a most brilliant and joyous company; but the fearful part of it was, that most of the guests resembled the ancestors of John's family, and were known to him by their resemblance to pictures which mouldered in the castle, or by traditionary description. At the head, the founder of the race, dressed like some mighty baron, or rather some Galwegian prince, sat with his lady. There was a difference of opinion between these ghostly personages concerning our honest John. The chief was inclined to receive him graciously; the lady considered him, from his mean marriage, as utterly unworthy of their name and board. The upshot is, that the chief discovers to his descendant the means of finding a huge treasure concealed in the castle; the lady assures him that the discovery shall never avail him.—In the morning no trace can be discovered of the singular personages who had occupied the hall. But John sought for and discovered the vault where the spoils of the Southrons were concealed, rolled away the covering stone, and feasted his eyes on a range of massy chests of iron, filled doubtless with treasure. As he deliberated on the best means of bringing them up, and descending into the vault, he observed it began slowly to fill with water. Bailing and pumping were resorted to, and when he had exhausted his own and his wife's strength, they summoned the assistance of the neighborhood. But the vengeance of the visionary lady was perfect; the waters of the lake had forced their way into the vault, and John, after a year or two spent in draining and so forth, died broken-hearted, the last Baron of Plenton.

Such is the tale, of which the incidents seem new, and the interest capable of being rendered striking; the story admits of the highest degree of decoration, both by poetry, music, and scenery, and I propose (in behalf of my godson) to take some pains in dramatizing it. As thus;—you shall play John, as you can speak a little Scotch; I will make him what the Baron of Bradwardine would have been in his circumstances, and he shall be alternately ridiculous from his family pride and prejudices, contrasted with his poverty, and respectable from his just and independent tone of feeling and character. I think Scotland is entitled to have something on the stage to balance Macklin's two worthies.[59] You understand the dialect will be only tinged with the national dialect—not that the baron is to speak broad Scotch, while all the others talk English. His wife and he shall have one child, a daughter, suitored unto by the conceited young parson or schoolmaster of the village, whose addresses are countenanced by her mother,—and by Halbert the hunter, a youth of unknown descent. Now this youth shall be the rightful heir and representative of the English owners of the treasure, of which they had been robbed by the baron's ancestors, for which unjust act, their spirits still walked the earth. These, with a substantial character or two, and the ghostly personages, shall mingle as they may—and the discovery of the youth's birth shall break the spell of the treasure-chamber. I will make the ghosts talk as never ghosts talked in the body or out of it; and the music may be as unearthly as you can get it. The rush of the shadows into the castle shall be seen through the window of the baron's apartment in the flat scene. The ghosts' banquet, and many other circumstances, may give great exercise to the scene-painter and dresser. If you like this plan, you had better suspend any other for the present. In my opinion it has the infinite merit of being perfectly new in plot and structure, and I will set about the sketch as soon as my strength is restored in some measure by air and exercise. I am sure I can finish it in a fortnight then. Ever yours truly,

    W. SCOTT.

About the time when this letter was written, a newspaper paragraph having excited the apprehension of two—or I should say three—of his dearest friends, that his life was in actual danger, Scott wrote to them as follows:—

TO J. B. S. MORRITT, ESQ., M. P., PORTLAND PLACE, LONDON.
EDINBURGH, 20th March, 1817.

MY DEAR MORRITT,—I hasten to acquaint you that I am in the land of life, and thriving, though I have had a slight shake, and still feel the consequences of medical treatment. I had been plagued all through this winter with cramps in my stomach, which I endured as a man of mould might, and endeavored to combat them by drinking scalding water, and so forth. As they grew rather unpleasantly frequent, I had reluctant recourse to Baillie. But before his answer arrived on the 5th, I had a most violent attack, which broke up a small party at my house, and sent me to bed roaring like a bull-calf. All sorts of remedies were applied, as in the case of Gil Blas's pretended colic, but such was the pain of the real disorder, that it outdevilled the Doctor hollow. Even heated salt, which was applied in such a state that it burned my shirt to rags, I hardly felt when clapped to my stomach. At length the symptoms became inflammatory, and dangerously so, the seat being the diaphragm. They only gave way to very profuse bleeding and blistering, which under higher assistance saved my life. My recovery was slow and tedious from the state of exhaustion. I could neither stir for weakness and giddiness, nor read for dazzling in my eyes, nor listen for a whizzing sound in my ears, nor even think for lack of the power of arranging my ideas. So I had a comfortless time of it for about a week. Even yet I by no means feel, as the copy-book hath it,

    "The lion bold, which the lamb doth hold—"

on the contrary, I am as weak as water. They tell me (of course) I must renounce every creature comfort, as my friend Jedediah calls it. As for dinner and so forth, I care little about it—but toast and water, and three glasses of wine, sound like hard laws to me. However, to parody the lamentation of Hassan, the camel-driver,

    "The lily health outvies the grape's bright ray,
And life is dearer than the usquebæ—"

so I shall be amenable to discipline. But in my own secret mind I suspect the state of my bowels more than anything else. I take enough of exercise and enough of rest; but unluckily they are like a Lapland year, divided as one night and one day. In the vacation I never sit down; in the session-time I seldom rise up. But all this must be better arranged in future; and I trust I shall live to weary out all your kindness.

I am obliged to break off hastily. I trust I shall be able to get over the Fell in the end of summer, which will rejoice me much, for the sound of the woods of Rokeby is lovely in mine ear. Ever yours,

    WALTER SCOTT.

TO MRS. MACLEAN CLEPHANE, OF TORLOISK, MULL.
EDINBURGH, 23d March, 1817.

MY DEAR MRS. AND MISS CLEPHANE,—Here comes to let you know you had nearly seen the last sight of me, unless I had come to visit you on my red beam like one of Fingal's heroes, which, Ossianic as you are, I trow you would readily dispense with. The cause was a cramp in my stomach, which, after various painful visits, as if it had been sent by Prospero, and had mistaken me for Caliban, at length chose to conclude by setting fire to its lodging, like the Frenchmen as they retreated through Russia, and placed me in as proper a state of inflammation as if I had had the whole Spafields committee in my unfortunate stomach. Then bleeding and blistering was the word; and they bled and blistered till they left me neither skin nor blood. However, they beat off the foul fiend, and I am bound to praise the bridge which carried me over. I am still very totterish, and very giddy, kept to panada, or rather to porridge, for I spurned at all foreign slops, and adhered to our ancient oatmeal manufacture.[60] But I have no apprehension of any return of the serious part of the malady, and I am now recovering my strength, though looking somewhat cadaverous upon the occasion.

I much approve of your going to Italy by sea; indeed it is the only way you ought to think of it. I am only sorry you are going to leave us for a while; but indeed the isle of Mull might be Florence to me in respect of separation, and cannot be quite Florence to you, since Lady Compton is not there. I lately heard her mentioned in a company where my interest in her was not known, as one of the very few English ladies now in Italy whom their acquirements, conduct, and mode of managing time, induce that part of foreign society, whose approbation is valuable, to consider with high respect and esteem. This I think is very likely; for, whatever folks say of foreigners, those of good education and high rank among them, must have a supreme contempt for the frivolous, dissatisfied, empty, gad-about manners of many of our modern belles. And we may say among ourselves, that there are few upon whom high accomplishments and information sit more gracefully.

John Kemble is here to take leave, acting over all his great characters, and with all the spirit of his best years. He played Coriolanus last night (the first time I have ventured out) fully as well as I ever saw him; and you know what a complete model he is of the Roman. He has made a great reformation in his habits; given up wine, which he used to swallow by pailfuls,—and renewed his youth like the eagles. He seems to me always to play best those characters in which there is a predominating tinge of some overmastering passion, or acquired habit of acting and speaking, coloring the whole man. The patrician pride of Coriolanus, the stoicism of Brutus and Cato, the rapid and hurried vehemence of Hotspur, mark the class of characters I mean. But he fails where a ready and pliable yielding to the events and passions of life makes what may be termed a more natural personage. Accordingly I think his Macbeth, Lear, and especially his Richard, inferior in spirit and truth. In Hamlet, the natural fixed melancholy of the prince places him within Kemble's range;— yet many delicate and sudden turns of passion slip through his fingers. He is a lordly vessel, goodly and magnificent when going large before the wind, but wanting the facility to go "*ready about*," so that he is sometimes among the breakers before he can wear ship. Yet we lose in him a most excellent critic, an accomplished scholar, and one who graced our forlorn drama with what little it has left of good sense and gentlemanlike feeling. And so exit he. He made me write some lines to speak when he withdraws, and he has been here criticising and correcting till he got them quite to his mind, which has rather tired me.

Most truly yours while
WALTER SCOTT.

On the 29th of March, 1817, John Philip Kemble, after going through the round of his chief parts, to the delight of the Edinburgh audience, took his final leave of them as Macbeth, and in the costume of that character delivered a farewell address, penned for him by Scott.[61] No one who witnessed that scene, and heard the lines as then recited, can ever expect to be again interested to the same extent by anything occurring within the walls of a theatre; nor was I ever present at any public dinner in all its circumstances more impressive than was that which occurred a few days afterwards, when Kemble's Scotch friends and admirers assembled around him—Francis Jeffrey being chairman, Walter Scott and John Wilson the croupiers.

Shortly before this time, Mr. William Laidlaw had met with misfortunes, which rendered it necessary for him to give up the lease of a farm, on which he had been for some years settled, in Mid-Lothian. He was now anxiously looking about him for some new establishment, and it occurred to Scott that it might be mutually advantageous, as well as agreeable, if his excellent friend would consent to come and occupy a house on his property,

61

and endeavor, under his guidance, to make such literary exertions as might raise his income to an amount adequate for his comfort. The prospect of obtaining such a neighbor was, no doubt, the more welcome to "Abbotsford and Kaeside," from its opening at this period of fluctuating health; and Laidlaw, who had for twenty years loved and revered him, considered the proposal with far greater delight than the most lucrative appointment on any noble domain in the island could have afforded him. Though possessed of a lively and searching sagacity as to things in general, he had always been as to his own worldly interests simple as a child. His tastes and habits were all modest; and when he looked forward to spending the remainder of what had not hitherto been a successful life, under the shadow of the genius that he had worshipped almost from boyhood, his gentle heart was all happiness. He surveyed with glistening eyes the humble cottage in which his friend proposed to lodge him, his wife, and his little ones, and said to himself that he should write no more sad songs on *Forest Flittings*.[62]

Scott's notes to him at this time afford a truly charming picture of thoughtful and respectful delicacy on both sides. Mr. Laidlaw, for example, appears to have hinted that he feared his friend, in making the proposal as to the house at Kaeside, might have perhaps in some degree overlooked the feelings of "Laird Moss," who, having sold his land several months before, had as yet continued to occupy his old homestead. Scott answers:—

TO MR. W. LAIDLAW.

EDINBURGH, April 5, 1817.

MY DEAR SIR,—Nothing can give me more pleasure than the prospect of your making yourself comfortable at Kaeside till some good thing casts up. I have not put Mr. Moss to any inconvenience, for I only requested an answer, giving him leave to sit if he had a mind—and of free will he leaves my premises void and redd at Whitsunday. I suspect the house is not in good order, but we shall get it brushed up a little. Without affectation I consider myself the obliged party in this matter—or at any rate it is a mutual benefit, and you shall have grass for a cow, and so forth—whatever you want. I am sure when you are so near I shall find some literary labor for you that will make ends meet. Yours, in haste,

W. SCOTT.

He had before this time made considerable progress in another historical sketch (that of the year 1815) for the Edinburgh Annual Register; and the first literary labor which he provided for Laidlaw appears to have been arranging for the same volume a set of newspaper articles, usually printed under the head of *Chronicle*, to which were appended some little extracts of new books of travels, and the like miscellanies. The Edinburgh Monthly Magazine, subsequently known by the name of its projector, Blackwood, commenced in April of this year; and one of its editors, Mr. Thomas Pringle, being a Teviotdale man and an old acquaintance of Laidlaw's, offered to the latter the care of its *Chronicle department* also,—not perhaps without calculating that, in case Laidlaw's connection with the new journal should become at all a strict one, Scott would be induced to give it occasionally the benefit of his own literary assistance. He accordingly did not write—being unwell at the time—but *dictated* to Pringle a collection of anecdotes concerning Scottish gypsies, which attracted a good deal of notice;[63] and, I believe, he also assisted Laidlaw in drawing up one or more articles on the subject of Scottish superstitions. But the bookseller and Pringle soon quarrelled, and the Magazine assuming, on the retirement of the latter, a high Tory character, Laidlaw's Whig feelings induced him to renounce its alliance; while Scott, having no kindness for Blackwood personally, and disapproving (though he chuckled over it) the reckless extravagance of juvenile satire which, by and by, distinguished his journal, appears to have easily acquiesced in the propriety of Laidlaw's determination. I insert meantime a few notes, which will show with what care and kindness he watched over Laidlaw's operations for the Annual Register.

TO MR. LAIDLAW, AT KAESIDE.

EDINBURGH, June 16, 1817.

DEAR SIR,—I enclose you "rare guerdon," better than remuneration,—namely, a cheque for £25, for the Chronicle part of the Register. The incidents selected should have some reference to amusement as well as information, and may be occasionally abridged in the narration; but, after all, paste and scissors form your principal materials. You must look out for two or three good original articles; and, if you would read and take pains to abridge one or two curious books of travels, I would send out the volumes. Could I once get the head of the concern fairly round before the wind again, I am sure I could make it £100 a year to you. In the present instance it will be at least £50.

Yours truly,

W. S.

TO THE SAME.

EDINBURGH, July 3, 1817.

MY DEAR SIR,—I send you Adam's and Riley's Travels. You will observe I don't want a review of the books, or a detail of these persons' adventures, but merely a short article expressing the light, direct or doubtful, which they have thrown on the interior of Africa. "Recent Discoveries in Africa" will be a proper title. I hope to find you materially amended, or rather quite stout, when I come out on Saturday. I am quite well this morning. Yours, in haste,

W. S.

P. S.—I add Mariner's Tonga Islands, and Campbell's Voyage. Pray take great care of them, as I am a coxcomb about my books, and hate specks or spots. Take care of yourself, and want for nothing that Abbotsford can furnish.

These notes have carried us down to the middle of the year. But I must now turn to some others, which show that before Whitsuntide, when Laidlaw settled at Kaeside, negotiations were on foot respecting another novel.

TO MR. JOHN BALLANTYNE, HANOVER STREET, EDINBURGH.

ABBOTSFORD, Monday. [April, 1817.]

DEAR JOHN,—I have a good subject for a work of fiction *in petto*. What do you think Constable would give for a smell of it? You ran away without taking leave the other morning, or I wished to have spoken to you about it. I don't mean a continuation of Jedediah, because there might be some delicacy in putting that by the original publishers. You may write if anything occurs to you on this subject. It will not interrupt my History. By the way, I have a great lot of the Register ready for delivery, and no man asks for it. I shall want to pay up some cash at Whitsunday, which will make me draw on my brains. Yours truly,

W. SCOTT.

TO THE SAME.

ABBOTSFORD, Saturday, May 3, 1817.

DEAR JOHN,—I shall be much obliged to you to come here with Constable on Monday, as he proposes a visit, and it will save time. By the way, you must attend that the usual quantity of stock is included in the arrangement—that is £600 for 6000 copies. My sum is £1700, payable in May—a round advance, by'r Lady, but I think I am entitled to it, considering what I have twined off hitherto on such occasions.

I make a point on your coming with Constable, health allowing. Yours truly,

W. S.

The result of this meeting is indicated in a note, scribbled by John Ballantyne at the bottom of the foregoing letter, before it was seen by his brother the printer:—

Half-past 3 o'clock, Tuesday.

DEAR JAMES,—I am at this moment returned from Abbotsford, with entire and full success. Wish me joy. I shall gain above £600—Constable taking my share of stock also. This title is *Rob Roy—by the Author of Waverley!!!* Keep this letter for me.

J. B.

On the same page there is written, in fresher ink, which marks, no doubt, the time when John pasted it into his collection of private papers now before me,—

N. B.—I did gain above £1200.—J. B.

The title of this novel was suggested by Constable, and he told me years afterwards the difficulty he had to get it adopted by the author. "What!" said he, "Mr. Accoucheur, must you be setting up for Mr. Sponsor too?—but let's hear it." Constable said the name of the real hero would be the best possible name for the book. "Nay," answered Scott, "never let me have to write up to a name. You well know I have generally adopted a title that told nothing."—The bookseller, however, persevered; and after the trio had dined, these scruples gave way.

On rising from table, according to Constable, they sallied out to the green before the door of the cottage, and all in the highest spirits enjoyed the fine May evening. John Ballantyne, hopping up and down in his glee, exclaimed, "Is Rob's gun here, Mr. Scott; would you object to my trying the auld barrel with a *few de joy*?"—"Nay, Mr. Puff," said Scott, "it would burst, and blow you to the devil before your time."—"Johnny, my man," said Constable, "what the mischief puts drawing at sight into *your* head?" Scott laughed heartily at this innuendo; and then observing that the little man felt somewhat sore, called attention to the notes of a bird in the adjoining shrubbery. "And by the bye," said he, as they continued listening, "'tis a long time, Johnny, since we have had the Cobbler of Kelso." Mr. Puff forthwith jumped up on a mass of stone, and seating himself in the proper attitude of one working with his awl, began a favorite interlude, mimicking a certain son of Crispin, at whose stall Scott and he had often lingered when they were schoolboys, and a blackbird, the only companion of his cell, that used to sing to him, while he talked and whistled to it all day long. With this performance Scott was always delighted: nothing could be richer than the contrast of the bird's wild sweet notes, some of which he imitated with wonderful skill, and the accompaniment of the Cobbler's hoarse cracked voice, uttering all manner of endearing epithets, which Johnny multiplied and varied in a style worthy of the Old Women in Rabelais at the birth of Pantagruel. I often wondered that Mathews, who borrowed so many good things from John Ballantyne, allowed this Cobbler, which was certainly the masterpiece, to escape him.

Scott himself had probably exceeded that evening the three glasses of wine sanctioned by his Sangrados. "I never," said Constable, "had found him so disposed to be communicative about what he meant to do. Though he had had a return of his illness but the day before, he continued for an hour or more to walk backwards and forwards on the green, talking and laughing—he told us he was sure he should make a hit in a Glasgow weaver, whom he would *ravel up with Rob*; and fairly outshone the Cobbler, in an extempore dialogue between the bailie and the cateran—something not unlike what the book gives us as passing in the Glasgow tolbooth."

Mr. Puff might well exult in the "full and entire success" of this trip to Abbotsford. His friend had made it a *sine qua non* with Constable that he should have a third share in the bookseller's moiety of the bargain—and though Johnny had no more trouble about the publishing or selling of Rob Roy than his own Cobbler of Kelso, this stipulation had secured him a *bonus* of £1200, before two years passed. Moreover, one must admire his adroitness in persuading Constable, during their journey back to Edinburgh, to relieve him of that fraction of his own old stock, with which his unhazardous share in the new transaction was burdened. Scott's kindness continued, as long as John Ballantyne lived, to provide for him a constant succession of similar advantages at the same easy rate; and Constable, from deference to Scott's wishes, and from his own liking for the humorous auctioneer, appears to have submitted with hardly a momentary grudge to this heavy tax on his most important ventures.

The same week Scott received Southey's celebrated letter to Mr. William Smith, M. P. for Norwich. The poet of Keswick had also forwarded to him somewhat earlier his Pilgrimage to Waterloo, which piece contains a touching allusion to the affliction the author had recently sustained in the death of a fine boy. Scott's letter on this occasion was as follows:—

TO ROBERT SOUTHEY, ESQ., KESWICK.

SELKIRK, May 9, 1817.

MY DEAR SOUTHEY,—I have been a strangely negligent correspondent for some months past, more especially as I have had you rarely out of my thoughts, for I think you will hardly doubt of my sincere sympathy in events which have happened since I have written. I shed sincere tears over the Pilgrimage to Waterloo. But in the crucible of human life, the purest gold is tried by the strongest heat, and I can only hope for the continuance of your present family blessings to one so well formed to enjoy the pure happiness they afford. My health has, of late, been very indifferent. I was very nearly succumbing under a violent inflammatory attack, and still feel the effects of the necessary treatment. I believe they took one third of the blood of my system, and blistered in proportion: so that both my flesh and my blood have been in a woefully reduced state. I got out here some weeks since, where, by dint of the insensible exercise which one takes in the country, I feel myself gathering strength daily, but am still obliged to observe a severe regimen. It was not to croak about myself, however, that I took up the pen, but to wish you joy of your triumphant answer to that coarse-minded William Smith. He deserved all he has got, and, to say the truth, you do not spare him, and have no cause. His attack seems to have proceeded from the vulgar insolence of a low mind desirous of attacking genius at disadvantage. It is the ancient and eternal strife of which the witch speaks in Thalaba. Such a man as he, feels he has no alliance with such as you, and his evil instincts lead him to treat as hostile whatever he cannot comprehend. I met Smith once during his stay in Edinburgh,[64] and had, what I seldom have with any one in society, a high quarrel with him. His mode of travelling had been from one gentleman's seat to another, abusing the well-known hospitality of the Highland lairds, by taking possession of their houses, even during their absence, domineering in them when they were present, and not only eating the dinner of to-day, but requiring that the dinner of to-morrow should also be made ready and carried forward with him, to save the expense of inns. All this was no business of mine, but when, in the middle of a company consisting of those to whom he had owed this hospitality, he abused the country, of which he knew little—the language, of which he knew nothing—and the people, who have their faults, but are a much more harmless, moral, and at the same time high-spirited population, than, I venture to say, he ever lived amongst—I thought it was really too bad, and so e'en took up the debate, and gave it him over the knuckles as smartly as I could. Your pamphlet, therefore, fed fat my ancient grudge against him as well as the modern one, for you cannot doubt that my blood boiled at reading the report of his speech. Enough of this gentleman, who, I think, will not walk out of the round in a hurry again, to slander the conduct of individuals.

I am at present writing at our head-court of freeholders—a set of quiet, unpretending, but sound-judging country gentlemen, and whose opinions may be very well taken as a fair specimen of those men of sense and honor, who are not likely to be dazzled by literary talent, which lies out of their beat, and who, therefore, cannot be of partial counsel in the cause; and I never heard an opinion more generally, and even warmly expressed, than that your triumphant vindication brands Smith as a slanderer in all time coming. I think you may not be displeased to know this, because what men of keen feelings and literary pursuits must have felt, cannot be unknown to you, and you may not have the same access to know the impression made upon the general class of society.

I have to thank you for the continuation of the History of Brazil—one of your gigantic labors; the fruit of a mind so active, yet so patient of labor. I am not yet far advanced in the second volume, reserving it usually for my hour's amusement in the evening, as children keep their dainties for *bonne bouche*: but as far as I have come, it possesses all the interest of the commencement, though a more faithless and worthless set than both Dutch and Portuguese I have never read of; and it requires your knowledge of the springs of human action, and your lively description of "hair-breadth 'scapes," to make one care whether the hog bites the dog, or the dog bites the hog. Both nations were in rapid declension from their short-lived age of heroism, and in the act of experiencing all those retrograde movements which are the natural consequence of selfishness on the one hand, and bigotry on the other.

I am glad to see you are turning your mind to the state of the poor. Should you enter into details on the subject of the best mode of assisting them, I would be happy to tell you the few observations I have made—not on a very small scale neither, considering my fortune, for I have kept about thirty of the laborers in my neighborhood in constant employment this winter. This I do not call charity, because they executed some extensive plantations and other works, which I could never have got done so cheaply, and which I always intended one day to do. But neither was it altogether selfish on my part, because I was putting myself to inconvenience in incurring the expense of several years at once, and certainly would not have done so, but to serve mine honest neighbors, who were likely to want work but for such exertion. From my observation, I am inclined greatly to doubt the salutary effect of the scheme generally adopted in Edinburgh and elsewhere for relieving the poor. At Edinburgh, they are employed on public works at so much a day—tenpence, I believe, or one shilling, with an advance to those who have families. This rate is fixed below that of ordinary wages, in order that no person may be employed but those who really cannot find work elsewhere. But it is attended with this bad effect, that the people regard it partly as charity, which is humiliating—and partly as an imposition, in taking their labor below its usual salable value; to which many add a third view of the subject—namely, that this sort of half-pay is not given them for the purpose of working, but to prevent their rising in rebellion. None of these misconceptions are favorable to hard labor, and the consequence is, that I never have seen such a set of idle *fainéants* as those employed on this system in the public works, and I am sure that, notwithstanding the very laudable intention of those who subscribed to form the fund, and the yet more praiseworthy, because more difficult, exertions of those who superintend it, the issue of the scheme will occasion full as much mischief as good to the people engaged in it. Private gentlemen, acting on something like a similar system, may make it answer better, because they have not the lazy dross of a metropolis to contend with—because they have fewer hands to manage—and, above all, because an individual always manages his own concerns better than those of the country can be managed. Yet all who have employed those who were distressed for want of work at under wages, have had, less or more, similar complaints to make. I think I have avoided this in my own case, by inviting the country people to do piece-work by the contract. Two things only are necessary—one is, that the nature of the work should be such as will admit of its being ascertained, when finished, to have been substantially executed. All sort of spade-work and hoe-work, with many other kinds of country labor, fall under this description, and the employer can hardly be cheated in the execution if he keeps a reasonable lookout. The other point is, to take care that the undertakers, in their anxiety for employment, do not take the job too cheap. A little acquaintance with country labor will enable one to regulate this; but it is an essential point, for if you do not keep them to their bargain, it is making a jest of the thing, and forfeiting the very advantage you have in view—that, namely, of inducing the laborer to bring his heart and spirit to his work. But this he will do where he has a fair bargain, which is to prove a good or bad one according to his own exertions. In this case you make the poor man his own friend, for the profits of his good conduct are all his own. It is astonishing how partial the people are to this species of contract, and how diligently they labor, acquiring or maintaining all the while those habits which render them honorable and useful members of society. I mention this to you, because the rich, much to their honor, do not, in general, require to be so much stimulated to benevolence, as to be directed in the most useful way to exert it.

I have still a word to say about the poor of our own parish of Parnassus. I have been applied to by a very worthy friend, Mr. Scott of Sinton, in behalf of an unfortunate Mr. Gilmour, who, it seems, has expended a little fortune in printing, upon his own account, poems which, from the sample I saw, seem exactly to answer the description of Dean Swift's country house:—

"Too bad for a blessing, too good for a curse,
I wish from my soul they were better or worse."

But you are the dean of our corporation, and, I am informed, take some interest in this poor gentleman. If you can point out any way in which I can serve him, I am sure my inclination is not wanting, but it looks like a very hopeless case. I beg my kindest respects to Mrs. Southey, and am always sincerely and affectionately yours,

WALTER SCOTT.

About this time Hogg took possession of Altrive Lake, and some of his friends in Edinburgh set on foot a subscription edition of his Queen's Wake (at a guinea each copy), in the hope of thus raising a sum adequate to the stocking of the little farm. The following letter alludes to this affair; and also to the death of Frances, Lady Douglas, sister to Duke Henry of Buccleuch, whose early kindness to Scott has been more than once mentioned.

TO THE RIGHT HON. LORD MONTAGU.

ABBOTSFORD, June 8, 1817.

MY DEAR LORD,—I am honored with your letter, and will not fail to take care that the Shepherd profits by your kind intentions, and those of Lady Montagu. This is a scheme which I did not devise, for I fear it will end in disappointment, but for which I have done, and will do, all I possibly can. There is an old saying of the seamen's, "Every man is not born to be a boatswain," and I think I have heard of men born under a sixpenny planet, and doomed never to be worth a groat. I fear something of this vile sixpenny influence had gleamed in at the cottage window when poor Hogg first came squeaking into the world. All that he made by his original book he ventured on a flock of sheep to drive into the Highlands to a farm he had taken there, but of which he could not get possession, so that all the stock was ruined and sold to disadvantage. Then he tried another farm, which proved too dear, so that he fairly broke upon it. Then put forth divers publications, which had little sale—and brought him accordingly few pence, though some praise. Then came this Queen's Wake, by which he might and ought to have made from £100 to £200—for there were, I think, three editions—when lo! his bookseller turned bankrupt, and paid him never a penny. The Duke has now, with his wonted generosity, given him a cosie bield, and the object of the present attack upon the public is to get if possible as much cash together as will stock it. But no one has loose guineas now to give poor poets, and I greatly doubt the scheme succeeding, unless it is more strongly patronized than can almost be expected. In bookselling matters, an author must either be the conjurer, who commands the devil, or the witch who serves him—and few are they whose situation is sufficiently independent to enable them to assume the higher character—and this is injurious to the indigent author in every respect, for not only is he obliged to turn his pen to every various kind of composition, and so to injure himself with the public by writing hastily, and on subjects unfitted for his genius; but, moreover, those honest gentlemen, the booksellers, from a natural association, consider the books as of least value, which they find they can get at least expense of copy-money, and therefore are proportionally careless in pushing the sale of the work. Whereas a good round sum out of their purse, like a moderate rise of rent on a farm, raises the work thus acquired in their own eyes, and serves as a spur to make them clear away every channel, by which they can discharge their quires upon the public. So much for bookselling, the most ticklish and unsafe and hazardous of all professions, scarcely with the exception of horse-jockeyship.

You cannot doubt the sincere interest I take in Lady Montagu's health. I was very glad to learn from the Duke, that the late melancholy event had produced no permanent effect on her constitution, as I know how much her heart must have suffered.[65] I saw our regretted friend for the last time at the Theatre, and made many schemes to be at Bothwell this next July. But thus the world glides from us, and those we most love and honor are withdrawn from the stage before us. I know not why it was that among the few for whom I had so much respectful regard, I never had associated the idea of early deprivation with Lady Douglas. Her excellent sense, deep information, and the wit which she wielded with so much good-humor, were allied apparently to a healthy constitution, which might have permitted us to enjoy, and be instructed by her society for many years. *Dis aliter visum*, and the recollection dwelling on all the delight which she afforded to society, and the good which she did in private life, is what now remains to us of her wit, wisdom, and benevolence. The Duke keeps his usual health, with always just so much of the gout, however, as would make me wish that he had more—a kind wish, for which I do not observe that he is sufficiently grateful. I hope to spend a few days at Drumlanrig Castle, when that ancient mansion shall have so far limited its courtesy as to stand covered in the presence of the wind and rain, which I believe is not yet the case. I am no friend to ceremony, and like a house as well when it does not carry its roof *en chapeau bras*. I heartily wish your Lordship joy of the new mansion at Ditton, and hope my good stars will permit me to pay my respects there one day. The discovery of the niches certainly bodes good luck to the house of Montagu, and as there are three of them, I presume it is to come threefold. From the care with which they were concealed, I presume they had been closed in the days of Cromwell, or a little before, and that the artist employed (like the General, who told his soldiers to fight bravely against the Pope, since they were Venetians before they were Christians) had more professional than religious zeal, and did not even, according to the practice of the time, think it necessary to sweep away Popery with the besom of destruction.[66] I am here on a stolen visit of two days, and find my mansion gradually enlarging. Thanks to Mr. Atkinson (who found out a practical use for our romantic theory), it promises to make a comfortable station for offering your Lordship and Lady Montagu a pilgrim's meal, when you next visit Melrose Abbey, and that without any risk of your valet (who I recollect is a substantial person) sticking between the wall of the parlor and the backs of the chairs placed round the table. This literally befell Sir Harry Macdougal's fat butler, who looked like a ship of the line in the loch at Bowhill, altogether unlike his master, who could glide wherever a weasel might make his way. Mr. Atkinson has indeed been more attentive than I can express, when I consider how valuable his time must be.[67] We are attempting no castellated conundrums to rival those Lord Napier used to have executed in sugar, when he was Commissioner, and no cottage neither, but an irregular somewhat—like an old English hall, in which your squire of £500 a year used to drink his ale in days of yore.

I am making considerable plantations (that is, considering), being greatly encouraged by the progress of those I formerly laid out. Read the veracious Gulliver's account of the Windsor Forest of Lilliput, and you will have some idea of the solemn gloom of my Druid shades. Your Lordship's truly faithful

WALTER SCOTT.

This is the 8th of June, and not an ash-tree in leaf yet. The country cruelly backward, and whole fields destroyed by the grub. I dread this next season.[Back to Contents]

CHAPTER XXXIX.

EXCURSION TO THE LENNOX, GLASGOW, AND DRUMLANRIG. — PURCHASE OF TOFTFIELD. — ESTABLISHMENT OF THE FERGUSON FAMILY AT HUNTLY BURN. — LINES WRITTEN IN ILLNESS. — VISITS OF WASHINGTON IRVING, LADY BYRON, AND SIR DAVID WILKIE. — PROGRESS OF THE BUILDING AT ABBOTSFORD. — LETTERS TO MORRITT, TERRY, ETC. — CONCLUSION OF ROB ROY.

1817.

During the summer term of 1817, Scott seems to have labored chiefly on his History of 1815 for the Register, which was published in August; but he also found time to draw up the Introduction for a richly embellished quarto, entitled Border Antiquities, which came out a month later. This valuable essay, containing large additions to the information previously embodied in the Minstrelsy, has been included in the late collection of his Miscellaneous Prose, and has thus obtained a circulation not to be expected for it in the original costly form.

Upon the rising of the Court in July, he made an excursion to the Lennox, chiefly that he might visit a cave at the head of Loch Lomond, said to have been a favorite retreat of his hero, Rob Roy. He was accompanied to the seat of his friend, Mr. Macdonald Buchanan, by Captain Adam Ferguson—the *long Linton* of the days of his apprenticeship; and thence to Glasgow, where, under the auspices of a kind and intelligent acquaintance, Mr. John Smith, bookseller, he refreshed his recollection of the noble cathedral, and other localities of the birthplace of Bailie Jarvie. Mr. Smith took care also to show the tourists the most remarkable novelties in the great manufacturing establishments of his flourishing city; and he remembers particularly the delight which Scott expressed on seeing the process of *singeing* muslin—that is, of divesting the finished web of all superficial knots and irregularities, by passing it, with the rapidity of lightning, over a bar of red-hot iron. "The man that imagined this," said Scott, "was *the Shakespeare of the Wabsters,—*

'Things out of hope are compass'd oft with vent'ring.'"[68]

The following note indicates the next stages of his progress:—

TO HIS GRACE THE DUKE OF BUCCLEUCH, DRUMLANRIG CASTLE.

SANQUHAR, 2 o'clock, July 30,[69] 1817.

From Ross, where the clouds on Benlomond are sleeping—
From Greenock, where Clyde to the Ocean is sweeping—
From Largs, where the Scotch gave the Northmen a drilling—
From Ardrossan, whose harbor cost many a shilling—
From Old Cumnock, where beds are as hard as a plank, sir—
From a chop and green pease, and a chicken in Sanquhar,
This eve, please the Fates, at Drumlanrig we anchor.

W. S.

The Poet and Captain Ferguson remained a week at Drumlanrig, and thence repaired together to Abbotsford. By this time, the foundations of that part of the existing house, which extends from the hall westwards to the original courtyard, had been laid; and Scott now found a new source of constant occupation in watching the proceedings of his masons. He had, moreover, no lack of employment further a-field,—for he was now negotiating with another neighboring landowner for the purchase of an addition, of more consequence than any he had hitherto made, to his estate. In the course of the autumn he concluded this matter, and became, for the price of £10,000, proprietor of the lands of *Toftfield*,[70] on which there had recently been erected a substantial mansion-house, fitted, in all points, for the accommodation of a genteel family. This circumstance offered a temptation which much quickened Scott's zeal for completing his arrangement. The venerable Professor Ferguson had died a year before; Captain Adam Ferguson was at home on half-pay; and Scott now saw the means of securing for himself, henceforth, the immediate neighborhood of the companion of his youth, and his amiable sisters. Ferguson, who had written, from the lines of Torres Vedras, his hopes of finding, when the war should be over, some sheltering cottage upon the Tweed, within a walk of Abbotsford, was delighted to see his dreams realized; and the family took up their residence next spring at the new house of Toftfield, on which Scott then bestowed, at the ladies' request, the name of Huntly Burn: this more harmonious designation being taken from the mountain brook which passes through its grounds and garden,—the same famous in tradition as the scene of Thomas the Rhymer's interviews with the Queen of Fairy. The upper part of the *Rhymer's Glen*, through which this brook finds its way from the Cauldshiels Loch to Toftfield, had been included in a previous purchase. He was now master of all these haunts of "True Thomas," and of the whole ground of the battle of Melrose, from *Skirmish-field* to *Turn-again*. His enjoyment of the new territories was, however, interrupted by various returns of his cramp, and the depression of spirit which always attended, in his case, the use of opium, the only medicine that seemed to have power over the disease.[71]

It was while struggling with such languor, on one lovely evening of this autumn, that he composed the following beautiful verses. They mark the very spot of their birth,—namely, the then naked height overhanging the northern side of the Cauldshiels Loch, from which Melrose Abbey to the eastward, and the hills of Ettrick and Yarrow to the west, are now visible over a wide range of rich woodland,—all the work of the poet's hand:—

"The sun upon the Weirdlaw Hill,
In Ettrick's vale, is sinking sweet;
The westland wind is hush and still—
The lake lies sleeping at my feet.
Yet not the landscape to mine eye
Bears those bright hues that once it bore;
Though evening, with her richest dye,
Flames o'er the hills of Ettrick's shore.

"With listless look along the plain
I see Tweed's silver current glide,
And coldly mark the holy fane
Of Melrose rise in ruin'd pride.
The quiet lake, the balmy air,
The hill, the stream, the tower, the tree,—
Are they still such as once they were,
Or is the dreary change in me?

"Alas! the warp'd and broken board,
How can it bear the painter's dye!
The harp of strain'd and tuneless chord,
How to the minstrel's skill reply!
To aching eyes each landscape lowers,
To feverish pulse each gale blows chill;

And Araby's or Eden's bowers
Were barren as this moorland hill."

He again alludes to his illness in a letter to Mr. Morritt:—

TO J. B. S. MORRITT, ESQ., M. P., ROKEBY.

ABBOTSFORD, August 11, 1817.

MY DEAR MORRITT,—I am arrived from a little tour in the west of Scotland, and had hoped, in compliance with your kind wish, to have indulged myself with a skip over the Border as far as Rokeby, about the end of this month. But my fate denies me this pleasure; for, in consequence of one or two blunders, during my absence, in executing my new premises, I perceive the necessity of remaining at the helm while they are going on. Our masons, though excellent workmen, are too little accustomed to the gimcracks of their art, to be trusted with the execution of a *bravura* plan, without constant inspection. Besides, the said laborers lay me under the necessity of laboring a little myself; and I find I can no longer with impunity undertake to make one week's hard work supply the omissions of a fortnight's idleness. Like you, I have abridged my creature-comforts,—as Old Mortality would call them,—renouncing beer and ale on all ordinary occasions; also pastry, fruit, etc., and all that tends to acidity. These are awkward warnings; but *sat est vixisse*. To have lived respected and regarded by some of the best men in our age is enough for an individual like me; the rest must be as God wills, and when He wills.

The poor-laws, into which you have ventured for the love of the country, form a sad quagmire. They are like John Bunyan's Slough of Despond, into which, as he observes, millions of cart-loads of good resolutions have been thrown, without perceptibly mending the way. From what you say, and from what I have heard from others, there is a very natural desire to trust to one or two empirical remedies, such as general systems of education, and so forth. But a man with a broken constitution might as well put faith in Spilsbury or Godbold. It is not the knowledge, but the use which is made of it, that is productive of real benefit. To say that the Scottish peasant is less likely than the Englishman to become an incumbrance on his parish, is saying, in other words, that this country is less populous,—that there are fewer villages and towns,—that the agricultural classes, from the landed proprietor down to the cottager, are individually more knit and cemented together;—above all, that the Scotch peasant has harder habits of life, and can endure from his infancy a worse fare and lodging than your parish almshouses offer.—There is a terrible evil in England to which we are strangers,—the number, to wit, of tippling-houses, where the laborer, as a matter of course, spends the overplus of his earnings. In Scotland there are few; and the Justices are commendably inexorable in rejecting all application for licenses where there appears no public necessity for granting them. A man, therefore, cannot easily spend much money in liquor, since he must walk three or four miles to the place of suction and back again, which infers a sort of *malice prepense* of which few are capable; and the habitual opportunity of indulgence not being at hand, the habits of intemperance, and of waste connected with it, are not acquired. If financiers would admit a general limitation of the ale-houses over England to one fourth of the number, I am convinced you would find the money spent in that manner would remain with the peasant, as a source of self-support and independence.

All this applies chiefly to the country;—in towns, and in the manufacturing districts, the evil could hardly be diminished by such regulations. There would, perhaps, be no means so effectual as that (which will never be listened to) of taxing the manufacturers according to the number of hands which they employ on an average, and applying the produce in maintaining the manufacturing poor. If it should be alleged that this would injure the manufacturers, I would boldly reply,—"And why not injure, or rather limit, speculations, the excessive stretch of which has been productive of so much damage to the principles of the country, and to the population, whom it has, in so many respects, degraded and demoralized?" For a great many years, manufactures, taken in a general point of view, have not partaken of the character of a regular profession, in which all who engaged with honest industry and a sufficient capital might reasonably expect returns proportional to their advances and labor—but have, on the contrary, rather resembled a lottery, in which the great majority of the adventurers are sure to be losers, although some may draw considerable advantage. Men continued for a great many years to exert themselves, and to pay extravagant wages, not in hopes that there could be a reasonable prospect of an orderly and regular demand for the goods they wrought up, but in order that they might be the first to take advantage of some casual opening which might consume their cargo, let others shift as they could. Hence extravagant wages on some occasions; for these adventurers who thus played at hit or miss, stood on no scruples while the chance of success remained open. Hence, also, the stoppage of work, and the discharge of the workmen, when the speculators failed of their object. All this while the country was the sufferer;—for whoever gained, the result, being upon the whole a loss, fell on the nation, together with the task of maintaining a poor, rendered effeminate and vicious by over-wages and over-living, and necessarily cast loose upon society. I cannot but think that the necessity of making some fund beforehand, for the provision of those whom they debauch, and render only fit for the almshouse, in prosecution of their own adventures, though it operated as a check on the increase of manufactures, would be a measure just in itself, and beneficial to the community. But it would never be listened to;—the weaver's beam, and the sons of Zeruiah, would be too many for the proposers.

This is the eleventh of August: Walter, happier than he will ever be again, perhaps, is preparing for the moors. He has a better dog than Trout, and rather less active. Mrs. Scott and all our family send kind love.

Yours ever,

W. S.

WASHINGTON IRVING
After the painting by Leslie.

Two or three days after this letter was written, Scott first saw Washington Irving, who has recorded his visit in a delightful Essay, which, however, having been penned nearly twenty years afterwards, betrays a good many slips of memory as to names and dates. Mr. Irving says he arrived at Abbotsford on the 27th of August, 1816; but he describes the walls of the new house as already overtopping the old cottage; and this is far from being the only circumstance he mentions which proves that he should have written 1817.[72] The picture which my amiable friend has drawn of his reception shows to all who remember the Scott and the Abbotsford of those days, how consistent accuracy as to essentials may be with forgetfulness of trifles.

Scott had received The History of New York by Knickerbocker, shortly after its appearance in 1812, from an accomplished American traveller, Mr. Brevoort; and the admirable humor of this early work had led him to anticipate the brilliant career which its author has since run. Mr. Thomas Campbell, being no stranger to Scott's high estimation of Irving's genius, gave him a letter of introduction, which, halting his chaise on the high-road above Abbotsford, he modestly sent down to the house, "with a card, on which he had written, that he was on his way to the ruins of Melrose, and wished to know whether it would be agreeable to Mr. Scott to receive a visit from him in the course of the morning." Scott's family well remember the delight with which he received this announcement:—he was at breakfast, and sallied forth instantly, dogs and children after him as usual, to greet the guest, and conduct him in person from the highway to the door.

"The noise of my chaise," says Irving, "had disturbed the quiet of the establishment. Out sallied the warder of the castle, a black greyhound, and leaping on one of the blocks of stone, began a furious barking. This alarm brought out the whole garrison of dogs, all open-mouthed and vociferous. In a little while, the lord of the castle himself made his appearance. I knew him at once, by the likenesses that had been published of him. He came limping up the gravel walk, aiding himself by a stout walking staff, but moving rapidly and with vigor. By his side jogged along a large iron-gray staghound, of most grave demeanor, who took no part in the clamor of the canine rabble, but seemed to consider himself bound, for the dignity of the house, to give me a courteous reception.

"Before Scott reached the gate, he called out in a hearty tone, welcoming me to Abbotsford, and asking news of Campbell. Arrived at the door of the chaise, he grasped me warmly by the hand: 'Come, drive down, drive down to the house,' said he; 'ye're just in time for breakfast, and afterwards ye shall see all the wonders of the Abbey.'

71

"I would have excused myself on the plea of having already made my breakfast. 'Hut, man,' cried he, 'a ride in the morning in the keen air of the Scotch hills is warrant enough for a second breakfast.'

"I was accordingly whirled to the portal of the cottage, and in a few moments found myself seated at the breakfast-table. There was no one present but the family, which consisted of Mrs. Scott; her eldest daughter, Sophia, then a fine girl about seventeen; Miss Anne Scott, two or three years younger; Walter, a well-grown stripling; and Charles, a lively boy, eleven or twelve years of age.

"I soon felt myself quite at home, and my heart in a glow, with the cordial welcome I experienced. I had thought to make a mere morning visit, but found I was not to be let off so lightly. 'You must not think our neighborhood is to be read in a morning like a newspaper,' said Scott; 'it takes several days of study for an observant traveller, that has a relish for auld-world trumpery. After breakfast you shall make your visit to Melrose Abbey; I shall not be able to accompany you, as I have some household affairs to attend to; but I will put you in charge of my son Charles, who is very learned in all things touching the old ruin and the neighborhood it stands in; and he and my friend Johnnie Bower will tell you the whole truth about it, with a great deal more that you are not called upon to believe, unless you be a true and nothing-doubting antiquary. When you come back, I'll take you out on a ramble about the neighborhood. To-morrow we will take a look at the Yarrow, and the next day we will drive over to Dryburgh Abbey, which is a fine old ruin, well worth your seeing.'—In a word, before Scott had got through with his plan, I found myself committed for a visit of several days, and it seemed as if a little realm of romance was suddenly open before me."

After breakfast, while Scott, no doubt, wrote a chapter of Rob Roy, Mr. Irving, under young Charles's guidance, saw Melrose Abbey, and Johnnie Bower the elder, whose son long since inherited his office as showman of the ruins, and all his enthusiasm about them and their poet. The senior on this occasion was loud in his praises of the affability of Scott. "He'll come here sometimes," said he, "with great folks in his company, and the first I'll know of it is hearing his voice calling out Johnnie!—Johnnie Bower!—and when I go out I'm sure to be greeted with a joke or a pleasant word. He'll stand and crack, an' laugh wi' me just like an auld wife,—and *to think that of a man that has such an awfu' knowledge o' history!*" [73]

On his return from the Abbey, Irving found Scott ready for a ramble. I cannot refuse myself the pleasure of extracting some parts of his description of it.

"As we sallied forth, every dog in the establishment turned out to attend us. There was the old staghound, Maida, that I have already mentioned, a noble animal, and Hamlet, the black greyhound, a wild thoughtless youngster, not yet arrived at the years of discretion; and Finette, a beautiful setter, with soft, silken hair, long pendent ears, and a mild eye, the parlor favorite. When in front of the house, we were joined by a superannuated greyhound, who came from the kitchen wagging his tail; and was cheered by Scott as an old friend and comrade. In our walks, he would frequently pause in conversation, to notice his dogs, and speak to them as if rational companions; and, indeed, there appears to be a vast deal of rationality in these faithful attendants on man, derived from their close intimacy with him. Maida deported himself with a gravity becoming his age and size, and seemed to consider himself called upon to preserve a great degree of dignity and decorum in our society. As he jogged along a little distance ahead of us, the young dogs would gambol about him, leap on his neck, worry at his ears, and endeavor to tease him into a gambol. The old dog would keep on for a long time with imperturbable solemnity, now and then seeming to rebuke the wantonness of his young companions. At length he would make a sudden turn, seize one of them, and tumble him in the dust, then giving a glance at us, as much as to say, 'You see, gentlemen, I can't help giving way to this nonsense,' would resume his gravity, and jog on as before. Scott amused himself with these peculiarities. 'I make no doubt,' said he, 'when Maida is alone with these young dogs, he throws gravity aside, and plays the boy as much as any of them; but he is ashamed to do so in our company, and seems to say—Ha' done with your nonsense, youngsters: what will the laird and that other gentleman think of me if I give way to such foolery?'

"Scott amused himself with the peculiarities of another of his dogs, a little shamefaced terrier, with large glassy eyes, one of the most sensitive little bodies to insult and indignity in the world. 'If ever he whipped him,' he said, 'the little fellow would sneak off and hide himself from the light of day in a lumber garret, from whence there was no drawing him forth but by the sound of the chopping-knife, as if chopping up his victuals, when he would steal forth with humiliated and downcast look, but would skulk away again if any one regarded him.'

"While we were discussing the humors and peculiarities of our canine companions, some object provoked their spleen, and produced a sharp and petulant barking from the smaller fry; but it was some time before Maida was sufficiently roused to ramp forward two or three bounds, and join the chorus with a deep-mouthed *bow wow*. It was but a transient outbreak, and he returned instantly, wagging his tail, and looking up dubiously in his master's face, uncertain whether he would receive censure or applause. 'Ay, ay, old boy!' cried Scott, 'you have done wonders; you have shaken the Eildon hills with your roaring: you may now lay by your artillery for the rest of the day. Maida,' continued he, 'is like the great gun at Constantinople; it takes so long to get it ready, that the smaller guns can fire off a dozen times first: but when it does go off, it plays the very devil.'

"These simple anecdotes may serve to show the delightful play of Scott's humors and feelings in private life. His domestic animals were his friends. Everything about him seemed to rejoice in the light of his countenance.

"Our ramble took us on the hills commanding an extensive prospect. 'Now,' said Scott, 'I have brought you, like the pilgrim in the Pilgrim's Progress, to the top of the Delectable Mountains, that I may show you all the goodly regions hereabouts. Yonder is Lammermuir, and Smailholm; and there you have Galashiels, and Torwoodlee, and Gala Water; and in that direction you see Teviotdale and the Braes of Yarrow, and Ettrick stream winding along like a silver thread, to throw itself into the Tweed.' He went on thus to call over names celebrated in Scottish song, and most of which had recently received a romantic interest from his own pen. In fact, I saw a great part of the Border country spread out before me, and could trace the scenes of those poems and romances which had in a manner bewitched the world.

"I gazed about me for a time with mute surprise, I may almost say with disappointment. I beheld a mere succession of gray waving hills, line beyond line, as far as my eye could reach, monotonous in their aspect, and so destitute of trees, that one could almost see a stout fly walking along their profile; and the far-famed Tweed appeared a naked stream, flowing between bare hills, without a tree or thicket on its banks; and yet such had been the magic web of poetry and romance thrown over the whole, that it had a greater charm for me than the richest scenery I had beheld in England. I could not help giving utterance to my thoughts. Scott hummed for a moment to himself, and looked grave; he had no idea of having his Muse complimented at the expense of his native hills. 'It may be pertinacity,' said he at length; 'but to my eye, these gray hills, and all this wild Border country, have beauties peculiar to themselves. I like the very nakedness of the land; it has something bold, and stern, and solitary about it. When I have been for some time in the rich scenery about Edinburgh, which is like ornamented garden land, I begin to wish myself back again among my own honest gray hills; and if I did not see the heather, at least once a year, *I think I should die!* The last words were said with an honest warmth, accompanied by a thump on the ground with his staff, by way of emphasis, that showed his heart was in his speech. He vindicated the Tweed, too, as a beautiful stream in itself; and observed that he did not dislike it for being bare of trees, probably from having been much of an angler in his time; and an angler does not like to have a stream overhung by trees, which embarrass him in the exercise of his rod and line.

"I took occasion to plead, in like manner, the associations of early life for my disappointment in respect to the surrounding scenery. I had been so accustomed to see hills crowned with forests, and streams breaking their way through a wilderness of trees, that all my ideas of romantic landscape were apt to be well wooded. 'Ay, and that's the great charm of your country,' cried Scott. 'You love the forest as I do the heather; but I would not have you think I do not feel the glory of a great woodland prospect. There is nothing I should like more than to be in the midst of one of your grand wild original forests, with the idea of hundreds of miles of untrodden forest around me. I once saw at Leith an immense stick of timber, just landed from America. It must have been an enormous tree when it stood in its native soil, at its full height, and with all its branches. I gazed at it with admiration; it seemed like one of the gigantic obelisks which are now and then brought from Egypt to shame the pigmy monuments of Europe; and, in fact, these vast aboriginal trees, that have sheltered the Indians before the intrusion of the white men, are the monuments and antiquities of your country.'

"The conversation here turned upon Campbell's poem of Gertrude of Wyoming, as illustrative of the poetic materials furnished by American scenery. Scott cited several passages of it with great delight. 'What a pity it is,' said he, 'that Campbell does not write more, and oftener, and give full sweep to his genius! He has wings that would bear him to the skies; and he does, now and then, spread them grandly, but folds them up again, and resumes his perch, as if he was afraid to launch away. What a grand idea is that,' said he, 'about prophetic boding, or, in common parlance, second sight—

"Coming events cast their shadows before!"—

The fact is,' added he, 'Campbell is, in a manner, a bugbear to himself. The brightness of his early success is a detriment to all his further efforts. *He is afraid of the shadow that his own fame casts before him.*'

"We had not walked much farther, before we saw the two Miss Scotts advancing along the hillside to meet us. The morning's studies being over, they had set off to take a ramble on the hills, and gather heather blossoms with which to decorate their hair for dinner. As they came bounding lightly like young fawns, and their dresses fluttering in the pure summer breeze, I was reminded of Scott's own description of his children, in his introduction to one of the cantos of Marmion:—

'My imps, though hardy, bold, and wild,
As best befits the mountain child,' etc.

As they approached, the dogs all sprang forward, and gambolled around them. They joined us with countenances full of health and glee. Sophia, the eldest, was the most lively and joyous, having much of her father's varied spirit in conversation, and seeming to catch excitement from his words and looks; Anne was of a quieter mood, rather silent, owing, in some measure, no doubt, to her being some years younger."[74]

Having often, many years afterwards, heard Irving speak warmly of William Laidlaw, I must not omit the following passage:—

"One of my pleasantest rambles with Scott about the neighborhood of Abbotsford was taken in company with Mr. William Laidlaw, the steward of his estate. This was a gentleman for whom Scott entertained a particular value. He had been born to a competency, had been well educated, his mind was richly stored with varied information, and he was a man of sterling moral worth. Having been reduced by misfortune, Scott had got him to take charge of his estate. He lived at a small farm, on the hillside above Abbotsford, and was treated by Scott as a cherished and confidential friend, rather than a dependant.

"That day at dinner we had Mr. Laidlaw and his wife, and a female friend who accompanied them. The latter was a very intelligent respectable person, about the middle age, and was treated with particular attention and courtesy by Scott. Our dinner was a most agreeable one, for the guests were evidently cherished visitors to the house, and felt that they were appreciated. When they were gone, Scott spoke of them in the most cordial manner. 'I wished to show you,' said he, 'some of our really excellent, plain Scotch people: not fine gentlemen and ladies, for such you can meet everywhere, and they are everywhere the same. The character of a nation is not to be learnt from its fine folks.' He then went on with a particular eulogium on the lady who had accompanied the Laidlaws. She was the daughter, he said, of a poor country clergyman, who had died in debt, and left her an orphan and destitute. Having had a good plain education, she immediately set up a child's school, and had soon a numerous flock under her care, by which she earned a decent maintenance. That, however, was not her main object. Her first care was to pay off her father's debts, that no ill word or ill will might rest upon his memory. This, by dint of Scotch economy, backed by filial reverence and pride, she accomplished, though in the effort she subjected herself to every privation. Not content with this, she in certain instances refused to take pay for the tuition of the children of some of her neighbors, who had befriended her father in his need, and had since fallen into poverty. 'In a word,' added Scott, 'she's a fine old Scotch girl, and I delight in her more than in many a fine lady I have known, and I have known many of the finest.'

"The evening passed away delightfully in a quaint-looking apartment, half study, half drawing-room. Scott read several passages from the old Romance of Arthur, with a fine deep sonorous voice, and a gravity of tone that seemed to suit the antiquated black-letter volume. It was a rich treat to hear such a work read by such a person, and in such a place; and his appearance, as he sat reading, in a large armchair, with his favorite hound Maida at his feet, and surrounded by books and reliques and Border trophies, would have formed an admirable and most characteristic picture. When I retired for the night, I found it almost impossible to sleep: the idea of being under the roof of Scott; of being on the Borders on the Tweed; in the very centre of that region which had, for some time past, been the favorite scene of romantic fiction; and, above all, the recollections of the ramble I had taken, the company in which I had taken it, and the conversation which had passed, all fermented in my mind, and nearly drove sleep from my pillow.

"On the following morning the sun darted his beams from over the hills through the low lattice of my window. I rose at an early hour, and looked out between the branches of eglantine which overhung the casement. To my surprise, Scott was already up, and forth, seated on a fragment of stone, and chatting with the workmen employed in the new building. I had supposed, after the time he had wasted upon me yesterday, he would be closely occupied this morning: but he appeared like a man of leisure, who had nothing to do but bask in the sunshine, and amuse himself. I soon dressed myself and joined him. He talked about his proposed plans of Abbotsford: happy would it have been for him could he have contented himself with his delightful little vine-covered cottage, and the simple, yet hearty and hospitable, style in which he lived at the time of my visit."[75]

Among other visitors who succeeded the distinguished American that autumn, were Lady Byron, the wife of the poet, and the great artist, Mr., now Sir David Wilkie, who then executed for Captain Ferguson that pleasing little picture, in which Scott and his family are represented as a group of peasants, while the gallant soldier himself figures by them in the character of a gamekeeper, or perhaps poacher. Mr. Irving has given, in the little work from which I have quoted so liberally, an amusing account of the delicate scruples of Wilkie about soliciting Scott to devote a morning to the requisite sitting, until, after lingering for several days, he at length became satisfied that, by whatever magic his host might contrive to keep Ballantyne's presses in full play, he had always abundance of leisure for matters less important than Ferguson's destined heirloom. I shall now, however, return to his correspondence; and begin with a letter to Joanna Baillie on Lady Byron's visit.

TO MISS JOANNA BAILLIE, HAMPSTEAD.

ABBOTSFORD, September 26, 1817.

MY DEAR MISS BAILLIE,—A series of little trinketty sort of business, and occupation, and idleness, have succeeded to each other so closely, that I have been scarce able, for some three weeks past, to call my time my own for half an hour together; but enough of apologies—they are vile things, and I know you will impute my negligence to anything rather than forgetting or undervaluing your friendship. You know, by this time, that we have had a visit from Lady Byron, delightful both on its own account, and because it was accompanied with good news and a letter from you. I regret we could not keep her longer than a day with us, which was spent on the banks of the Yarrow, and I hope and believe she was pleased with us, because I am sure she will be so with everything that is intended to please her: meantime her visit gave me a most lawyer-like fit of the bile. I have lived too long to be surprised at any instance of human caprice, but still it vexes me. Now, one would suppose Lady Byron, young, beautiful, with birth, and rank, and fortune, and taste, and high accomplishments, and admirable good sense, qualified to have made happy one whose talents are so high as Lord Byron's, and whose marked propensity it is to like those who are qualified to admire and understand his talents; and yet it has proved otherwise. I can safely

75

say my heart ached for her all the time we were together; there was so much patience and decent resignation to a situation which must have pressed on her thoughts, that she was to me one of the most interesting creatures I had seen for a score of years. I am sure I should not have felt such strong kindness towards her had she been at the height of her fortune, and in the full enjoyment of all the brilliant prospects to which she seemed destined.—You will wish to hear of my complaint. I think, thank God, that it is leaving me—not suddenly, however, for I have had some repetitions, but they have become fainter and fainter, and I have not been disturbed by one for these three weeks. I trust, by care and attention, my stomach will return to its usual tone, and I am as careful as I can. I have taken hard exercise with good effect, and am often six hours on foot without stopping or sitting down, to which my plantations and enclosures contribute not a little. I have, however, given up the gun this season, finding myself unable to walk up to the dogs; but Walter has taken it in hand, and promises to be a first-rate shot; he brought us in about seven or eight brace of birds the evening Lady Byron came to us, which papa was of course a little proud of. The blackcocks are getting very plenty on our moor-ground at Abbotsford, but I associate them so much with your beautiful poem,[76] that I have not the pleasure I used to have in knocking them down. I wish I knew how to send you a brace. I get on with my labors here; my house is about to be roofed in, and a comical concern it is.

Yours truly,

W. S.

The next letter refers to the Duke of Buccleuch's preparations for a cattle-show at Bowhill, which was followed by an entertainment on a large scale to his Grace's Selkirkshire neighbors and tenantry, and next day by a fox-hunt, after Dandie Dinmont's fashion, among the rocks of the Yarrow. The Sheriff attended *with his tail on*; and Wilkie, too, went with him. It was there that Sir David first saw Hogg, and the Shepherd's greeting was graceful. He eyed the great painter for a moment in silence, and then stretching out his hand, said: "Thank God for it. I did not know that you were so young a man!"

TO THE DUKE OF BUCCLEUCH, ETC., ETC., ETC., DRUMLANRIG CASTLE.

MY DEAR LORD DUKE,—I am just honored with your Grace's of the 27th. The posts, which are as cross as pie-crust, have occasioned some delay. Depend on our attending at Bowhill on the 20th, and staying over the show. I have written to Adam Ferguson, who will come with a whoop and a hollo. So will the Ballantynes—flageolet[77] and all—for the festival, and they shall be housed at Abbotsford. I have an inimitably good songster in the person of Terence Magrath, who teaches my girls. He beats almost all whom I have ever heard attempt Moore's songs, and I can easily cajole him also out to Abbotsford for a day or two. In jest or earnest, I never heard a better singer in a room, though his voice is not quite full enough for a concert; and for an after-supper song, he almost equals Irish Johnstone.[78]

Trade of every kind is recovering, and not a loom idle in Glasgow. The most faithful respects of this family attend the Ladies and all at Drumlanrig. I ever am your Grace's truly obliged and grateful

WALTER SCOTT.

Given from my Castle of Grawacky, this second day of the month called October, One Thousand Eight Hundred and Seventeen Years.

There is a date nearly as long as the letter.

I hope we shall attack the foxes at Bowhill. I will hazard Maida.

We have some allusions to this Bowhill party in another letter; the first of several which I shall now insert according to their dates, leaving them, with a few marginal notes, to tell out the story of 1817:—

TO DANIEL TERRY, ESQ., LONDON.

ABBOTSFORD, October 24, 1817.

DEAR TERRY,—Bullock has not gone to Skye, and I am very glad he has not, for to me who knew the Hebrides well, the attempt seemed very perilous at this season. I have considerably enlarged my domains since I wrote to you, by the purchase of a beautiful farm adjacent. The farmhouse, which is new and excellent, I have let to Adam Ferguson and his sisters. We will be within a pleasant walk of each other, and hope to end our lives, as they began, in each other's society. There is a beautiful brook, with remnants of natural wood, which would make Toftfield rival Abbotsford, but for the majestic Tweed. I am in treaty for a field or two more; one of which contains the only specimen of a Peel-house, or defensive residence of a small proprietor, which remains in this neighborhood. It is an orchard, in the hamlet of Darnick, to which it gives a most picturesque effect. Blore admires it very much. We are all well here, but crowded with company. I have been junketing this week past at Bowhill. Mr. Magrath has been with us these two or three days, and has seen his ward, Hamlet, behave most *princelike* on Newark Hill and elsewhere. He promises to be a real treasure.[79] Notwithstanding, Mr. Magrath went to Bowhill with me one day, where his vocal talents gave great pleasure, and I hope will procure him the notice and protection of the Buccleuch family. The Duke says my building engrosses, as a common centre, the thoughts of Mr. Atkinson and Mr. Bullock, and wishes he could make them equally anxious in his own behalf. You may believe this flatters me not a little.

P. S.—I agree with you that the tower will look rather rich for the rest of the building; yet you may be assured, that with diagonal chimneys and notched gables, it will have a very fine effect, and is in Scotch architecture by no means incompatible. My house has been like a *cried fair*, and extreme the inconvenience of having no corner sacred to my own use, and free from intrusion.

Ever truly yours,

W. S.

TO THE SAME.

ABBOTSFORD, 29th October, 1817.

MY DEAR TERRY,—I enclose a full sketch of the lower story, with accurate measurements of rooms, casements, doorways, chimneys, etc., that Mr. Atkinson's good will may not want means to work upon. I will speak to the subjects of your letters separately, that I may omit none of them. *1st*, I cannot possibly surrender the window to the west in the library,[80] although I subscribe to all you urge about it. Still it is essential in point of light to my old eyes, and the single northern aspect will not serve me. Above all, it looks into the yard, and enables me to summon Tom Purdie without the intervention of a third party. Indeed, as I can have but a few books about me, it is of the less consequence. *2dly*, I resign the idea of *coving* the library to your better judgment, and I think the Stirling Heads[81] will be admirably disposed in the glass of the armory window. I have changed my mind as to having doors on the book-presses, which is, after all, a great bore. No person will be admitted into my sanctum, and I can have the door locked during my absence. *3dly*, I expect Mr. Bullock here every day, and should be glad to have the drawings for the dining-room wainscot, as he could explain them to the artists who are to work them. This (always if quite convenient) would be the more desirable, as I must leave this place in a fortnight at farthest,—the more 's the pity,—and, consequently, the risk of blunders will be considerably increased. I should like if the panelling of the wainscot could admit of a press on each side of the sideboard. I don't mean a formal press with a high door, but some crypt, or, to speak vulgarly, *cupboard*, to put away bottles of wine, etc. You know I am my own butler, and such accommodation is very convenient. We begin roofing to-morrow. Wilkie admires the whole as a composition, and that is high authority. I agree that the fountain shall be out of doors in front of the greenhouse; there may be an enclosure for it with some ornamented mason work, as in old gardens, and it will occupy an angle, which I should be puzzled what to do with, for turf and gravel would be rather meagre, and flowers not easily kept. I have the old fountain belonging to the Cross of Edinburgh, which flowed with wine at the coronation of our kings and on other occasions of public rejoicing. I send a sketch of this venerable relic, connected as it is with a thousand associations. It is handsome in its forms and proportions—a freestone basin about three feet in diameter, and five inches and a half in depth, very handsomely hollowed. A piece has been broken off one edge, but as we have the fragment, it can easily be restored with cement. There are four openings for pipes in the circumference—each had been covered with a Gothic masque, now broken off and defaced, but which may be easily restored. Through these the wine had fallen into a larger and lower reservoir. I intend this for the centre of my fountain. I do not believe I should save £100 by retaining Mrs. Redford, by the time she was raised, altered, and beautified, for, like the Highlandman's gun, she wants stock, lock, and barrel, to put her into repair. In the mean time, "the cabin is convenient." Yours ever,

W. S.

TO MR. WILLIAM LAIDLAW, KAESIDE.

EDINBURGH, November 15, 1817.

DEAR WILLIE,—I have no intention to let the Whitehaugh without your express approbation, and I wish you to act as my adviser and representative in these matters. I would hardly have ventured to purchase so much land without the certainty of your counsel and coöperation.... On the other side you will find a small order on the banker at Galashiels, to be renewed half yearly; not by way of recompensing your friendship "with a load of barren money," but merely to ease my conscience in some degree for the time which I must necessarily withdraw from the labor which is to maintain your family. Believe me, dear Willie, yours truly,

W. SCOTT.

TO THE SAME.

EDINBURGH, 19th November, 1817.

DEAR WILLIE,—I hope you will not quarrel with my last. Believe me that, to a sound-judging, and philosophical mind, this same account of Dr. and Cr., which fills up so much time in the world, is comparatively of very small value. When you get rich, unless I thrive in the same proportion, I will request your assistance for less, for little, or for nothing, as the case may require; but while I wear my seven-leagued boots to stride in triumph over moss and muir, it would be very silly in either of us to let a cheque twice a year of £25 make a difference between us. But all this we will talk over when we meet. I meditate one day a *coup-de-maître*, which will make my friend's advice and exertion essential—indeed worthy of much better remuneration. When you come, I hope you will bring us information of all my rural proceedings. Though so lately come to town, I still remember, at my waking hours, that I can neither see Tom Purdie nor Adam Paterson,[82] and rise with the more unwillingness. I was unwell on Monday and Tuesday, but am quite recovered.

Yours truly,

W. S.

TO THOMAS SCOTT, ESQ., PAYMASTER, 70TH REGIMENT, KINGSTON, CANADA.

EDINBURGH, 13th December, 1817.

MY DEAR TOM,—I should be happy to attend to your commission about a dominie for your boy, but I think there will be much risk in yoking yourself with one for three or four years. You know what sort of black cattle these are, and how difficult it is to discern their real character, though one may give a guess at their attainments. When they get good provender in their guts, they are apt to turn out very different animals from what they were in their original low condition, and get frisky and troublesome. I have made several inquiries, however, and request to know what salary you would think reasonable, and also what acquisitions he ought to possess. There is no combating the feelings which you express for the society of your son, otherwise I really think that a Scottish education would be highly desirable; and should you at any time revert to this plan, you may rely on my bestowing the same attention upon him as upon my own boys.

I agree entirely with you on the necessity of your remaining in the regiment while it is stationary, and retiring on half-pay when it marches; but I cannot so easily acquiesce in your plan of settling in Canada. On the latter event taking place, on the contrary, I think it would be highly advisable that you should return to your native country. In the course of nature you must soon be possessed of considerable property, now life-rented by our mother, and I should think that even your present income would secure you comfort and independence here. Should you remain in Canada, you must consider your family as settlers in that state, and as I cannot believe that it will remain very long separated from America, I should almost think this equal to depriving them of the advantages of British subjects—at least of those which they might derive from their respectable connections in this country. With respect to your son, in particular, I have little doubt that I could be of considerable service to him in almost any line of life he might chance to adopt here, but could of course have less influence on his fortunes were he to remain on the Niagara. I certainly feel anxious on this subject, because the settlement of your residence in America would be saying, in other words, that we two, the last remains of a family once so numerous, are never more to meet upon this side of time. My own health is very much broken up by the periodical recurrence of violent cramps in the stomach, which neither seem disposed to yield to medicine nor to abstinence. The complaint, the doctors say, is not dangerous in itself, but I cannot look forward to its continued recurrence, without being certain that it is to break my health, and anticipate old age in cutting me short. Be it so, my dear Tom—*Sat est vixisse*—and I am too much of a philosopher to be anxious about protracted life, which, with all its infirmities and deprivations, I have never considered as a blessing. In the years which may be before me, it would be a lively satisfaction to me to have the pleasure of seeing you in this country, with the prospect of a comfortable settlement. I have but an imperfect account to render of my doings here. I have amused myself with making an addition to my cottage in the country. One little apartment is to be fitted up as an armory for my old relics and curiosities. On the wicket I intend to mount your *deer's foot*[83]—as an appropriate knocker. I hope the young ladies liked their watches, and that all your books, stationery, etc., came safe to hand. I am told you have several kinds of the oak peculiar to America. If you can send me a few good acorns, with the names of the kinds they belong to, I will have them reared with great care and attention. The heaviest and smoothest acorns should be selected, as one would wish them, sent from such a distance, to succeed, which rarely happens unless they are particularly well ripened. I shall be as much obliged to you as Sancho was to the Duchess, or, to speak more correctly, the Duchess to Sancho, for a similar favor. Our mother keeps her health surprisingly well now, nor do I think there is any difference, unless that her deafness is rather increased. My eldest boy is upwards of six feet high; therefore born, as Sergeant Kite says, to be a great man. I should not like such a rapid growth, but that he carries strength along with it; my youngest boy is a very sharp little fellow—and the girls give us great satisfaction. Ever affectionately yours,

WALTER SCOTT.

The following note is without date. It accompanied, no doubt, the last proof sheet of Rob Roy, and was therefore in all probability written about ten days before the 31st of December, 1817—on which day the novel was published.

TO MR. JAMES BALLANTYNE, ST. JOHN STREET.

DEAR JAMES,—

With great joy
I send you Roy.
'T was a tough job,
But we're done with Rob.

I forget if I mentioned Terry in my list of Friends. Pray send me two or three copies as soon as you can. It were pity to make the Grinder[84] pay carriage.

Yours ever,

W. S.

The novel had indeed been "a tough job"—for lightly and airily as it reads, the author had struggled almost throughout with the pains of cramp or the lassitude of opium. Calling on him one day to dun him for copy, James Ballantyne found him with a clean pen and a blank sheet before him, and uttered some rather solemn exclamation of surprise. "Ay, ay, Jemmy," said he, "'tis easy for you to bid me get on, but how the deuce can I make Rob Roy's wife speak, with such a *curmurring* in my guts?"[Back to Contents]

CHAPTER XL.

1818.

Rob Roy and his wife, Bailie Nicol Jarvie and his housekeeper, Die Vernon and Rashleigh Osbaldistone—these boldly drawn and happily contrasted personages—were welcomed as warmly as the most fortunate of their predecessors.[85] Constable's resolution to begin with an edition of 10,000 proved to have been as sagacious as brave; for within a fortnight a second impression of 3000 was called for; and the subsequent sale of this novel has considerably exceeded 40,000 more.

Scott, however, had not waited for this new burst of applause. As soon as he came within view of the completion of Rob Roy, he desired John Ballantyne to propose to Constable and Co. a second series of the Tales of my Landlord, to be comprised, like the first, in four volumes, and ready for publication by "the King's birthday;" that is, the 4th of June, 1818. "I have hungered and thirsted," he wrote, "to see the end of those shabby borrowings among friends; they have all been wiped out except the good Duke's £4000— and I will not suffer either new offers of land or anything else to come in the way of that clearance. I expect that you will be able to arrange this resurrection of Jedediah, so that £5000 shall be at my order."

Mr. Rigdum used to glory in recounting that he acquitted himself on this occasion with a species of dexterity not contemplated in his commission. He well knew how sorely Constable had been wounded by seeing the first Tales of Jedediah published by Murray and Blackwood—and that the utmost success of Rob Roy would only double his anxiety to keep them out of the field, when the hint should be dropt that a second MS. from Gandercleuch might shortly be looked for. John therefore took a convenient opportunity to mention the new scheme as if casually—so as to give Constable the impression that the author's purpose was to divide the second series also between his old rival in Albemarle Street, of whom his jealousy was always sensitive, and his neighbor Blackwood, whom, if there had been no other grudge, the recent conduct and rapidly increasing sale of his Magazine would have been sufficient to make Constable hate with a perfect hatred. To see not only his old "Scots Magazine" eclipsed, but the authority of the Edinburgh Review itself bearded on its own soil by this juvenile upstart, was to him gall and wormwood; and, moreover, he himself had come in for his share in some of those grotesque *jeux d'esprit* by which, at this period, Blackwood's young Tory wags delighted to assail their elders and betters of the Whig persuasion. To prevent the proprietor of this new journal from acquiring anything like a hold on the author of Waverley, and thus competing with himself not only in periodical literature, but in the highest of the time, was an object for which, as John Ballantyne shrewdly guessed, Constable would have made at that moment almost any sacrifice. When, therefore, the haughty but trembling bookseller—"The Lord High Constable" (as he had been dubbed by these jesters)—signified his earnest hope that the second Tales of my Landlord were destined to come out under the same auspices with Rob Roy, the plenipotentiary answered with an air of deep regret, that he feared it would be impossible for the author to dispose of the work—unless to publishers who should agree to take with it *the whole* of the remaining stock of "John Ballantyne and Co.;" and Constable, pertinaciously as he had stood out against many more modest propositions of this nature, was so worked upon by his jealous feelings, that his resolution at once gave way. He agreed on the instant to do all that John seemed to shrink from asking—and at one sweep cleared the Augean stable in Hanover Street of unsalable rubbish to the amount of £5270! I am assured by his surviving partner, that when he had finally redisposed of the stock, he found himself a loser by fully two thirds of this sum.

Burthened with this heavy condition, the agreement for the sale of 10,000 copies of the embryo series was signed before the end of November, 1817; and on the 7th January, 1818, Scott wrote as follows to his noble friend:—

TO THE DUKE OF BUCCLEUCH, ETC., ETC.

MY DEAR LORD DUKE,—I have the great pleasure of enclosing the discharged bond which your Grace stood engaged in for me, and on my account. The accommodation was of the greatest consequence to me, as it enabled me to retain possession of some valuable literary property, which I must otherwise have suffered to be sold at a time when the booksellers had no money to buy it. My dear Lord, to wish that all your numerous and extensive acts of kindness may be attended with similar advantages to the persons whom you oblige, is wishing you what to your mind will be the best recompense; and to wish that they may be felt by all as gratefully as by me, though you may be careless to hear about that part of the story, is only wishing what is creditable to human nature. I have this moment your more than kind letter, and congratulate your Grace that, in one sense of the word, you can be what you never will be in any other,*ambidexter.* But I am sorry you took so much trouble, and I fear *pains* besides, to display your new talent.

Ever your Grace's truly faithful,
WALTER SCOTT.

The closing sentence of this letter refers to a fit of the gout which had disabled the Duke's right hand, but not cooled his zeal on a subject which, throughout January, 1818, occupied, I firmly believe, much more of his correspondent's thoughts by day and dreams by night, than any one, or perhaps than all others, besides. The time now approached when a Commission to examine the Crown-room in the Castle of Edinburgh, which had sprung from one of Scott's conversations with the Prince Regent in 1815, was at length to be acted upon. The minstrel of the "Rough Clan" had taken care that the name of his chief should stand at the head of the document; but the Duke's now precarious health ultimately prevented him from being present at the discovery of the long buried and almost forgotten Regalia of Scotland. The two following letters on this subject are of the same date— Edinburgh, 14th January, 1818.

TO THE DUKE OF BUCCLEUCH, ETC., ETC., BOWHILL.

MY DEAR LORD,—You will hear from the Advocate that the Commission for opening the Regalia is arrived, and that the Commissioners held their first meeting yesterday. They have named next Wednesday (in case your Grace can attend) for opening the mysterious chest. So this question will be put to rest forever.

I remember among the rebel company which debauched my youth, there was a drunken old Tory, who used to sing a ballad made about these same Regalia at the time of the Union, in which they were all destined to the basest uses; the crown, for example,
"To make a can for Brandy Nan
To puke in when she's tipsy."
The rest of the song is in a tone of equally pure humor; the chorus ran:—
"Farewell, thou ancient kingdom—
Farewell, thou ancient kingdom.
Who sold thyself for English pelf—
Was ever such a thing done?"
I hope your Grace feels yourself sufficiently interested in the recovery of these ancient symbols of national independence, so long worn by your forefathers, and which were never profaned by the touch of a monarch of a foreign dynasty. Here is fine planting weather. I trust it is as good in the Forest and on Tweedside.

Ever your Grace's truly faithful
WALTER SCOTT.

TO J. B. S. MORRITT, ESQ., M. P., ROKEBY.

DEAR MORRITT,—Our fat friend has remembered a petition which I put up to him, and has granted a Commission to the Officers of State and others (my unworthy self included)—which trusty and well-beloved persons are to institute a search after the Regalia of Scotland. There has an odd mystery hung about the fate of these royal symbols of national independence. The spirit of the Scotch at the Union clung fondly to these emblems; and to soothe their jealousy it was specially provided by an article of the Union, that the Regalia should never be removed, under any pretext, from the kingdom of Scotland. Accordingly they were deposited, with much ceremony, as an authentic instrument bears, in a strong chest, secured by many locks, and the chest itself placed in a strong room, which again was carefully bolted up and secured, leaving to national pride the satisfaction of pointing to the barred window, with the consciousness that there lay the Regalia of Scotland. But this gratification was strangely qualified by a surmise, which somehow became generally averred, stating, that the Regalia had been sent to London; and you may remember that we saw at the Jewel Office a crown, *said to be* the ancient Crown of Scotland. If this transfer (by the way, highly illegal) was ever made, it must have been under some secret warrant; for no authority can be traced for such a proceeding in the records of the Secretary of State's Office. Fifteen or twenty years ago, the Crown-room, as it is called, was opened by certain Commissioners, under authority of a sign-manual. They saw the fatal chest, strewed with the dust of an hundred years, about six inches thick: a coating of like thickness lay on the floor; and I have heard the late President Blair say, that the uniform and level appearance of the dust warranted them to believe that the chest, if opened at all after 1707, must have been violated within a short time of that date, since, had it been opened at a later period, the dust accumulated on the lid, and displaced at opening it, must have been lying around the chest. But the Commissioners did not think their warrant entitled them to force this chest, for which no keys could be found; especially as their warrant only entitled them to search for *records*—not for crowns and sceptres.

The mystery, therefore, remained unpenetrated; and public curiosity was left to console itself with the nursery rhyme:—

"On Tintock tap there is a mist,
And in the mist there is a kist."

Our fat friend's curiosity, however, goes to the point at once, authorizing and enjoining an express search for the Regalia. Our friend of Buccleuch is at the head of the Commission, and will, I think, be as keen as I or any one, to see the issue.

I trust you have read Rob by this time. I think he smells of the cramp. Above all, I had too much flax on my distaff; and as it did not consist with my patience or my plan to make a fourth volume, I was obliged at last to draw a rough, coarse, and hasty thread. But the book is well liked here, and has reeled off in great style. I have two stories on the anvil, far superior to Rob Roy in point of interest. Ever yours,

WALTER SCOTT.

The Commissioners, who finally assembled on the 4th of February, were, according to the record, "the Right Hon. Charles Hope, Lord President of the Court of Session; the Right Hon. David Boyle, Lord Justice-Clerk; the Right Hon. William Adam, Lord Chief Commissioner of the Jury Court; Major-General John Hope (Commanding the Forces in Scotland); the Solicitor-General (James Wedderburn, Esq.); the Lord Provost of Edinburgh (Kincaid Mackenzie, Esq.); William Clerk, Esq., Principal Clerk of the Jury Court; Henry Jardine, Esq., Deputy Remembrancer in the Exchequer; Thomas Thomson, Esq., Deputy Clerk-Register of Scotland; and Walter Scott, Esq., one of the Principal Clerks of Session."

Of the proceedings of this day, the reader has a full and particular account in an Essay which Scott penned shortly afterwards, and which is included in his Prose Miscellanies (vol. vii.). But I must not omit the contemporaneous letters in which he announced the success of the quest to his friend the Secretary of the Admiralty, and through him to the Regent:—

TO J. W. CROKER, ESQ., M. P., ETC., ETC., ADMIRALTY, LONDON.

EDINBURGH, 4th February, 1818.

MY DEAR CROKER,—I have the pleasure to assure you the Regalia of Scotland were this day found in perfect preservation. The Sword of State and Sceptre showed marks of hard usage at some former period; but in all respects agree with the description in Thomson's work.[86] I will send you a complete account of the opening to-morrow, as the official account will take some time to draw up. In the mean time, I hope you will remain as obstinate in your unbelief as St. Thomas, because then you will come down to satisfy yourself. I know nobody entitled to earlier information, save ONE, to whom you can perhaps find the means of communicating the result of our researches. The post is just going off.

Ever yours truly,
WALTER SCOTT.

TO THE SAME.

EDINBURGH, 5th February, 1818.

MY DEAR CROKER,—I promised I would add something to my report of yesterday, and yet I find I have but little to say. The extreme solemnity of opening sealed doors of oak and iron, and finally breaking open a chest which had been shut since 7th March, 1707, about a hundred and eleven years, gave a sort of interest to our researches, which I can hardly express to you, and it would be very difficult to describe the intense eagerness with which we watched the rising of the lid of the chest, and the progress of the workmen in breaking it open, which was neither an easy nor a speedy task. It sounded very hollow when they worked on it with their tools, and I began to lean to your faction of the Little Faiths. However, I never could assign any probable or feasible reason for withdrawing these memorials of ancient independence; and my doubts rather arose from the conviction that many absurd things are done in public as well as in private life, merely out of a hasty impression of passion or resentment. For it was evident the removal of the Regalia might have greatly irritated people's minds here, and offered a fair pretext of breaking the Union, which for thirty years was the predominant wish of the Scottish nation.

The discovery of the Regalia has interested people's minds much more strongly than I expected, and is certainly calculated to make a pleasant and favorable impression upon them in respect to the kingly part of the constitution. It would be of the utmost consequence that they should be occasionally shown to them, under proper regulations, and for a small fee. The Sword of State is a most beautiful piece of workmanship, a present from Pope Julius II. to James IV. The scabbard is richly decorated with filigree work of silver, double gilded, representing oak leaves and acorns, executed in a taste worthy that classical age in which the arts revived. A draughtsman has been employed to make sketches of these articles, in order to be laid before his Royal Highness. The fate of these Regalia, which his Royal Highness's goodness has thus restored to light and honor, has on one or two occasions been singular enough. They were, in 1652, lodged in the Castle of Dunnottar, the seat of the Earl Marischal, by whom, according to his ancient privilege, they were kept. The castle was defended by George Ogilvie of Barra, who, apprehensive of the progress which the English made in reducing the strong places in Scotland, became anxious for the safety of these valuable memorials. The ingenuity of his lady had them conveyed out of the castle in a bag on a woman's back, among some *hards*, as they are called, of lint. They were carried to the Kirk of Kinneff, and entrusted to the care of the clergyman, named Grainger, and his wife, and buried under the pulpit. The Castle of Dunnottar, though very strong and faithfully defended, was at length under necessity of surrendering, being the last strong place in Britain on which the royal flag floated in those calamitous times. Ogilvie and his lady were threatened with the utmost extremities by the Republican General Morgan, unless they should produce the Regalia. The governor stuck to it that he knew nothing of them, as in fact they had been carried away without his knowledge. The lady maintained she had given them to John Keith, second son of the Earl Marischal, by whom, she said, they had been carried to France. They suffered a long imprisonment, and much ill usage. On the Restoration, the old Countess Marischal, founding upon the story Mrs. Ogilvie had told to screen her husband, obtained for her own son, John Keith, the earldom of Kintore, and the post of Knight Marischal, with £400 a year, as if he had been in truth the preserver of the Regalia. It soon proved that this reward had been too hastily given, for Ogilvie of Barra produced the Regalia, the honest clergyman refusing to deliver them to any one but those from whom he received them. Ogilvie was made a Knight Baronet, however, and got a new charter of the lands, acknowledging the good service. Thus it happened oddly enough, that Keith, who was abroad during the transaction, and had nothing to do with it, got the earldom, pension, etc., Ogilvie only inferior honors, and the poor clergyman nothing whatever, or, as we say, *the hare's foot to lick*. As for Ogilvie's lady, she died before the Restoration, her health being ruined by the hardships she endured from the Cromwellian satellites. She was a Douglas, with all the high spirit of that proud family. On her deathbed, and not till then, she told her husband where the honors were concealed, charging him to suffer death rather than betray them. Popular tradition says, not very probably, that Grainger and his wife were *booted* (that is, tortured with the engine called the boots). I think that the Knight Marischal's office rested in the Kintore family until 1715, when it was resumed on account of the bearded Earl's accession to the Insurrection of that year. He escaped well, for they might have taken his estate and his earldom. I must save post, however, and conclude abruptly. Yours ever,

WALTER SCOTT.

On the 5th, after the foregoing letter had been written at the Clerk's table, Scott and several of his brother Commissioners revisited the Castle, accompanied by some of the ladies of their families. His daughter tells me that her father's conversation had worked her feelings up to such a pitch, that when the lid was again removed, she nearly fainted, and drew back from the circle. As she was retiring, she was startled by his voice exclaiming, in a tone of the deepest emotion, "something between anger and despair," as she expresses it,— "By G—, No!" One of the Commissioners, not quite entering into the solemnity with which Scott regarded this business, had, it seems, made a sort of motion as if he meant to put the crown on the head of one of the young ladies near him, but the voice and aspect of the Poet were more than sufficient to make the worthy gentleman understand his error; and, respecting the enthusiasm with which he had not been taught to sympathize, he laid down the ancient diadem with an air of painful embarrassment. Scott whispered, "Pray, forgive me;" and turning round at the moment, observed his daughter deadly pale, and leaning by the door. He immediately drew her out of the room, and when the air had somewhat recovered her, walked with her across the Mound to Castle Street. "He never spoke all the way home," she says, "but every now and then I felt his arm tremble; and from that time I fancied he began to treat me more like a woman than a child. I thought he liked me better, too, than he had ever done before."

These little incidents may give some notion of the profound seriousness with which his imagination had invested this matter. I am obliged to add, that in the society of Edinburgh at the time, even in the highest Tory circles, it did not seem to awaken much even of curiosity—to say nothing of any deeper feeling. There was, however, a great excitement among the common people of the town, and a still greater among the peasantry, not only in the neighborhood, but all over Scotland; and the Crown-room, becoming thenceforth one of the established *lions* of a city much resorted to, moreover, by stranger tourists, was likely, on the most moderate scale of admission-fee, to supply a revenue sufficient for remunerating responsible and respectable guardianship. This post would, as Scott thought, be a very suitable one for his friend, Captain Adam Ferguson; and he exerted all his zeal for that purpose. The Captain was appointed: his nomination, however, did not take place for some months after; and the postscript of a letter to the Duke of Buccleuch, dated May 14, 1818, plainly indicates the interest on which Scott mainly relied for its completion: "If you happen," he writes, "to see Lord Melville, pray give him a jog about Ferguson's affair; but between ourselves, I depend chiefly on the kind offices of Willie Adam, who is an auld sneck-drawer." The Lord Chief-Commissioner, at all times ready to lend Scott his influence with the Royal Family, had, on the present occasion, the additional motive of warm and hereditary personal regard for Ferguson.

I have placed together such letters as referred principally to the episode of the Regalia; but shall now give, in the order of time, a few which will sufficiently illustrate the usual course of his existence, while The Heart of Mid-Lothian was in progress. It appears that he resumed, in the beginning of this year, his drama of Devorgoil. His letters to Terry are of course full of that subject, but they contain, at the same time, many curious indications of his views and feelings as to theatrical affairs in general—and mixed up with these a most characteristic record of the earnestness with which he now watched the interior fitting up, as he had in the season before the outward architecture, of the new edifice at Abbotsford. Meanwhile it will be seen that he found leisure hours for various contributions to periodical works,—among others, an article on Kirkton's Church History, and another on (of all subjects in the world) *military bridges*, for the Quarterly Review; a spirited version of the old German ballad on the Battle of Sempach, and a generous criticism on Mrs. Shelley's romance of Frankenstein, for Blackwood's Magazine. This being the first winter and spring of Laidlaw's establishment at Kaeside, communications as to the affairs of the farm were exchanged weekly whenever Scott was in Edinburgh, and they afford delightful evidence of that paternal solicitude for the well-being of his rural dependents, which all along kept pace with Scott's zeal as to the economical improvement, and the picturesque adornment of his territories.

TO D. TERRY, ESQ., LONDON.

EDINBURGH, 23d January, 1818.

MY DEAR TERRY,—You have by this time the continuation of the drama, down to the commencement of the third act, as I have your letter on the subject of the first. You will understand that I only mean them as sketches; for the first and second acts are too short, and both want much to combine them with the third. I can easily add music to Miss Devorgoil's part. As to Braham, he is a beast of an actor, though an angel of a singer, and truly I do not see what he could personify. Let me know, however, your thoughts and wishes, and all shall be moulded to the best of my power to meet them: the point is to make it *take* if we can; the rest is all leather and prunella. A great many things must occur to you technically better, in the way of alteration and improvement, and you know well that, though too indolent to amend things on my own conviction, I am always ready to make them meet my friends' wishes if possible. We shall both wish it better than I can make it, but there is no reason why we should not do for it all that we can. I advise you to take some sapient friend into your counsels, and let me know the result, returning the MS. at the same time.

I am now anxious to complete Abbotsford. I think I told you I mean to do nothing whatever to the present house, but to take it away altogether at some future time, so that I finish the upper story without any communication with Mrs. Redford's *ci-devant* mansion, and shall place the opening in the lower story, wherever it will be most suitable for the new house, without regard to defacing the temporary drawing-room. I am quite feverish about the armory. I have two pretty complete suits of armor—one Indian one, and a cuirassier's, with boots, casque, etc.; many helmets, corselets, and steel caps, swords and poniards without end, and about a dozen of guns, ancient and modern. I have besides two or three battle-axes and maces, pikes and targets, a Highlander's accoutrement complete, a great variety of branches of horns, pikes, bows and arrows, and the clubs and creases of Indian tribes. Mr. Bullock promised to give some hint about the fashion of disposing all these matters; and now our spring is approaching, and I want but my plans to get on. I have reason to be proud of the finishing of my castle, for even of the tower, for which I trembled, not a stone has been shaken by the late terrific gale, which blew a roof clear off in the neighborhood. It was lying in the road like a saddle, as Tom Purdie expressed it. Neither has a slate been lifted, though about two yards of slating were stripped from the stables in the haugh, which you know were comparatively less exposed.

I am glad to hear of Mrs. Terry's improved health and good prospects. As for young Master Mumblecrust, I have no doubt he will be a credit to us all.

Yours ever truly,

W. SCOTT.

As the letters to Mr. Laidlaw did not travel by post, but in the basket which had come laden with farm-produce for the use of the family in Edinburgh, they have rarely any date but the day of the week. This is, however, of no consequence.

TO MR. LAIDLAW, KAESIDE.

Wednesday. [January, 1818.]

DEAR WILLIE,—Should the weather be rough, and you nevertheless obliged to come to town, do not think of riding, but take the Blucher.[87] Remember, your health is of consequence to your family. Pray talk generally with the notables of Darnick—I mean Rutherford, and so forth—concerning the best ordering of the road to the marle; and also of the foot-road. It appears to me some route might be found more convenient than the present, but that which is most agreeable to those interested shall also be most agreeable for me. As a patriotic member of the community of Darnick, I consider their rights equally important as my own.

I told you I should like to convert the present steading at Beechland into a little hamlet of laborers, which we will name Abbotstown. The art of making people happy is to leave them much to their own guidance, but some little regulation is necessary. In the first place, I should like to have active and decent people there; then it is to be considered on what footing they should be. I conceive the best possible is, that they should pay for their cottages, and cow-grass, and potato ground, and be paid for their labor at the ordinary rate. I would give them some advantages sufficient to balance the following conditions, which, after all, are conditions in my favor: *1st*, That they shall keep their cottages and little gardens, and doors, tolerably neat; and *2d*, That the men shall on no account shoot, or the boys break timber or take birds' nests, or go among the planting. I do not know any other restrictions, and these are easy. I should think we might settle a few families very happily here, which is an object I have much at heart, for I have no notion of the proprietor who is only ambitious to be lord of the "beast and the brute," and chases the human face from his vicinity. By the bye, could we not manage to have a piper among the colonists?

We are delighted to hear that your little folks like the dells. Pray, in your walks try to ascertain the locality of St. John's Well, which cures the botts, and which John Moss claims for Kaeside; also the true history of the Carline's Hole. Ever most truly yours,

W. SCOTT.

I hope Mrs. Laidlaw does not want for anything that she can get from the garden or elsewhere.

TO DANIEL TERRY, ESQ.

8th February, 1818.

MY DEAR TERRY,—Yours arrived, unluckily, just half an hour after my packet was in the post-office, so this will cost you 9*d*., for which I grieve. To answer your principal question first,—the drama is

"Yours, Terry, yours in every thought."

I should never have dreamed of making such an attempt in my own proper person; and if I had such a vision, I should have been anxious to have made it something of a legitimate drama, such as a literary man, uncalled upon by any circumstance to connect himself with the stage, might have been expected to produce. Now this is just what any gentleman in your situation might run off, to give a little novelty to the entertainment of the year, and as such will meet a mitigated degree of criticism, and have a better chance of that *productive* success, which is my principal object in my godson's behalf. If any time should come when you might wish to disclose the secret, it will be in your power, and our correspondence will always serve to show that it was only at my earnest request, annexed as the condition of bringing the play forward, that you gave it your name—a circumstance which, with all the attending particulars, will prove plainly that there was no assumption on your part.

A beautiful drama might be made on the concealment of the Scotch Regalia during the troubles. But it would interfere with the democratic spirit of the times, and would probably

—— "By party rage,

Or right or wrong, be hooted from the stage."

I will never forgive you if you let any false idea of my authorial feelings prevent your acting in this affair as if you were the real parent, not the godfather of the piece. Our facetious friend J. B. knows nought of such a matter being *en train*, and never will know. I am delighted to hear my windows are finished. Yours very truly,

WALTER SCOTT.

TO MR. LAIDLAW, KAESIDE.

Wednesday. [February, 1818.]

DEAR WILLIE,—I am not desirous to buy more land at present, unless I were to deal with Mr. Rutherford or Heiton, and I would rather deal with them next year than this, when I would have all my payments made for what I am now buying. Three or four such years as the last would enable me with prudence and propriety to ask Nicol[89] himself to flit and remove.

I like the idea of the birch-hedge much, and if intermixed with holly and thorns, I think it might make an impenetrable thicket, having all the advantages of a hedge without the formality. I fancy you will also need a great number of (black) Italian poplars—which are among the most useful and best growers, as well as most beautiful of plants which love a wet soil.

I am glad the saws are going.[90] We may begin by and by with wrights, but I cannot but think that a handy laborer might be taught to work at them. I shall insist on Tom learning the process perfectly himself.

As to the darkness of the garrets, they are intended for the accommodation of travelling geniuses, poets, painters, and so forth, and a little obscurity will refresh their shattered brains. I dare say Lauchie[91] will *shave* his knoll, if it is required—it may to the barber's with the Laird's hebdomadal beard—and Packwood would have thought it the easier job of the two.

I saw Blackwood yesterday, and Hogg the day before, and I understand from them you think of resigning the Chronicle department of the Magazine. Blackwood told me that if you did not like that part of the duty, he would consider himself accountable for the same sum he had specified to you for any other articles you might communicate from time to time. He proposes that Hogg should do the Chronicle: He will not do it so well as you, for he wants judgment and caution, and likes to have the appearance of eccentricity where eccentricity is least graceful; that, however, is Blackwood's affair. If you really do not like the Chronicle, there can be no harm in your giving it up. What strikes me is, that there is a something certain in having such a department to conduct, whereas you may sometimes find yourself at a loss when you have to cast about for a subject every month. Blackwood *is* rather in a bad pickle just now—sent to Coventry by the trade, as the booksellers call themselves, and all about the parody of the two beasts.[92] Surely these gentlemen think themselves rather formed of porcelain clay than of common potter's ware. Dealing in satire against all others, their own dignity suffers so cruelly from an ill-imagined joke! If B. had good books to sell, he might set them all at defiance. His Magazine does well, and beats Constable's: but we will talk of this when we meet.[93]

As for Whiggery in general, I can only say, that as no man can be said to be utterly overset until his rump has been higher than his head, so I cannot read in history of any free state which has been brought to slavery until the rascal and uninstructed populace had had their short hour of anarchical government, which naturally leads to the stern repose of military despotism. Property, morals, education, are the proper qualifications for those who should hold political rights, and extending them very widely greatly lessens the chance of these qualifications being found in electors. Look at the sort of persons chosen at elections where the franchise is very general, and you will find either fools who are content to flatter the passions of the mob for a little transient popularity, or knaves who pander to their follies, that they may make their necks a footstool for their own promotion. With these convictions, I am very jealous of Whiggery, under all modifications; and I must say, my acquaintance with the total want of principle in some of its warmest professors does not tend to recommend it. Somewhat too much of this. My compliments to the goodwife. Yours truly,

WALTER SCOTT.

TO THE SAME.

Wednesday. [February, 1818.]

DEAR WILLIE,—I have no idea Usher[94] will take the sheepland again, nor would I press it on him. As my circumstances stand, immediate revenue is much less my object than the real improvement of this property, which amuses me besides; our wants are amply supplied by my £1600 a year official income: nor have we a wish or a motive to extend our expenses beyond that of the decencies and hospitality of our station in life; so that my other resources remain for buying land in future, or improving what we have. No doubt Abbotsford, in maintaining our establishment during the summer, may be reckoned £150 or £200 saved on what we must otherwise buy; and if we could arrange to have mutton and beef occasionally from the farm in winter, it would be a still greater saving. All this you will consider: for Tom, thoroughly honest and very clever in his way, has no kind of generalizing, and would often like to save sixpence in his own department at the expense of my paying five shillings in another. This is his fault, and when you join to it a Scotch slovenliness which leads him to see things half-finished without pain or anxiety, I do not know any other he has—but such as they are, these must be guarded against. For our housemaid (for housekeeper we must not call her), I should like much a hawk of a nest so good as that you mention: but would not such a place be rather beneath her views? Her duty would be to look to scrupulous cleanliness within doors, and employ her leisure in spinning, or plain-work, as wanted. When we came out for a blink, she would be expected to cook a little in a plain way, and play maid of all work; when we were stationary, she would assist the housemaid and superintend the laundry. Probably your aunt's granddaughter will have pretensions to something better than this; but as we are to be out on the 12th March, we will talk it over.

Assuredly a well-connected steady person would be of the greatest consequence to us. I like your plan of pitting much; and to compromise betwixt you and Tom, do one half with superior attention, and slit in the others for mere nurses. But I am no friend to that same slitting.

I adhere to trying a patch or two of larches, of a quarter of an acre each, upon the Athole plan, by way of experiment. We can plant them up if they do not thrive. On the whole, three-and-a-half feet is, I think, the right distance. I have no fear of the ground being impoverished. Trees are not like arable crops, which necessarily derive their sustenance from the superficial earth—the roots of trees go far and wide, and, if incommoded by a neighbor, they send out suckers to procure nourishment elsewhere. They never hurt each other till their tops interfere, which may be easily prevented by timely weeding.

I rejoice in the sawmill. Have you settled with Harper?—and how do Og and Bashan[95] come on? I cannot tell you how delighted I am with the account Hogg gives me of Mr. Grieve. The great Cameron was chaplain in the house of my great something grandfather, and so I hope Mr. Grieve will be mine. If, as the King of Prussia said to Rousseau, "a little persecution is necessary to make his home entirely to his mind," he shall have it; and what persecutors seldom promise, I will stop whenever he is tired of it. I have a pair of thumbikins also much at his service, if he requires their assistance to glorify God and the Covenant. Sincerely, I like enthusiasm of every kind so well, especially when united with worth of character, that I shall be delighted with this old gentleman. Ever yours,

W. SCOTT.

The last paragraph of this letter refers to an uncle of Laidlaw's (the father of Hogg's friend, John Grieve), who at this time thought of occupying a cottage on Scott's estate. He was a preacher of the Cameronian sect, and had long ministered to a very small remnant of "the hill-folk" scattered among the wilds of Ettrick. He was a very good man, and had a most venerable and apostolical benignity of aspect; but his prejudices were as extravagant as those of Cameron, his patriarch, himself could have been. The project of his removal to Tweedside was never realized.

The following admirable letter was written at the request of Messrs. Constable, who had, on Scott's recommendation, undertaken the publication of Mr. Maturin's novel, Women, or *Pour et Contre*. The reverend author's Bertram had, it may be remembered, undergone some rather rough usage in Coleridge's Biographia Literaria; and he was now desirous to revenge himself by a preface of the polemical sort:—

TO THE REV. C. R. MATURIN, DUBLIN.

26th February, 1818.

DEAR SIR,—I am going to claim the utmost and best privilege of sincere friendship and good-will, that of offering a few words of well-meant advice; and you may be sure that the occasion seems important to induce me to venture so far upon your tolerance. It respects the preface to your work, which Constable and Co. have sent to me. It is as well written as that sort of thing can be; but will you forgive me if I say—it is too much in the tone of the offence which gave rise to it, to be agreeable either to good taste or to general feeling. Coleridge's work has been little read or heard of, and has made no general impression whatever—certainly no impression unfavorable to you or your play. In the opinion, therefore, of many, you will be resenting an injury of which they are unacquainted with the existence. If I see a man beating another unmercifully, I am apt to condemn him upon the first blush of the business, and hardly excuse him though I may afterwards learn he had ample provocation. Besides, your diatribe is not*hujus loci*. We take up a novel for amusement, and this current of controversy breaks out upon us like a stream of lava out of the side of a beautiful green hill; men will say you should have reserved your disputes for reviews or periodical publications, and they will sympathize less with your anger, because they will not think the time proper for expressing it. We are bad judges, bad physicians, and bad divines in our own case; but, above all, we are seldom able, when injured or insulted, to judge of the degree of sympathy which the world will bear in our resentment and our retaliation. The instant, however, that such degree of sympathy is exceeded, we hurt ourselves, and not our adversary. I am so convinced of this, and so deeply fixed in the opinion, that besides the uncomfortable feelings which are generated in the course of literary debate, a man lowers his estimation in the public eye by engaging in such controversy, that, since I have been dipped in ink, I have suffered no personal attacks (and I have been honored with them of all descriptions) to provoke me to reply. A man will certainly be vexed on such occasions, and I have wished to have the knaves *where the muircock was the bailie*—or, as *you* would say, *upon the sod*—but I never let the thing cling to my mind, and always adhered to my resolution, that if my writings and tenor of life did not confute such attacks, my words never should. Let me entreat you to view Coleridge's violence as a thing to be contemned, not retaliated—the opinion of a British public may surely be set in honest opposition to that of one disappointed and wayward man. You should also consider, *en bon Chrétien*, that Coleridge has had some room to be spited at the world, and you are, I trust, to continue to be a favorite with the public—so that you should totally neglect and despise criticism, however virulent, which arises out of his bad fortune and your good.

I have only to add that Messrs. Constable and Co. are seriously alarmed for the effects of the preface upon the public mind as unfavorable to the work. In this they must be tolerable judges, for their experience as to popular feeling is very great; and as they have met your wishes, in all the course of the transaction, perhaps you will be disposed to give some weight to their opinion upon a point like this. Upon my own part I can only say that I have no habits of friendship, and scarce those of acquaintance with Coleridge—I have not even read his Autobiography—but I consider him as a man of genius, struggling with bad habits and difficult circumstances. It is, however, entirely upon your account that I take the liberty of stating an opinion on a subject of such delicacy. I should wish you to give your excellent talents fair play, and to ride this race without carrying any superfluous weight; and I am so well acquainted with my old friend the public, that I could bet a thousand pounds to a shilling, that the preface (if that controversial part of it is not cancelled) will greatly prejudice your novel.

I will not ask your forgiveness for the freedom I have used, for I am sure you will not suspect me of any motives but those which arise from regard to your talents and person; but I shall be glad to hear (whether you follow my advice or no) that you are not angry with me for having volunteered to offer it.

My health is, I think, greatly improved; I have had some returns of my spasmodic affection, but tolerable in degree, and yielding to medicine. I hope gentle exercise and the air of my hills will set me up this summer. I trust you will soon be out now. I have delayed reading the sheets in progress after Vol. I., that I might enjoy them when collected. Ever yours, etc.,

WALTER SCOTT.

TO MR. LAIDLAW.

EDINBURGH, Wednesday. [March, 1818.]

DEAR WILLIE,—I am delighted to hear the plantings get on so well. The weather here has been cruelly changeable—fresh one day—frost the next—snow the third. This morning the snow lay three inches thick, and before noon it was gone, and blowing a tempest. Many of the better ranks are ill of the typhus fever, and some deaths. How do your poor folks come on? Let Tom advance you money when it is wanted. I do not propose, like the heroine of a novel, to convert the hovels of want into the abodes of elegant plenty, but we have enough to spare to relieve actual distress, and do not wish to economize where we can find out (which is difficult) where the assistance is instantly useful.

Don't let Tom forget hedgerow trees, which he is very unwilling to remember; and also to plant birches, oaks, elms, and such like round-headed trees along the verges of the Kaeside plantations; they make a beautiful outline, and also a sort of fence, and were not planted last year because the earth at the sunk fences was too newly travelled. This should be mixed with various bushes, as hollies, thorns, so as to make a wild hedge, or thickety obstruction to the inroads of cattle. A few sweetbriers, alders, honeysuckles, laburnums, etc., should be thrown in. A verdant screen may be made in this way, of the wildest and most beautiful description, which should never be clipt, only pruned, allowing the loose branches to drop over those that are taken away. Tom is very costive about trees, and talks only of 300 poplars. I shall send at least double that number; also some hagberries, etc. He thinks he is saving me money when he is starving my projects; but he is a pearl of honesty and good intention, and I like him the better for needing driving where expense is likely. Ever yours,

W. SCOTT.

TO JOHN MURRAY, ESQ., ALBEMARLE STREET, LONDON.

ABBOTSFORD, 23d March, 1818.

DEAR MURRAY,—

"Grieve not for me, my dearest dear,
I am not dead but sleepeth here."—

I have little to plead for myself, but the old and vile apologies of laziness and indisposition. I think I have been so unlucky of late as to have always the will to work when sitting at the desk hurts me, and the irresistible propensity to be lazy, when I might, like the man whom Hogarth introduces into Bridewell with his hands strapped up against the wall, "better work than stand thus." I laid Kirkton[96] aside half finished, from a desire to get the original edition of the lives of Cameron, etc., by Patrick Walker, which I had not seen since a boy, and now I have got it, and find, as I suspected, that some curious *morceaux* have been cut out by subsequent editors.[97] I will, without loss of time, finish the article, which I think you will like. Blackwood kidnapped an article for his Magazine on the Frankenstein story,[98] which I intended for you. A very old friend and school companion of mine, and a gallant soldier, if ever there was one, Sir Howard Douglas, has asked me to review his work on Military Bridges. I must get a friend's assistance for the scientific part, and add some balaam of mine own (as printers' devils say) to make up four or five pages. I have no objection to attempt Lord Orford if I have time, and find I can do it with ease. Though far from admiring his character, I have always had a high opinion of his talents, and am well acquainted with his works. The letters you have published are, I think, his very best—lively, entertaining, and unaffected.[99] I am greatly obliged to you for these and other literary treasures which I owe to your goodness from time to time. Although not thankfully acknowledged as they should be in course, these things are never thanklessly received.

I could have sworn that Beppo was founded on Whistlecraft, as both were on Anthony Hall,[100] who, like Beppo, had more wit than grace.

I am not, however, in spirits at present for treating either these worthies, or my friend Rose,[101] though few have warmer wishes to any of the trio. But this confounded changeable weather has twice within this fortnight brought back my cramp in the stomach. Adieu. My next shall be with a packet.—Yours truly,

W. Scott.

In the next letter we have Scott's lamentation over the death of Mrs. Murray Keith— the Mrs. Bethune Baliol of his Chronicles of the Canongate. The person alluded to under the designation of "Prince of the Black Marble Islands" was Mr. George Bullock, already often mentioned as, with Terry and Mr. Atkinson, consulted about all the arrangements of the rising house at Abbotsford. Scott gave him this title from the Arabian Nights, on occasion of his becoming the lessee of some marble quarries in the Isle of Anglesea.

TO D. TERRY, ESQ., LONDON.

April 30, 1818—SELKIRK.

MY DEAR TERRY,—Your packet arrived this morning. I was much disappointed not to find the Prince of the Black Islands' plan in it, nor have I heard a word from him since anent it, or anent the still more essential articles of doors and windows. I heard from Hector Macdonald Buchanan, that the said doors and windows were packing a fortnight since, but there are no news of them. Surely our friend's heart has grown as hard as his materials; or the spell of the enchantress, which confined itself to the extremities of his predecessor, has extended over his whole person. Mr. Atkinson has kept tryst charmingly, and the ceiling of the dining-room will be superb. I have got I know not how many casts, from Melrose and other places, of pure Gothic antiquity. I must leave this on the 12th, and I could bet a trifle the doors, etc., will arrive the very day I set out, and be all put up *à la bonne aventure*. Meantime I am keeping open house, not much to my convenience, and I am afraid I shall be stopped in my plastering by the want of these matters. The exposed state of my house has led to a mysterious disturbance. The night before last we were awaked by a violent noise, like drawing heavy boards along the new part of the house. I fancied something had fallen, and thought no more about it. This was about *two* in the morning. Last night, at the same witching hour, the very same noise occurred. Mrs. S., as you know, is rather *timbersome*, so up got I, with Beardie's broadsword under my arm,

"So bolt upright,
And ready to fight."

But nothing was out of order, neither can I discover what occasioned the disturbance. However, I went to bed, grumbling against Tenterden Street,[102] and all its works. If there was no entrance but the keyhole, I should warrant myself against the ghosts. We have a set of idle fellows called workmen about us, which is a better way of accounting for nocturnal noises than any that is to be found in Baxter or Glanville.

When you see Mr. Atkinson, will you ask him how far he is satisfied with the arch between the armory and the ante-room, and whether it pleases him as it now stands? I have a brave old oaken cabinet, as black as ebony, 300 years old at least, which will occupy one side of the ante-room for the present. It is seven feet and a half long, about eighteen inches deep, and upwards of six feet high—a fine stand for china, etc.

You will be sorry to hear that we have lost our excellent old friend, Mrs. Murray Keith. She enjoyed all her spirits and excellent faculties till within two days of her death, when she was seized with a feverish complaint, which eighty-two years were not calculated to resist. Much tradition, and of the very best kind, has died with this excellent old lady; one of the few persons whose spirits and cleanliness, and freshness of mind and body, made old age lovely and desirable. In the general case, it seems scarce endurable.

It seems odd to me that Rob Roy[103] should have made good fortune; pray let me know something of its history. There is in Jedediah's present work a thing capable of being woven out a *bourgeoise* tragedy. I think of contriving that it shall be in your hands some time before the public see it, that you may try to operate upon it yourself. This would not be difficult, as vol. 4, and part of 3d, contain a different story. *Avowedly* I will never write for the stage; if I do, "call me *horse.*" And indeed I feel severely the want of knowledge of theatrical business and effect: however, something we will do. I am writing in the noise and babble of a head-court of freeholders; therefore my letter is incoherent, and therefore it is written also on long paper; but therefore, moreover, it will move by frank, as the member is here, and stands upon his popularity. Kind compliments to Mrs. Terry and Walter.

Yours very truly,
WALTER SCOTT.

On the morning that Mr. Terry received the foregoing letter in London, Mr. William Erskine was breakfasting with him; and the chief subject of their conversation was the sudden death of George Bullock, which had occurred on the same night, and, as nearly as they could ascertain, at the very hour when Scott was roused from his sleep by the "mysterious disturbance" here described, and sallied from his chamber with old Beardie's Killiecrankie claymore in his hand. This coincidence, when Scott received Erskine's minute detail of what had happened in Tenterden Street, made a much stronger impression on his mind than might be gathered from the tone of an ensuing communication.

TO D. TERRY, ESQ., LONDON.

ABBOTSFORD, 4th May, 1818.

DEAR TERRY,—I received with the greatest surprise, and the most sincere distress, the news of poor George Bullock's death. In the full career of honorable industry,— distinguished by his uncommon taste and talent,—esteemed by all who transacted business with him,—and loved by those who had the pleasure of his more intimate acquaintance,—I can scarce conceive a more melancholy summons. It comes as a particular shock to me, because I had, particularly of late, so much associated his idea with the improvements here, in which his kind and enthusiastic temper led him to take such interest; and in looking at every unfinished or projected circumstance, I feel an impression of melancholy which will for some time take away the pleasure I have found in them. I liked George Bullock because he had no trumpery selfishness about his heart, taste, or feelings. Pray let me know about the circumstances of his family, etc. I feel most sincerely interested in all that concerns him. It must have been a dreadful surprise to Mr. Atkinson and you who lived with him so much. I need not, I am sure, beg you to be in no hurry about my things. The confusion must be cruelly great, without any friend adding to it; and in fact, at this moment, I am very indifferent on the subject. The poor kind fellow! He took so much notice of little Charles, and was so domesticated with us all, that I really looked with a schoolboy's anxiety for his being here in the season, to take his own quiet pleasures, and to forward mine. But God's will be done. All that surviving friends can do upon such a loss is, if possible, to love each other still better.—I beg to be kindly remembered to Mrs. Terry and Monsieur Walter. Ever most truly yours,

WALTER SCOTT.

TO THE SAME.

EDINBURGH, 16th May, 1818.

MY DEAR TERRY,—Mr. Nasmyth[104] has obligingly given me an opportunity of writing to you a few lines, as he is setting out for London. I cannot tell you how much I continue to be grieved for our kind-hearted and enthusiastic friend Bullock. I trust he has left his family comfortably settled, though, with so many plans which required his active and intelligent mind to carry them through, one has natural apprehensions upon that score. When you can with propriety make inquiry how my matters stand, I should be glad to know. Hector Macdonald tells me that my doors and windows were ready packed, in which case, perhaps, the sooner they are embarked the better, not only for safety, but because they can only be in the way, and the money will now be the more acceptable. Poor Bullock had also the measures for my chimney-pieces, for grates of different kinds, and orders for beds, dining-room tables and chairs. But how far these are in progress of being executed, or whether they can now be executed, I must leave to your judgment and inquiry. Your good sense and delicacy will understand the *façon de faire* better than I can point it out. I shall never have the pleasure in these things that I expected.

I have just left Abbotsford to attend the Summer session—left it when the leaves were coming out—the most delightful season for a worshipper of the country like me. The Home-bank, which we saw at first green with turnips, will now hide a man somewhat taller than Johnny Ballantyne in its shades. In fact, the trees cover the ground, and have a very pretty bosky effect; from six years to ten or twelve, I think wood is as beautiful as ever it is afterwards until it figures as aged and magnificent. Your hobbledehoy tree of twenty-five years' standing is neither so beautiful as in its infancy, nor so respectable as in its age.

Counsellor Erskine is returned, much pleased with your hospitality, and giving an excellent account of you. Were you not struck with the fantastical coincidence of our nocturnal disturbances at Abbotsford with the melancholy event that followed? I protest to you the noise resembled half-a-dozen men hard at work putting up boards and furniture, and nothing can be more certain than that there was nobody on the premises at the time. With a few additional touches, the story would figure in Glanville or Aubrey's Collection. In the mean time you may set it down with poor Dubisson's warnings,[105] as a remarkable coincidence coming under your own observation. I trust we shall see you this season. I think we could hammer a neat *comédie bourgeoise* out of The Heart of Mid-Lothian. Mrs. Scott and family join in kind compliments to Mrs. Terry; and I am ever yours truly,

WALTER SCOTT.

It appears from one of these letters to Terry, that, so late as the 30th of April, Scott still designed to include two separate stories in the second series of the Tales of my Landlord. But he must have changed his plan soon after that date; since the four volumes, entirely occupied with The Heart of Mid-Lothian, were before the public in the course of June. The story thus deferred, in consequence of the extent to which that of Jeanie Deans grew on his hands, was The Bride of Lammermoor.[Back to Contents]

CHAPTER XLI.

DINNER AT MR. HOME DRUMMOND'S. — SCOTT'S EDINBURGH DEN. — DETAILS OF HIS DOMESTIC LIFE IN CASTLE STREET. — HIS SUNDAY DINNERS. — HIS EVENING DRIVES, ETC. — HIS CONDUCT IN THE GENERAL SOCIETY OF EDINBURGH. — DINNERS AT JOHN BALLANTYNE'S VILLA, AND AT JAMES BALLANTYNE'S IN ST. JOHN STREET, ON THE APPEARANCE OF A NEW NOVEL. — ANECDOTES OF THE BALLANTYNES, AND OF CONSTABLE.

1818.

On the 12th of May, as we have seen, Scott left Abbotsford, for the summer session in Edinburgh.

At this moment, his position, take it for all in all, was, I am inclined to believe, what no other man had ever won for himself by the pen alone. His works were the daily food, not only of his countrymen, but of all educated Europe. His society was courted by whatever England could show of eminence. Station, power, wealth, beauty, and genius, strove with each other in every demonstration of respect and worship—and, a few political fanatics and envious poetasters apart—wherever he appeared in town or in country, whoever had Scotch blood in him, "gentle or simple," felt it move more rapidly through his veins when he was in the presence of Scott. To descend to what many looked on as higher things, he considered himself, and was considered by all about him, as rapidly consolidating a large fortune: the annual profits of his novels alone had, for several years, been not less than £10,000: his domains were daily increased—his castle was rising—and perhaps few doubted that erelong he might receive from the just favor of his Prince some distinction in the way of external rank, such as had seldom before been dreamt of as the possible consequence of a mere literary celebrity. It was about this time that the compiler of these pages first had the opportunity of observing the plain easy modesty which had survived the many temptations of such a career; and the kindness of heart pervading, in all circumstances, his gentle deportment, which made him the rare, perhaps the solitary, example of a man signally elevated from humble beginnings, and loved more and more by his earliest friends and connections, in proportion as he had fixed on himself the homage of the great, and the wonder of the world.

It was during the sitting of the General Assembly of the Kirk in May, 1818, that I first had the honor of meeting him in private society: the party was not a large one, at the house of a much-valued common friend—Mr. Home Drummond of Blair Drummond, the grandson of Lord Kames. Mr. Scott, ever apt to consider too favorably the literary efforts of others, and more especially of very young persons, received me, when I was presented to him, with a cordiality which I had not been prepared to expect from one filling a station so exalted. This, however, is the same story that every individual, who ever met him under similar circumstances, has had to tell. When the ladies retired from the dinner-table, I happened to sit next him; and he, having heard that I had lately returned from a tour in Germany, made that country and its recent literature the subject of some conversation. In the course of it, I told him that when, on reaching the inn at Weimar, I asked the waiter whether Goethe was then in the town, the man stared as if he had not heard the name before; and that on my repeating the question, adding *Goethe der grosse dichter* (the great poet), he shook his head as doubtfully as before—until the landlady solved our difficulties, by suggesting that perhaps the traveller might mean "the *Herr Geheimer-Rath* (Privy Counsellor) *Von Goethe*." Scott seemed amused with this, and said, "I hope you will come one of these days and see me at Abbotsford; and when you reach Selkirk or Melrose, be sure you ask even the landlady for nobody but *the Sheriff*." He appeared particularly interested when I described Goethe as I first saw him, alighting from a carriage, crammed with wild plants and herbs which he had picked up in the course of his morning's botanizing among the hills above Jena. "I am glad," said he, "that my old master has pursuits somewhat akin to my own. I am no botanist, properly speaking; and though a dweller on the banks of the Tweed, shall never be knowing about Flora's beauties;[106] but how I should like to have a talk with him about trees!" I mentioned how much any one must be struck with the majestic beauty of Goethe's countenance (the noblest certainly by far that I have ever yet seen): "Well," said he, "the grandest demigod I ever saw was Dr. Carlyle, minister of Musselburgh, commonly called *Jupiter Carlyle*, from having sat more than once for the king of gods and men to Gavin Hamilton—and a shrewd, clever old carle was he, no doubt, but no more a poet than his precentor. As for poets, I have seen, I believe, all the best of our own time and country—and, though Burns had the most glorious eyes imaginable, I never thought any of them would come up to an artist's notion of the character, except Byron." A reverend gentleman present (I think, Principal Nicoll of St. Andrews) expressed his regret that he had never seen Lord Byron. "And the prints," resumed Scott, "give one no impression of him— the lustre is there, Doctor, but it is not lighted up. Byron's countenance is *a thing to dream of*.

93

A certain fair lady, whose name has been too often mentioned in connection with his, told a friend of mine, that when she first saw Byron, it was in a crowded room, and she did not know who it was, but her eyes were instantly nailed, and she said to herself, *that pale face is my fate*. And, poor soul, if a godlike face and godlike powers could have made any excuse for devilry, to be sure she had one." In the course of this talk, an old friend and schoolfellow of Scott's[107] asked him across the table if he had any faith in the antique busts of Homer. "No, truly," he answered, smiling, "for if there had been either limners or stuccoyers worth their salt in those days, the owner of such a headpiece would never have had to trail the poke. They would have alimented the honest man decently among them for a lay-figure."

A few days after this, I received a communication from the Messrs. Ballantyne, to the effect that Mr. Scott's various avocations had prevented him from fulfilling his agreement with them as to the historical department of the Edinburgh Annual Register for 1816, and that it would be acceptable to him as well as them, if I could undertake to supply it in the course of the autumn. This proposal was agreed to on my part, and I had consequently occasion to meet him pretty often during that summer session. He told me, that if the war had gone on, he should have liked to do the historical summary as before; but that the prospect of having no events to record but radical riots, and the passing or rejecting of corn bills and poor bills, sickened him; that his health was no longer what it had been; and that though he did not mean to give over writing altogether—(here he smiled significantly, and glanced his eye towards a pile of MS. on the desk by him)—he thought himself now entitled to write nothing but what would rather be an amusement than a fatigue to him—"*Juniores ad labores*."

He at this time occupied as his *den* a square small room, behind the dining parlor in Castle Street. It had but a single Venetian window, opening on a patch of turf not much larger than itself, and the aspect of the place was on the whole sombrous. The walls were entirely clothed with books; most of them folios and quartos, and all in that complete state of repair which at a glance reveals a tinge of bibliomania. A dozen volumes or so, needful for immediate purposes of reference, were placed close by him on a small movable frame—something like a dumb-waiter. All the rest were in their proper niches, and wherever a volume had been lent, its room was occupied by a wooden block of the same size, having a card with the name of the borrower and date of the loan, tacked on its front. The old bindings had obviously been retouched and regilt in the most approved manner; the new, when the books were of any mark, were rich, but never gaudy—a large proportion of blue morocco—all stamped with his *device* of the portcullis, and its motto, *clausus tutus ero*—being an anagram of his name in Latin. Every case and shelf was accurately lettered, and the works arranged systematically; history and biography on one side—poetry and the drama on another—law books and dictionaries behind his own chair. The only table was a massive piece of furniture which he had had constructed on the model of one at Rokeby, with a desk and all its appurtenances on either side, that an amanuensis might work opposite to him when he chose; and with small tiers of drawers, reaching all round to the floor. The top displayed a goodly array of session papers, and on the desk below were, besides the MS. at which he was working, sundry parcels of letters, proof sheets, and so forth, all neatly done up with red tape. His own writing apparatus was a very handsome old box, richly carved, lined with crimson velvet, and containing ink-bottles, taper-stand, etc., in silver—the whole in such order that it might have come from the silversmith's window half an hour before. Besides his own huge elbow-chair, there were but two others in the room, and one of these seemed, from its position, to be reserved exclusively for the amanuensis. I observed, during the first evening I spent with him in this *sanctum*, that while he talked, his hands were hardly ever idle—sometimes he folded letter-covers—sometimes he twisted paper into matches, performing both tasks with great mechanical expertness and nicety; and when there was no loose paper fit to be so dealt with, he snapped his fingers, and the noble Maida aroused himself from his lair on the hearth-rug, and laid his head across his master's knees, to be caressed and fondled. The room had no space for pictures except one, an original portrait of Claverhouse, which hung over the chimney-piece, with a Highland target on either side, and broadswords and dirks (each having its own story), disposed star-fashion round them. A few green tin-boxes, such as solicitors keep title-deeds in, were piled over each other on one side of the window; and on the top of these lay a fox's tail, mounted on an antique silver handle, wherewith, as often as he had occasion to take down a book, he gently brushed the dust off the upper leaves before opening it. I think I have mentioned all the furniture of the room except a sort of ladder, low, broad, well carpeted, and strongly guarded with oaken rails, by which he helped himself to books from his higher shelves. On the top step of this convenience, Hinse of Hinsfeldt, (so called from one of the German *Kinder-märchen*,) a venerable tom-cat, fat and sleek, and no longer very locomotive, usually lay watching the proceedings of his master and Maida with an air of dignified equanimity; but when Maida chose to leave the party, he signified his inclinations by thumping the door with his huge paw, as violently as ever a fashionable footman handled a knocker in Grosvenor Square; the Sheriff rose and opened it for him with courteous alacrity,—and then Hinse came down purring from his perch, and mounted guard by the footstool,*vice* Maida absent upon furlough.[108] Whatever discourse might be passing, was broken every now and then by some affectionate apostrophe to these four-footed friends. He said they understood everything he said to them—and I believe they did understand a great deal of it. But at all events, dogs and cats, like children, have some infallible tact for discovering at once who is and who is not really fond of their company; and I venture to say, Scott was never five minutes in any room before the little pets of the family, whether dumb or lisping, had found out his kindness for all their generation.

I never thought it lawful to keep a journal of what passes in private society, so that no one need expect from the sequel of this narrative any detailed record of Scott's familiar talk. What fragments of it have happened to adhere to a tolerably retentive memory, and may be put into black and white without wounding any feelings which my friend, were he alive, would have wished to spare, I shall introduce as the occasion suggests or serves. But I disclaim on the threshold anything more than this; and I also wish to enter a protest once for all against the general fidelity of several literary gentlemen who have kindly forwarded to me private lucubrations of theirs, designed to *Boswellize*Scott, and which they may probably publish hereafter. To report conversations fairly, it is a necessary prerequisite that we should be completely familiar with all the interlocutors, and understand thoroughly all their minutest relations, and points of common knowledge and common feeling with each other. He who does not, must be perpetually in danger of misinterpreting sportive allusion into serious statement; and the man who was only recalling, by some jocular phrase or half-phrase, to an old companion, some trivial reminiscence of their boyhood or youth, may be represented as expressing, upon some person or incident casually tabled, an opinion which he had never framed, or if he had, would never have given words to in any mixed assemblage—not even among what the world calls *friends* at his own board. In proportion as a man is witty and humorous, there will always be about him and his a widening maze and wilderness of cues and catchwords, which the uninitiated will, if they are bold enough to try interpretation, construe, ever and anon, egregiously amiss—not seldom into arrant falsity. For this one reason, to say nothing of many others, I consider no man justified in journalizing what he sees and hears in a domestic circle where he is not thoroughly at home; and I think there are still higher and better reasons why he should not do so where he is.

Before I ever met Scott in private, I had, of course, heard many people describe and discuss his style of conversation. Everybody seemed to agree that it overflowed with hearty good-humor, as well as plain unaffected good sense and sagacity; but I had heard not a few persons of undoubted ability and accomplishment maintain that the genius of the great poet and novelist rarely, if ever, revealed itself in his talk. It is needless to say, that the persons I allude to were all his own countrymen, and themselves imbued, more or less, with the conversational habits derived from a system of education in which the study of metaphysics occupies a very large share of attention. The best table-talk of Edinburgh was, and probably still is, in a very great measure made up of brilliant disquisition—such as might be transferred without alteration to a professor's note-book, or the pages of a critical Review— and of sharp word-catchings, ingenious thrusting and parrying of dialectics, and all the quips and quibblets of bar pleading. It was the talk of a society to which lawyers and lecturers had, for at least a hundred years, given the tone. From the date of the Union, Edinburgh ceased to be the headquarters of the Scotch nobility—and long before the time of which I speak, they had all but entirely abandoned it as a place of residence. I think I never knew above two or three of the Peerage to have houses there at the same time—and these were usually among the poorest and most insignificant of their order. The wealthier gentry had followed their example. Very few of that class ever spent any considerable part of the year in Edinburgh, except for the purposes of educating their children, or superintending the progress of a lawsuit; and these were not more likely than a score or two of comatose and lethargic old Indians, to make head against the established influences of academical and forensic celebrity. Now Scott's tastes and resources had not much in common with those who had inherited and preserved the chief authority in this provincial hierarchy of rhetoric. He was highly amused with watching their dexterous logomachies—but his delight in such displays arose mainly, I cannot doubt, from the fact of their being, both as to subject-matter and style and method, remote *a Scævolæ studiis*. He sat by, as he would have done at a stage-play or a fencing-match, enjoying and applauding the skill exhibited, but without feeling much ambition to parade himself as a rival either of the foil or the buskin. I can easily believe, therefore, that in the earlier part of his life—before the blaze of universal fame had overawed local prejudice, and a new generation, accustomed to hear of that fame from their infancy, had grown up—it may have been the commonly adopted creed in Edinburgh, that Scott, however distinguished otherwise, was not to be named as a table-companion in the same day with this or that master of luminous dissertation or quick rejoinder, who now sleeps as forgotten as his grandmother. It was natural enough that persons brought up in the same circle with him, who remembered all his beginnings, and had but slowly learned to acquiesce in the justice of his claim to unrivalled honor in literature, should have clung all the closer for that late acquiescence to their original estimate of him as inferior to themselves in other titles to admiration. It was also natural that their prejudice on that score should be readily taken up by the young aspirants who breathed, as it were, the atmosphere of their professional renown. Perhaps, too, Scott's steady Toryism, and the effect of his genius and example in modifying the intellectual sway of the long dominant Whigs in the north, may have had some share in this matter. However all that may have been, the substance of what I had been accustomed to hear certainly was, that Scott had a marvellous stock of queer stories, which he often told with happy effect, but that, bating these drafts on a portentous memory, set off with a simple old-fashioned *naïveté* of humor and pleasantry, his strain of talk was remarkable neither for depth of remark nor felicity of illustration; that his views and opinions on the most important topics of practical interest were hopelessly perverted by his blind enthusiasm for the dreams of bygone ages; and that, but for the grotesque phenomenon presented by a great writer of the nineteenth century gravely uttering sentiments worthy of his own Dundees and Invernahyles, the main texture of his discourse would be pronounced, by any enlightened member of modern society, rather bald and poor than otherwise. I think the epithet most in vogue was *commonplace*.

It will easily be believed that, in companies such as I have been alluding to, made up of, or habitually domineered over, by voluble Whigs and political economists, Scott was often tempted to put forth his Tory doctrines and antiquarian prejudices in an exaggerated shape—in colors, to say the truth, altogether different from what they assumed under other circumstances, or which had any real influence upon his mind and conduct on occasions of practical moment. But I fancy it will seem equally credible, that the most sharp-sighted of these social critics may not always have been capable of tracing, and doing justice to, the powers which Scott brought to bear upon the topics which they, not he, had chosen for discussion. In passing from a gas-lit hall into a room with wax candles, the guests sometimes complain that they have left splendor for gloom; but let them try by what sort of light it is most satisfactory to read, write, or embroider, or consider at leisure under which of the two, either men or women look their best.

The strongest, purest, and least observed of all lights, is, however, daylight; and his talk was commonplace, just as sunshine is, which gilds the most indifferent objects, and adds brilliancy to the brightest. As for the old-world anecdotes which these clever persons were condescending enough to laugh at as pleasant extravagances, serving merely to relieve and set off the main stream of debate, they were often enough, it may be guessed, connected with the theme in hand by links not the less apt that they might be too subtle to catch their bedazzled and self-satisfied optics. There might be keener knowledge of human nature than was "dreamt of in their philosophy"—which passed with them for *commonplace*, only because it was clothed in plain familiar household words, not dressed up in some pedantic masquerade of antithesis. "There are people," says Landor, "who think they write and speak finely, merely because they have forgotten the language in which their fathers and mothers used to talk to them;" and surely there are a thousand homely old proverbs, which many a dainty modern would think it beneath his dignity to quote either in speech or writing, any one of which condenses more wit (take that word in any of its senses) than could be extracted from all that was ever said or written by the *doctrinaires* of the Edinburgh school. Many of those gentlemen held Scott's conversation to be commonplace exactly for the same reason that a child thinks a perfectly limpid stream, though perhaps deep enough to drown it three times over, must needs be shallow. But it will be easily believed that the best and highest of their own idols had better means and skill of measurement: I can never forget the pregnant expression of one of the ablest of that school and party—Lord Cockburn—who, when some glib youth chanced to echo in his hearing the consolatory tenet of local mediocrity, answered quietly: "I have the misfortune to think differently from you—in my humble opinion, Walter Scott's *sense* is a still more wonderful thing than his *genius*."

Indeed I have no sort of doubt that, long before 1818, full justice was done to Scott, even in these minor things, by all those of his Edinburgh acquaintance, whether Whig or Tory, on whose personal opinion he could have been supposed to set much value. With few exceptions, the really able lawyers of his own or nearly similar standing had ere that time attained stations of judicial dignity, or were in the springtide of practice; and in either case they were likely to consider general society much in his own fashion, as the joyous relaxation of life, rather than the theatre of exertion and display. Their tables were elegantly, some of them sumptuously spread; and they lived in a pretty constant interchange of entertainments upon a large scale, in every circumstance of which, conversation included, it was their ambition to imitate those voluptuous metropolitan circles, wherein most of them had from time to time mingled, and several of them with distinguished success. Among such prosperous gentlemen, like himself past the *mezzo cammin*, Scott's picturesque anecdotes, rich easy humor, and gay involuntary glances of mother-wit, were, it is not difficult to suppose, appreciated above contributions of a more ambitious stamp; and no doubt his London *réputation de salon* (which had by degrees risen to a high pitch, although he cared nothing for it) was not without its effect in Edinburgh. But still the old prejudice lingered on in the general opinion of the place, especially among the smart praters of *the Outer-House*, whose glimpses of the social habits of their superiors were likely to be rare, and their gall-bladders to be more distended than their purses.

In truth, it was impossible to listen to Scott's oral narrations, whether gay or serious, or to the felicitous fun with which he parried absurdities of all sorts, without discovering better qualities in his talk than *wit*—and of a higher order; I mean especially a power of *vivid painting*—the true and primary sense of what is called *Imagination*. He was like Jaques—though not a "Melancholy Jaques;" and "moralized" a common topic "into a thousand similitudes." Shakespeare and the banished Duke would have found him "full of matter." He disliked mere disquisitions in Edinburgh, and prepared *impromptus* in London; and puzzled the promoters of such things sometimes by placid silence, sometimes by broad merriment. To such men he seemed *commonplace*—not so to the most dexterous masters in what was to some of them almost a science; not so to Rose, Hallam, Moore, or Rogers,—to Ellis, Mackintosh, Croker, or Canning.

Scott managed to give and receive such great dinners as I have been alluding to, at least as often as any other private gentleman in Edinburgh; but he very rarely accompanied his wife and daughters to the evening assemblies, which commonly ensued under other roofs—for *early to rise*, unless in the case of spare-fed anchorites, takes for granted *early to bed*. When he had no dinner engagement, he frequently gave a few hours to the theatre; but still more frequently, when the weather was fine, and still more, I believe, to his own satisfaction, he drove out with some of his family, or a single friend, in an open carriage; the favorite rides being either to the Blackford Hills, or to Ravelston, and so home by Corstorphine; or to the beach of Portobello, where Peter was always instructed to keep his horses as near as possible to the sea. More than once, even in the first summer of my acquaintance with him, I had the pleasure of accompanying him on these evening excursions; and never did he seem to enjoy himself more fully than when placidly surveying, at such sunset or moonlight hours, either the massive outlines of his "own romantic town," or the tranquil expanse of its noble estuary. He delighted, too, in passing, when he could, through some of the quaint windings of the ancient city itself, now deserted, except at mid-day, by the upper world. How often have I seen him go a long way round about, rather than miss the opportunity of halting for a few minutes on the vacant esplanade of Holyrood, or under the darkest shadows of the Castle rock, where it overhangs the Grassmarket, and the huge slab that still marks where the gibbet of Porteous and the Covenanters had its station. His coachman knew him too well to move at a Jehu's pace amidst such scenes as these. No funeral hearse crept more leisurely than did his landau up the Canongate or the Cowgate; and not a queer tottering gable but recalled to him some long-buried memory of splendor or bloodshed, which, by a few words, he set before the hearer in the reality of life. His image is so associated in my mind with the antiquities of his native place, that I cannot now revisit them without feeling as if I were treading on his gravestone.

Whatever might happen on the other evenings of the week, he always dined at home on Sunday, and usually some few friends were then with him, but never any person with whom he stood on ceremony. These were, it may be readily supposed, the most agreeable of his entertainments. He came into the room rubbing his hands, his face bright and gleesome, like a boy arriving at home for the holidays, his Peppers and Mustards gambolling about his heels, and even the stately Maida grinning and wagging his tail in sympathy. Among the most regular guests on these happy evenings were, in my time, as had long before been the case, Mrs. Maclean Clephane of Torloisk (with whom he agreed cordially on all subjects except the authenticity of Ossian), and her daughters, whose guardian he had become, at their own choice. The eldest of them had been for some years married to the Earl Compton (now Marquis of Northampton), and was of course seldom in the north; but the others had much of the same tastes and accomplishments which so highly distinguished the late Lady Northampton; and Scott delighted especially in their proficiency in the poetry and music of their native isles. Mr. and Mrs. Skene of Rubislaw were frequent attendants—and so were the Macdonald-Buchanans of Drumakiln, whose eldest daughter, Isabella, was his chief favorite among all his *nieces* of the Clerk's table—as was, among the *nephews*, my own dear friend and companion, Joseph Hume, a singularly graceful young man, rich in the promise of hereditary genius, but, alas, cut off in the early bloom of his days. The well-beloved Erskine was seldom absent; and very often Terry or James Ballantyne came with him—sometimes, though less frequently, Constable. Among other persons who now and then appeared at these "dinners without the silver dishes," as Scott called them, I may mention—to say nothing of such old cronies as Mr. Clerk, Mr. Thomson, and Mr. Kirkpatrick Sharpe—Sir Alexander Boswell of Auchinleck, who had all his father *Bozzy's* cleverness, good-humor, and joviality, without one touch of his meaner qualities,—wrote Jenny dang the Weaver, and some other popular songs, which he sang capitally—and was moreover a thorough bibliomaniac; the late Sir Alexander Don of Newton, in all courteous and elegant accomplishments the model of a cavalier; and last, not least, William Allan, R. A., who had shortly before this time returned to Scotland from several years of travel in Russia and Turkey. At one of these plain hearty dinners, however, the company rarely exceeded three or four, besides the as yet undivided family.

SCOTT'S HOUSE IN CASTLE STREET
After the drawing by J. M. W. Turner.

Scott had a story of a topping goldsmith on the Bridge, who prided himself on being the mirror of Amphitryons, and accounted for his success by stating that it was his invariable custom to set his own stomach at ease, by a beefsteak and a pint of port in his back-shop, half an hour before the arrival of his guests. But the host of Castle Street had no occasion to imitate this prudent arrangement, for his appetite at dinner was neither keen nor nice. Breakfast was his chief meal. Before that came, he had gone through the severest part of his day's work, and he then set to with the zeal of Crabbe's Squire Tovell—

"And laid at once a pound upon his plate."

No fox-hunter ever prepared himself for the field by more substantial appliances. His table was always provided, in addition to the usually plentiful delicacies of a Scotch breakfast, with some solid article, on which he did most lusty execution—a round of beef—a pasty, such as made Gil Blas's eyes water—or, most welcome of all, a cold sheep's head, the charms of which primitive dainty he has so gallantly defended against the disparaging sneers of Dr. Johnson and his bear-leader.[109] A huge brown loaf flanked his elbow, and it was placed upon a broad wooden trencher, that he might cut and come again with the bolder knife. Often did the *Clerks' coach*, commonly called among themselves *the Lively*—which trundled round every morning to pick up the brotherhood, and then deposited them at the proper minute in the Parliament Close—often did this lumbering hackney arrive at his door before he had fully appeased what Homer calls "the sacred rage of hunger;" and vociferous was the merriment of the learned *uncles*, when the surprised poet swung forth to join them, with an extemporized sandwich, that looked like a ploughman's luncheon, in his hand. But this robust supply would have served him in fact for the day. He never tasted anything more before dinner, and at dinner he ate almost as sparingly as Squire Tovell's niece from the boarding-school,—

—"Who cut the sanguine flesh in frustums fine,
And marvelled much to see the creatures dine."

The only dishes he was at all fond of were the old-fashioned ones to which he had been accustomed in the days of Saunders Fairford; and which really are excellent dishes,— such, in truth, as Scotland borrowed from France before Catherine de' Medici brought in her Italian *virtuosi* to revolutionize the kitchen like the court. Of most of these, I believe, he has in the course of his novels found some opportunity to record his esteem. But, above all, who can forget that his King Jamie, amidst the splendors of Whitehall, thinks himself an ill-used monarch unless his first course includes *cocky-leeky*?

It is a fact, which some philosophers may think worth setting down, that Scott's organization, as to more than one of the senses, was the reverse of exquisite. He had very little of what musicians call an ear; his smell was hardly more delicate. I have seen him stare about, quite unconscious of the cause, when his whole company betrayed their uneasiness at the approach of an overkept haunch of venison; and neither by the nose nor the palate could he distinguish corked wine from sound. He could never tell Madeira from sherry,—nay, an Oriental friend having sent him a butt of *sheeraz*, when he remembered the circumstance some time afterwards, and called for a bottle to have Sir John Malcolm's opinion of its quality, it turned out that his butler, mistaking the label, had already served up half the bin as *sherry*. Port he considered as physic: he never willingly swallowed more than one glass of it, and was sure to anathematize a second, if offered, by repeating John Home's epigram:—

"Bold and erect the Caledonian stood,
Old was his mutton, and his claret good;
Let him drink port, the English statesman cried—
He drank the poison, and his spirit died."

In truth, he liked no wines except sparkling champagne and claret; but even as to this last he was no connoisseur; and sincerely preferred a tumbler of whiskey-toddy to the most precious "liquid ruby" that ever flowed in the cup of a prince. He rarely took any other potation when quite alone with his family; but at the Sunday board he circulated the champagne briskly during dinner, and considered a pint of claret each man's fair share afterwards. I should not omit, however, that his Bordeaux was uniformly preceded by a small libation of the genuine *mountain dew*, which he poured with his own hand, *more majorum*, for each guest—making use for the purpose of such a multifarious collection of ancient Highland *quaighs* (little cups of curiously dovetailed wood, inlaid with silver) as no Lowland sideboard but his was ever equipped with—but commonly reserving for himself one that was peculiarly precious in his eyes, as having travelled from Edinburgh to Derby in the canteen of Prince Charlie. This relic had been presented to "the wandering Ascanius" by some very careful follower, for its bottom is of glass, that he who quaffed might keep his eye the while upon the dirk hand of his companion.

The sound of music (even, I suspect, of any sacred music but psalm-singing) would be considered indecorous in the streets of Edinburgh on a Sunday night; so, upon the occasions I am speaking of, the harp was silent, and Otterburne and The Bonnie House of Airlie must needs be dispensed with. To make amends, after tea in the drawing-room, Scott usually read some favorite author for the amusement of his little circle; or Erskine, Ballantyne, or Terry, did so, at his request. He himself read aloud high poetry with far greater simplicity, depth, and effect, than any other man I ever heard; and in Macbeth or Julius Cæsar, or the like, I doubt if Kemble could have been more impressive. Yet the changes of intonation were so gently managed, that he contrived to set the different interlocutors clearly before us, without the least approach to theatrical artifice. Not so the others I have mentioned; they all read cleverly and agreeably, but with the decided trickery of stage recitation. To them he usually gave the book when it was a comedy, or, indeed, any other drama than Shakespeare's or Joanna Baillie's. Dryden's Fables, Johnson's two Satires, and certain detached scenes of Beaumont and Fletcher, especially that in The Lover's Progress, where the ghost of the musical innkeeper makes his appearance, were frequently selected. Of the poets, his contemporaries, however, there was not one that did not come in for his part. In Wordsworth, his pet pieces were, I think, the Song for Brougham Castle, the Laodamia, and some of the early sonnets; in Southey, Queen Orraca, Fernando Ramirez, the Lines on the Holly Tree—and, of his larger poems, the Thalaba. Crabbe was perhaps, next to Shakespeare, the standing resource; but in those days Byron was pouring out his spirit fresh and full: and, if a new piece from his hand had appeared, it was sure to be read by Scott the Sunday evening afterwards, and that with such delighted emphasis as showed how completely the elder bard had kept all his enthusiasm for poetry at the pitch of youth, all his admiration of genius, free, pure, and unstained by the least drop of literary jealousy. Rare and beautiful example of a happily constituted and virtuously disciplined mind and character!

Very often something read aloud by himself or his friends suggested an old story of greater compass than would have suited a dinner-table—and he told it, whether serious or comical, or, as more frequently happened, part of both, exactly in every respect in the tone and style of the notes and illustrations to his novels. A great number of his best oral narratives have, indeed, been preserved in those parting lucubrations; and not a few in his letters. Yet very many there were of which his pen has left no record—so many, that, were I to task my memory, I could, I believe, recall the outlines at least of more than would be sufficient to occupy a couple of these volumes. Possibly, though well aware how little justice I could do to such things, rather than think of their perishing forever, and leaving not even a shadow behind, I may at some future day hazard the attempt.

Let me turn, meanwhile, to some dinner-tables very different from his own, at which, from this time forward, I often met Scott. It is very true of the societies I am about to describe, that he was "among them, not of them;" and it is also most true that this fact was apparent in all the demeanor of his bibliopolical and typographical allies towards him whenever he visited them under their roofs—not a bit less so than when they were received at his own board; but still, considering how closely his most important worldly affairs were connected with the personal character of the Ballantynes, I think it a part, though neither a proud nor a very pleasing part, of my duty as his biographer, to record my reminiscences of them and their doings in some detail.

James Ballantyne then lived in St. John Street, a row of good, old-fashioned, and spacious houses, adjoining the Canongate and Holyrood, and at no great distance from his printing establishment. He had married a few years before the daughter of a wealthy farmer in Berwickshire—a quiet, amiable woman, of simple manners, and perfectly domestic habits: a group of fine young children were growing up about him; and he usually, if not constantly, had under his roof his aged mother, his and his wife's tender care of whom it was most pleasing to witness. As far as a stranger might judge, there could not be a more exemplary household, or a happier one; and I have occasionally met the poet in St. John Street when there were no other guests but Erskine, Terry, George Hogarth,[110] and another intimate friend or two, and when James Ballantyne was content to appear in his own true and best colors, the kind head of his family, the respectful but honest schoolfellow of Scott, the easy landlord of a plain, comfortable table. But when any great event was about to take place in the business, especially on the eve of a new novel, there were doings of a higher strain in St. John Street; and to be present at one of those scenes was truly a rich treat, even—if not especially—for persons who, like myself, had no more *knowledge* than the rest of the world as to the authorship of Waverley. Then were congregated about the printer all his own literary allies, of whom a considerable number were by no means personally familiar with "THE GREAT UNKNOWN:"—who, by the way, owed to him that widely adopted title;—and He appeared among the rest with his usual open aspect of buoyant good-humor—although it was not difficult to trace, in the occasional play of his features, the diversion it afforded him to watch all the procedure of his swelling confidant, and the curious neophytes that surrounded the well-spread board.

The feast was, to use one of James's own favorite epithets, *gorgeous;* an aldermanic display of turtle and venison, with the suitable accompaniments of iced punch, potent ale, and generous Madeira. When the cloth was drawn, the burly preses arose, with all he could muster of the port of John Kemble, and spouted with a sonorous voice the formula of Macbeth:—

"Fill full!
I drink to the general joy of the whole table!"

This was followed by "The King, God bless him!" and second came—"Gentlemen, there is another toast which never has been nor shall be omitted in this house of mine—I give you the health of Mr. Walter Scott with three times three!" All honor having been done to this health, and Scott having briefly thanked the company with some expressions of warm affection to their host, Mrs. Ballantyne retired; the bottles passed round twice or thrice in the usual way; and then James rose once more, every vein on his brow distended, his eyes solemnly fixed upon vacancy, to propose, not as before in his stentorian key, but with "'bated breath," in the sort of whisper by which a stage conspirator thrills the gallery,— *"Gentlemen, a bumper to the immortal Author of Waverley!"* The uproar of cheering, in which Scott made a fashion of joining, was succeeded by deep silence, and then Ballantyne proceeded—

"In his Lord Burleigh look, serene and serious,
A something of imposing and mysterious"—

to lament the obscurity in which his illustrious but too modest correspondent still chose to conceal himself from the plaudits of the world, to thank the company for the manner in which the *nominis umbra* had been received, and to assure them that the Author of Waverley would, when informed of the circumstance, feel highly delighted—"the proudest hour of his life," etc., etc. The cool, demure fun of Scott's features during all this mummery was perfect; and Erskine's attempt at a gay*nonchalance* was still more ludicrously meritorious. Aldiborontiphoscophornio, however, bursting as he was, knew too well to allow the new novel to be made the subject of discussion. Its name was announced, and success to it crowned another cup; but after that, no more of Jedediah. To cut the thread, he rolled out unbidden some one of his many theatrical songs, in a style that would have done no dishonor to almost any orchestra—The Maid of Lodi—or perhaps, The Bay of Biscay, O!— or The Sweet Little Cherub that Sits up Aloft. Other toasts followed, interspersed with ditties from other performers;—old George Thomson, the friend of Burns, was ready, for one, with The Moorland Wedding, or Willie Brew'd a Peck o' Maut;—and so it went on, until Scott and Erskine, with any clerical or very staid personage that had chanced to be admitted, saw fit to withdraw. Then the scene was changed. The claret and olives made way for broiled bones and a mighty bowl of punch; and when a few glasses of the hot beverage had restored his powers, James opened *ore rotundo* on the merits of the forthcoming romance. "One chapter, one chapter only," was the cry. After *"Nay, by'r Lady, nay!"* and a few more coy shifts, the proof sheets were at length produced, and James, with many a prefatory hem, read aloud what he considered as the most striking dialogue they contained.

The first I heard so read was the interview between Jeanie Deans, the Duke of Argyle, and Queen Caroline, in Richmond Park; and notwithstanding some spice of the pompous tricks to which he was addicted, I must say he did the inimitable scene great justice. At all events, the effect it produced was deep and memorable, and no wonder that the exulting typographer's *one bumper more to Jedediah Cleishbotham* preceded his parting stave, which was uniformly The Last Words of Marmion, executed certainly with no contemptible rivalry of Braham.

What a different affair was a dinner, although probably including many of the same guests, at the junior partner's! He in those days retained, I think, no private apartments attached to his auction-rooms in Hanover Street, over the door of which he still kept emblazoned "John Ballantyne and Company, Booksellers." At any rate, such of his entertainments as I ever saw Scott partake of, were given at his villa near to the Frith of Forth, by Trinity;—a retreat which the little man had named "Harmony Hall," and invested with an air of dainty voluptuous finery, contrasting strikingly enough with the substantial citizen-like snugness of his elder brother's domestic appointments. His house was surrounded by gardens so contrived as to seem of considerable extent, having many a shady tuft, trellised alley, and mysterious alcove, interspersed among their bright parterres. It was a fairy-like labyrinth, and there was no want of pretty Armidas, such as they might be, to glide half-seen among its mazes. The sitting-rooms opened upon gay and perfumed conservatories, and John's professional excursions to Paris and Brussels in quest of objects of *virtu*, had supplied both the temptation and the means to set forth the interior in a fashion that might have satisfied the most fastidious *petite maîtresse* of Norwood or St. Denis. John, too, was a married man: he had, however, erected for himself a private wing, the accesses to which, whether from the main building or the *bosquet*, were so narrow that it was physically impossible for the handsome and portly lady who bore his name to force her person through any one of them. His dinners were in all respects Parisian, for his wasted palate disdained such John Bull luxuries as were all in all with James. The piquant pasty of Strasburg or Perigord was never to seek; and even the *pièce de résistance* was probably a boar's head from Coblentz, or a turkey ready stuffed with truffles from the Palais Royal. The pictures scattered among John's innumerable mirrors were chiefly of theatrical subjects—many of them portraits of beautiful actresses—the same Peg Woffingtons, Bellamys, Kitty Clives, and so forth, that found their way in the sequel to Charles Mathews's gallery at Highgate. Here that exquisite comedian's own mimicries and parodies were the life and soul of many a festival, and here, too, he gathered from his facetious host not a few of the richest materials for his *at homes* and *monopolylogues*. But, indeed, whatever actor or singer of eminence visited Edinburgh, of the evenings when he did not perform several were sure to be reserved for Trinity. Here Braham quavered, and here Liston drolled his best—here Johnstone, and Murray, and Yates mixed jest and stave—here Kean revelled and rioted—and here the Roman Kemble often played the Greek from sunset to dawn. Nor did the popular *cantatrice* or *danseuse* of the time disdain to freshen her roses, after a laborious week, amidst these Paphian arbors of Harmony Hall.

Johnny had other tastes that were equally expensive. He had a well-furnished stable, and followed the foxhounds whenever the cover was within an easy distance. His horses were all called after heroes in Scott's poems or novels; and at this time he usually rode up to his auction on a tall milk-white hunter, yclept *Old Mortality*, attended by a leash or two of greyhounds,—Die Vernon, Jenny Dennison, and so forth, by name. The featherweight himself appeared uniformly, hammer-in-hand, in the half-dress of some sporting club—a light gray frock, with emblems of the chase on its silver buttons, white cord breeches, and jockey-boots in Meltonian order. Yet he affected in the pulpit rather a grave address; and was really one of the most plausible and imposing of the Puff tribe. Probably Scott's presence overawed his ludicrous propensities; for the poet was, when sales were going on, almost a daily attendant in Hanover Street, and himself not the least energetic of the numerous competitors for Johnny's uncut *fifteeners*, Venetian lamps, Milanese cuirasses, and old Dutch cabinets. Maida, by the way, was so well aware of his master's habits, that about the time when the Court of Session was likely to break up for the day, he might usually be seen couched in expectation among Johnny's own *tail* of greyhounds at the threshold of the mart.

It was at one of those Trinity dinners this summer that I first saw Constable. Being struck with his appearance, I asked Scott who he was, and he told me—expressing some surprise that anybody should have lived a winter or two in Edinburgh without knowing, by sight at least, a citizen whose name was so familiar to the world. I happened to say that I had not been prepared to find the great bookseller a man of such gentlemanlike and even distinguished bearing. Scott smiled, and answered, "Ay, Constable is indeed a grand-looking chield. He puts me in mind of Fielding's apology for Lady Booby—to wit, that Joseph Andrews had an air which, to those who had not seen many noblemen, would give an idea of nobility." I had not in those days been much initiated in the private jokes of what is called, by way of excellence, *the trade*, and was puzzled when Scott, in the course of the dinner, said to Constable, "Will your Czarish Majesty do me the honor to take a glass of champagne?" I asked the master of the feast for an explanation. "Oh!" said he, "are you so green as not to know that Constable long since dubbed himself *The Czar of Muscovy*, John Murray, *The Emperor of the West*, and Longman and his string of partners *The Divan?*" "And what title," I asked, "has Mr. John Ballantyne himself found in this new *almanach imperial?*"—"Let that flee stick to the wa'," quoth Johnny: "When I set up for a bookseller, The Crafty christened me *The Dey of Alljeers*—but he now considers me as next thing to dethroned." He added, "His Majesty the autocrat is too fond of these nicknames. One day a partner of the house of Longman was dining with him in the country, to settle an important piece of business, about which there occurred a good deal of difficulty. 'What fine swans you have in your pond there!' said the Londoner, by way of parenthesis.—'Swans!' cried Constable; 'they are only geese, man. There are just five of them, if you please to observe, and their names are Longman, Hurst, Rees, Orme, and Brown.' This skit cost The Crafty a good bargain."

It always appeared to me that James Ballantyne felt his genius rebuked in the presence of Constable: his manner was constrained, his smile servile, his hilarity elaborate. Not so with Johnny: the little fellow never seemed more airily frolicsome than when he capered for the amusement of the Czar.[111] I never, however, saw those two together, where, I am told, the humors of them both were exhibited to the richest advantage—I mean at the dinners with which Constable regaled, among others, his own circle of literary serfs, and when "Jocund Johnny" was very commonly his croupier. There are stories enough of practical jokes upon such occasions, some of them near akin to those which the author of Humphrey Clinker has thought fit to record of his own suburban villa, in the most diverting of young Melford's letters to Sir Watkin Philips. I have heard, for example, a luculent description of poor *Allister Campbell*, and another drudge of the same class, running a race after dinner for a new pair of breeches, which Mr. David Bridges, tailor in ordinary to this northern potentate,—himself a wit, a virtuoso, and the croupier on that day in lieu of Rigdum,—had been instructed to bring with him, and display before the threadbare rivals. But I had these pictures from John Ballantyne, and I dare say they might be overcharged. That Constable was a most bountiful and generous patron to the ragged tenants of Grub Street, there can, however, be no doubt: and as little that John himself acted on all occasions by them in the same spirit, and this to an extent greatly beyond what prudence (if he had ever consulted that guide in anything) would have dictated.

When I visited Constable, as I often did at a period somewhat later than that of which I now speak, and for the most part in company with Scott, I found the bookseller established in a respectable country gentleman's seat, some six or seven miles out of Edinburgh, and doing the honors of it with all the ease that might have been looked for had he been the long-descended owner of the place; there was no foppery, no show, no idle luxury, but to all appearance the plain abundance and simple enjoyment of hereditary wealth. His conversation was manly and vigorous, abounding in Scotch anecdotes of the old time, which he told with a degree of spirit and humor only second to his great author's. No man could more effectually control, when he had a mind, either the extravagant vanity which, on too many occasions, made him ridiculous, or the despotic temper, which habitually held in fear and trembling all such as were in any sort dependent on his Czarish Majesty's pleasure. In him I never saw (at this period) anything but the unobtrusive sense and the calm courtesy of a well-bred gentleman. His very equipage kept up the series of contrasts between him and the two Ballantynes. Constable went back and forward between the town and Polton in a deep-hung and capacious green barouche, without any pretence at heraldic blazonry, drawn by a pair of sleek, black, long-tailed horses, and conducted by a grave old coachman in plain blue livery. The Printer of the Canongate drove himself and his wife about the streets and suburbs in a snug machine, which did not overburthen one powerful and steady cob; while the gay auctioneer, whenever he left the saddle for the box, mounted a bright blue dogcart, and rattled down the Newhaven road with two high-mettled steeds, prancing *tandem* before him, and most probably—especially if he was on his way to the races at Musselburgh—with some "sweet singer of Israel" flaming, with all her feathers, beside him. On such occasions, by the bye, Johnny sometimes had a French horn with him, and he played on it with good skill, and with an energy by no means prudent in the state of his lungs.

The Sheriff told with peculiar unction the following anecdote of this spark. The first time he went over to pick up curiosities at Paris, it happened that he met, in the course of his traffickings, a certain brother bookseller of Edinburgh, as unlike him as one man could well be to another—a grave, dry Presbyterian, rigid in all his notions as the buckle of his wig. This precise worthy having ascertained John's address, went to call on him, a day or two afterwards, with the news of some richly illuminated missal, which he might possibly be glad to make prize of. On asking for his friend, a smiling *laquais de place* informed him that *Monsieur* had gone out, but that *Madame* was at home. Not doubting that Mrs. Ballantyne had accompanied her husband on his trip, he desired to pay his respects to *Madame*, and was ushered in accordingly. "But oh, Mr. Scott!" said, or rather groaned, the austere elder, on his return from this modern Babylon, "oh, Mr. Scott, there was nae Mrs. John yonder, but a painted Jezebel sittin' up in her bed, wi' a wheen impudent French limmers like hersel', and twa or three whiskered blackguards, takin' their collation o' knickknacks and champagne wine! I ran out o' the house as if I had been shot. What judgment will this wicked warld come to! The Lord pity us!" Scott was a severe enough censor in the general of such levities, but somehow, in the case of Rigdumfunnidos, he seemed to regard them with much the same toleration as the naughty tricks of a monkey in the "Jardin des Plantes."

Why did Scott persist in mixing up all his most important concerns with such people as I have been describing? I asked myself that question too unceremoniously at a long subsequent period, and in due time the reader shall see the answer I received; but it left the main question, to my apprehension, as much in the dark as ever. I shall return to the sad subject hereafter more seriously; but in the mean time let it suffice to say, that he was the most patient, long-suffering, affectionate, and charitable of mankind; that in the case of both the Ballantynes he could count, after all, on a sincerely, nay, a passionately devoted attachment to his person; that, with the greatest of human beings, use is in all but unconquerable power; and that he who so loftily tossed aside the seemingly most dangerous assaults of flattery, the blandishment of dames, the condescension of princes, the enthusiasm of crowds—had still his weak point, upon which two or three humble besiegers, and one unwearied, though most frivolous underminer, well knew how to direct their approaches. It was a favorite saw of his own, that the wisest of our race often reserve the average stock of folly to be all expended upon some one flagrant absurdity.[Back to Contents]

CHAPTER XLII.

PUBLICATION OF THE HEART OF MID-LOTHIAN. — ITS RECEPTION IN EDINBURGH AND IN ENGLAND. — ABBOTSFORD IN OCTOBER. — MELROSE ABBEY, DRYBURGH, ETC. — LION-HUNTERS FROM AMERICA. — TRAGEDY OF THE CHEROKEE LOVERS. — SCOTT'S DINNER TO THE SELKIRKSHIRE YEOMEN.

1818.

Hoping to be forgiven for a long digression, the biographer willingly returns to the thread of Scott's story. The Heart of Mid-Lothian appeared, as has been mentioned, before the close of June, 1818, and among the letters which he received soon afterwards from the friends by this time in the secret, there is one which (though I do not venture to name the writer) I am tempted to take the liberty of quoting:[112]—

"Now for it, dear Mr. Scott. I can speak to the purpose, as I have not only read it myself, but am in a house where everybody is tearing it out of each other's hands, and talking of nothing else. So much for its success—the more flattering, because it overcomes a prejudice. People were beginning to say the author would wear himself out; it was going on too long in the same key, and no striking notes could possibly be produced. On the contrary, I think the interest is stronger here than in any of the former ones—(always excepting my first-love Waverley)—and one may congratulate you upon having effected what many have tried to do, and nobody yet succeeded in, making the perfectly good character the most interesting. Of late days, especially since it has been the fashion to write moral and even religious novels, one might almost say of some of the wise good heroines, what a lively girl once said to [me] of her well-meaning aunt—'Upon my word she is enough to make anybody wicked.' And though beauty and talents are heaped on the right side, the writer, in spite of himself, is sure to put agreeableness on the wrong; the person from whose errors he means you should take warning, runs away with your secret partiality in the mean time. Had this very story been conducted by a common hand, Effie would have attracted all our concern and sympathy—Jeanie only cold approbation. Whereas Jeanie, without youth, beauty, genius, warm passions, or any other novel-perfection, is here our object from beginning to end. This is 'inlisting the affections in the cause of virtue' ten times more than ever Richardson did; for whose male and female pedants, all-excelling as they are, I never could care half so much as I found myself inclined to do for Jeanie before I finished the first volume....

"You know I tell you my opinion just as I should do to a third person, and I trust the freedom is not unwelcome. I was a little tired of your Edinburgh lawyers in the introduction; English people in general will be more so, as well as impatient of the passages alluding to Scotch law throughout. Mr. Saddletree will not entertain them. The latter part of the fourth volume unavoidably flags to a certain degree; after Jeanie is happily settled at Roseneath, we have no more to wish for. But the chief fault I have to find relates to the reappearance and shocking fate of the boy. I hear on all sides, 'Oh, I do not like that!' I cannot say what I would have had instead; but I do not like it either; it is a lame, huddled conclusion. I know you so well in it, by the bye!—you grow tired yourself, want to get rid of the story, and hardly care how. Sir George Staunton finishes his career very fitly; he ought not to die in his bed, and for Jeanie's sake one would not have him hanged. It is unnatural, though, that he should ever have gone within twenty miles of the Tolbooth, or shown his face in the streets of Edinburgh, or dined at a public meeting, if the Lord Commissioner had been his brother. Here ends my *per contra* account. The opposite page would make my letter too long if I entered equally into particulars. Carlisle and Corby Castles in Waverley did not affect me more deeply than the prison and trial scenes. The end of poor Madge Wildfire is also most pathetic. The meeting at Muschat's Cairn tremendous. Dumbiedikes and Rory Bean are delightful. And I shall own that my prejudices were secretly gratified by the light in which you place [Uncle] John of Argyle, whom Mr. Coxe so ran down to please Lord Orford. You have drawn him to the very life. I heard so much of him in my youth, so many anecdotes, so often 'as the Duke of Argyle used to say'—that I really believe I am almost as good a judge as if I had seen and lived with him.... [My beloved mother] has told me, that when she married, [in 1737, the very time], he was still remarkably handsome; with manners more graceful and engaging than she ever saw in any one else; the most agreeable person in conversation, the best teller of a story. When fifty-seven thus captivates eighteen, the natural powers of pleasing must be extraordinary. You have likewise colored Queen Caroline exactly right—but I was bred up in another creed about Lady Suffolk, of whom, as a very old deaf woman, I have some faint recollection. [My mother] knew her intimately, and never would allow she had been the King's mistress, though she owned it was currently believed. She said he had just enough liking for her to make the Queen very civil to her, and very jealous and spiteful; the rest remained always uncertain at most, like a similar scandal in our days, where I, for one, imagine love of seeming influence on one side, and love of lounging, of an easy house and a good dinner on the other, to be all the criminal passions concerned. However, I confess, [my mother] had that in herself which made her not ready to think the worst of her fellow-women.

"Did you ever hear the history of John, Duke of Argyle's marriage, and constant attachment, before and after, to a woman not handsomer or much more elegant than Jeanie Deans, though very unlike her in understanding? I can give it you, if you wish it, for it is at my fingers' ends. [I was so much the youngest of a numerous family that I had no playfellow, and for that reason listened with all my ears to the grown people's conversation, most especially when my mother and the friends of her youth got upon old stories; nor did I lose my taste for them when I grew old enough to converse with her on equal terms, and enquire into particulars.] Now I am [an] ancient [tabby] myself, I should be a great treasure of anecdote to anybody who had the same humor,—but I meet with few who have. They read vulgar tales in books, Wraxall, and so forth, what the footmen and maids only gave credit to at the moment, but they desire no farther information. I dare swear many of your readers never heard of the Duke of Argyle before. 'Pray, who was Sir Robert Walpole,' they ask me, 'and when did he live?'—or perhaps—'Was not the great Lord Chatham in Queen Anne's days?'[113]

"[Amongst the persons most pleased here is Lady Charlotte Lindsay. She has the true North humor, and love of humor, and she does enjoy it heartily. They] have, to help [them], an exemplification on two legs in [their] country apothecary, whom you have painted over and over without the honor of knowing him; an old, dry, arguing, prosing, obstinate Scotchman, very shrewd, rather sarcastic, a sturdy Whig and Presbyterian, *tirant un peu sur le démocrate*. Your books are birdlime to him, however; he hovers about the house to obtain a volume when others have done with it. I long to ask him whether Douce Davie was any way *sib* to him. He acknowledges he would not *now* go to Muschat's Cairn at night for any money—he had such a horror of it 'sixty years ago' when a laddie. But I am come to the end of my fourth page, and will not tire you with any more scribbling....

"P. S.—If I had known nothing, and the whole world had told me the contrary, I should have found you out in that one parenthesis,—'for the man was mortal, and had been a schoolmaster.'"

This letter was addressed from a great country house in the south[114]; and may, I presume, be accepted as a fair index of the instantaneous English popularity of Jeanie Deans. From the choice of localities, and the splendid blazoning of tragical circumstances that had left the strongest impression on the memory and imagination of every inhabitant, the reception of this tale in Edinburgh was a scene of all-engrossing enthusiasm, such as I never witnessed there on the appearance of any other literary novelty. But the admiration and delight were the same all over Scotland. Never before had he seized such really noble features of the national character as were canonized in the person of his homely heroine: no art had ever devised a happier running contrast than that of her and her sister, or interwoven a portraiture of lowly manners and simple virtues, with more graceful delineations of polished life, or with bolder shadows of terror, guilt, crime, remorse, madness, and all the agony of the passions.

In the introduction and notes to The Heart of Mid-Lothian, drawn up in 1830, we are presented with details concerning the suggestion of the main plot, and the chief historical incidents made use of, to which I can add nothing of any moment.

The 12th of July restored the author as usual to the supervision of his trees and carpenters; but he had already told the Ballantynes that the story which he had found it impossible to include in the recent series of Jedediah should be forthwith taken up as the opening one of a third; and instructed John to embrace the first favorable opportunity of offering Constable the publication of this, on the footing of 10,000 copies again forming the first edition; but now at length without any more stipulations connected with the unfortunate "old stock" of the Hanover Street Company.

Before he settled himself to his work, however, he made a little tour of the favorite description with his wife and children—halting for a few days at Drumlanrig, thence crossing the Border to Carlisle and Rokeby, and returning by way of Alnwick. On the 17th August he writes thus to John Ballantyne from Drumlanrig: "This is heavenly weather, and I am making the most of it, as I shall have a laborious autumn before me. I may say of my head and fingers as the farmer of his mare, when he indulged her with an extra feed,—

'Ye ken that Maggie winna sleep
For that or Simmer.'

We have taken our own horses with us, and I have my pony, and ride when I find it convenient."

The following seems to have been among the first letters he wrote after his return:—

TO J. B. S. MORRITT, ESQ., M. P., ROKEBY.

ABBOTSFORD, 10th September, 1818.

MY DEAR MORRITT,—We have been cruising to and fro since we left your land of woods and streams. Lord Melville wished me to come and stay two days with him at Melville

Castle, which has broken in upon my time a little, and interrupted my purpose of telling you as how we arrived safe at Abbotsford, without a drop of rain, thus completing a tour of three weeks in the same fine weather in which we commenced it—a thing which never fell to my lot before. Captain Ferguson is inducted into the office of Keeper of the Regalia, to the great joy, I think, of all Edinburgh. He has entered upon a farm (of eleven acres) in consequence of this advancement, for you know it is a general rule, that whenever a Scotsman gets his head *above water*, he immediately turns it to *land*. As he has already taken all the advice of all the *notables* in and about the good village of Darnick, we expect to see his farm look like a tailor's book of patterns, a snip of every several opinion which he has received occupying its appropriate corner. He is truly what the French call *un drôle de corps*.

I wish you would allow your coachman to look out for me among your neighbors a couple of young colts (rising three would be the best age) that would match for a carriage some two years hence. I have plenty of grass for them in the mean while, and should never know the expense of their keep at Abbotsford. He seemed to think he could pick them up at from £25 to £30, which would make an immense saving hereafter. Peter Matheson and he had arranged some sort of plan of this kind. For a pair of very ordinary carriage-horses in Edinburgh they ask £140 or more; so it is worth while to be a little provident. Even then you only get one good horse, the other being usually a brute. Pray you excuse all this palaver,—

"These little things are great to little men."

Our harvest is almost all in, but as farmers always grumble about something, they are now growling about the lightness of the crop. All the young part of our household are wrapt up in uncertainty concerning the Queen's illness—for—if her Majesty parts cable, there will be no Forest Ball, and that is a terrible prospect. On Wednesday (when no post arrives from London) Lord Melville chanced to receive a letter with a black seal by express, and as it was of course argued to contain the expected intelligence of poor Charlotte, it sold a good many ells of black cloth and stuffs before it was ascertained to contain no such information. Surely this came within the line of high treason, being an imagining of the Queen's death.

Ever yours truly,
WALTER SCOTT.

P. S.—Once more *anent* the colts. I am indifferent about color; but, *cæteris paribus*, would prefer black or brown, to bright bay or gray. I mention two off—as the age at which they can be best judged of by the buyer.

Of the same date I find written in pencil, on what must have been the envelope of some sheriff's-process, this note, addressed to Mr. Charles Erskine, the Sheriff-Substitute of Selkirkshire:—

September 10, 1818.

DEAR CHARLES,—I have read these papers with all attention this morning—but think you will agree with me that there must be an Eke to the Condescendence. Order the Eke against next day.—Tom leaves with this packet a blackcock, and (more's the pity) a gray hen. Yours,

W. S.

And again he thus writes by post to James Ballantyne:

ABBOTSFORD, September 10, 1818.

DEAR JAMES,—I am quite satisfied with what has been done as to the London bills. I am glad the presses move. I have been interrupted sadly since my return by tourist gazers. This day a confounded pair of Cambridge boys have robbed me of two good hours, and you of a sheet of copy—though whether a good sheet or no, deponent saith not. The story is a dismal one, and I doubt sometimes whether it will bear working out to much length after all. Query, if I shall make it so effective in two volumes as my mother does in her quarter of an hour's crack by the fireside? But *nil desperandum*. You shall have a bunch to-morrow or next day—and when the proofs come in, my pen must and shall step out. By the bye, I want a supply of pens—and ditto of ink. Adieu for the present, for I must go over to Toftfield, to give orders *anent* the dam and the footpath, and see *item* as to what should be done *anent* steps at the Rhymer's Waterfall, which I think may be made to turn out a decent bit of a linn, as would set True Thomas his worth and dignity. Ever yours,

W. S.

It must, I think, be allowed that these careless scraps, when combined, give a curious picture of the man who was brooding over the first chapters of The Bride of Lammermoor. One of his visitors of that month was Mr. R. Cadell, who was of course in all the secrets of the house of Constable; and observing how his host was harassed with lion-hunters, and what a number of hours he spent daily in the company of his work-people, he expressed, during one of their walks, his wonder that Scott should ever be able to write books at all while in the country. "I know," he said, "that you contrive to get a few hours in your own room, and that may do for the mere pen-work; but when is it that you think?" "Oh," said Scott, "I lie *simmering* over things for an hour or so before I get up—and there's the time I am dressing to overhaul my half-sleeping, half-waking *projet de chapitre*—and when I get the paper before me, it commonly runs off pretty easily.—Besides, I often take a doze in the plantations, and while Tom marks out a dyke or a drain as I have directed, one's fancy may be running its ain riggs in some other world."

JOHN GIBSON LOCKHART
After the painting by Pickersgill.
    It was in the month following that I first saw Abbotsford. He invited my friend John Wilson (now Professor of Moral Philosophy at Edinburgh) and myself to visit him for a day or two on our return from an excursion to Mr. Wilson's beautiful villa on the Lake of Windermere, but named the particular day (October 8) on which it would be most convenient for him to receive us; and we discovered on our arrival that he had fixed it from a good-natured motive. We found him walking in one of his plantations, at no great distance from the house, with five or six young people, and his friends Lord Melville and Captain Ferguson. Having presented us to the First Lord of the Admiralty, he fell back a little and said, "I am glad you came to-day, for I thought it might be of use to you both, some time or other, to be known to my old schoolfellow here, who is, and I hope will long continue to be, the great giver of good things in the Parliament House. I trust you have had enough of certain pranks with your friend Ebony, and if so, Lord Melville will have too much sense to remember them."[115] We then walked round the plantation, as yet in a very young state, and came back to the house by a formidable work which he was constructing for the defence of his*haugh* against the wintry violences of the Tweed; and he discoursed for some time with keen interest upon the comparative merits of different methods of embankment, but stopped now and then to give us the advantage of any point of view in which his new building on the eminence above pleased his eye. It had a fantastic appearance—being but a fragment of the existing edifice—and not at all harmonizing in its outline with "Mother Retford's" original tenement to the eastward. Scott, however, expatiated *con amore* on the rapidity with which, being chiefly of darkish granite, it was assuming a "time-honored" aspect. Ferguson, with a grave and respectful look, observed, "Yes, it really has much the air of some old fastness hard by the river Jordan." This allusion to the Chaldee MS., already quoted, in the manufacture of which Ferguson fancied Wilson and myself to have had a share, gave rise to a burst of laughter among Scott's merry young folks and their companions, while he himself drew in his nether lip, and rebuked the Captain with "Toots, Adam! toots, Adam!" He then returned to his embankment, and described how a former one had been entirely swept away in one night's flood. But the Captain was ready with another verse of the Chaldee MS., and groaned out, by way of echo, "Verily my fine gold hath perished!" Whereupon the "Great Magician" elevated his huge oaken staff as if to lay it on the waggish soldier's back—but flourished it gayly over his own head, and laughed louder than the youngest of the company. As we walked and talked, the Pepper and Mustard terriers kept snuffing about among the bushes and heather near us, and started every five minutes a hare, which scudded away before them and the ponderous staghound Maida—the Sheriff and all his tail hollowing and cheering, in perfect confidence that the dogs could do no more harm to poor puss than the venerable tom-cat, Hinse of Hinsfeldt, who pursued the vain chase with the rest.
    At length we drew near *Peterhouse*, and found sober Peter himself, and his brother-in-law, the facetious factotum Tom Purdie, superintending, pipe in mouth, three or four sturdy laborers busy in laying down the turf for a bowling-green. "I have planted hollies all round it,

108

you see," said Scott, "and laid out an arbor on the right-hand side for the laird; and here I mean to have a game at bowls after dinner every day in fine weather—for I take that to have been among the indispensables of our old *vie de château*." But I must not forget the reason he gave me some time afterwards for having fixed on that spot for his bowling-green. "In truth," he then said, "I wished to have a smooth walk, and a canny seat for myself within ear-shot of Peter's evening psalm." The coachman was a devout Presbyterian, and many a time have I in after-years accompanied Scott on his evening stroll, when the principal object was to enjoy, from the bowling-green, the unfailing melody of this good man's family worship—and heard him repeat, as Peter's manly voice led the humble choir within, that beautiful stanza of Burns's Saturday Night:—

"They chaunt their artless notes in simple guise;
They tune their hearts, by far the noblest aim," etc.

It was near the dinner-hour before we reached the house, and presently I saw assembled a larger company than I should have fancied to be at all compatible with the existing accommodations of the place; but it turned out that Captain Ferguson, and the friends whom I have not as yet mentioned, were to find quarters elsewhere for the night. His younger brother, Captain John Ferguson of the Royal Navy (a favorite lieutenant of Lord Nelson's), had come over from Huntly Burn; there were present, also, Mr. Scott of Gala, whose residence is within an easy distance; Sir Henry Hay Macdougal of Mackerstoun, an old baronet, with gay, lively, and highly polished manners, related in the same degree to both Gala and the Sheriff; Sir Alexander Don, the member for Roxburghshire, whose elegant social qualities have been alluded to in the preceding chapter; and Dr. Scott of Darnlee, a modest and intelligent gentleman, who having realized a fortune in the East India Company's medical service, had settled within two or three miles of Abbotsford, and, though no longer practising his profession, had kindly employed all the resources of his skill in the endeavor to counteract his neighbor's recent liability to attacks of cramp. Our host and one or two others appeared, as was in those days a common fashion with country gentlemen, in the lieutenancy uniform of their county. How fourteen or fifteen people contrived to be seated in the then dining-room of Abbotsford I know not—for it seemed quite full enough when it contained only eight or ten; but so it was—nor, as Sir Harry Macdougal's fat valet, warned by former experience, did not join the train of attendants, was there any perceptible difficulty in the detail of the arrangements. Everything about the dinner was, as the phrase runs, in excellent style; and in particular the *potage à la Meg Merrilies*, announced as an attempt to imitate a device of the Duke of Buccleuch's celebrated cook,—by name Monsieur Florence,—seemed, to those at least who were better acquainted with the Kaim of Derncleugh than with the *cuisine* of Bowhill,[116] a very laudable specimen of the art. The champagne circulated nimbly—and I never was present at a gayer dinner. It had advanced a little beyond the soup when it received an accompaniment which would not, perhaps, have improved the satisfaction of southern guests, had any such been present. A tall and stalwart bagpiper, in complete Highland costume, appeared pacing to and fro on the green before the house, and the window being open, it seemed as if he might as well have been straining his lungs within the parlor. At a pause of his strenuous performance, Scott took occasion to explain that *John of Skye* was a recent acquisition to the rising hamlet of Abbotstown; that the man was a capital hedger and ditcher, and only figured with the pipe and philabeg on high occasions in the after-part of the day; "but indeed," he added, laughing, "I fear John will soon be discovering that the hook and mattock are unfavorable to his chanter hand." When the cloth was drawn, and the never-failing salver of *quaighs* introduced, John of Skye, upon some well-known signal, entered the room, but *en militaire*, without removing his bonnet, and taking his station behind the landlord, received from his hand the largest of the Celtic bickers brimful of Glenlivet. The man saluted the company in his own dialect, tipped off the contents (probably a quarter of an English pint of raw aqua vitæ) at a gulp, wheeled about as solemnly as if the whole ceremony had been a movement on parade, and forthwith recommenced his pibrochs and gatherings, which continued until long after the ladies had left the table, and the autumnal moon was streaming in upon us so brightly as to dim the candles.

I had never before seen Scott in such buoyant spirits as he showed this evening—and I never saw him in higher afterwards; and no wonder, for this was the first time that he, Lord Melville, and Adam Ferguson, daily companions at the High School of Edinburgh, and partners in many joyous scenes of the early volunteer period, had met since the commencement of what I may call the serious part of any of their lives. The great poet and novelist was receiving them under his own roof, when his fame was at its *acme*, and his fortune seemed culminating to about a corresponding height—and the generous exuberance of his hilarity might have overflowed without moving the spleen of a Cynic. Old stories of *the Yards* and *the Cross-causeway* were relieved by sketches of real warfare, such as none but Ferguson (or Charles Mathews, had he been a soldier) could ever have given; and they toasted the memory of *Green-breeks* and the health of *the Beau* with equal devotion.

When we rose from table, Scott proposed that we should all ascend his western turret, to enjoy a moonlight view of the valley. The younger part of his company were too happy to do so: some of the seniors, who had tried the thing before, found pretexts for hanging back. The stairs were dark, narrow, and steep; but the Sheriff piloted the way, and at length there were as many on the top as it could well afford footing for. Nothing could be more lovely than the panorama; all the harsher and more naked features being lost in the delicious moonlight; the Tweed and the Gala winding and sparkling beneath our feet; and the distant ruins of Melrose appearing, as if carved of alabaster, under the black mass of the Eildons. The poet, leaning on his battlement, seemed to hang over the beautiful vision as if he had never seen it before. "If I live," he exclaimed, "I will build me a higher tower, with a more spacious platform, and a staircase better fitted for an old fellow's scrambling." The piper was heard re-tuning his instrument below, and he called to him for Lochaber no More. John of Skye obeyed, and as the music rose, softened by the distance, Scott repeated in a low key the melancholy words of the song of exile.

On descending from the tower, the whole company were assembled in the new dining-room, which was still under the hands of the carpenters, but had been brilliantly illuminated for the occasion. Mr. Bruce took his station, and old and young danced reels to his melodious accompaniment until they were weary, while Scott and the Dominie looked on with gladsome faces, and beat time now and then, the one with his staff, the other with his wooden leg. A tray with mulled wine and whiskey punch was then introduced, and Lord Melville proposed a bumper, with all the honors, to the *Roof-tree*. Captain Ferguson having sung Johnnie Cope, called on the young ladies for Kenmure's On and Awa'; and our host then insisted that the whole party should join, standing in a circle hand-in-hand*more majorum*, in the hearty chorus of

"Weel may we a' be,
Ill may we never see,
God bless the king and the gude companie!"

—which being duly performed, all dispersed. Such was *the handsel* (for Scott protested against its being considered as *the house-heating*) of the new Abbotsford.

When I began this chapter, I thought it would be a short one, but it is surprising how, when one digs into his memory, the smallest details of a scene that was interesting at the time, shall by degrees come to light again. I now recall, as if I had seen and heard them yesterday, the looks and words of eighteen years ago. Awakening between six and seven next morning, I heard Scott's voice close to me, and looking out of the little latticed window of the then detached cottage called *the chapel*, saw him and Tom Purdie pacing together on the green before the door, in earnest deliberation over what seemed to be a rude daub of a drawing; and every time they approached my end of their parade, I was sure to catch the words *Blue Bank*. It turned out in the course of the day, that a field of clay near Toftfield went by this name, and that the draining of it was one of the chief operations then in hand. My friend Wilson meanwhile, who lodged also in the chapel, tapped at my door, and asked me to rise and take a walk with him by the river, for he had some angling project in his head. He went out and joined in the consultation about the Blue Bank, while I was dressing; presently Scott hailed me at the casement, and said he had observed a volume of a new edition of Goethe on my table—would I lend it him for a little? He carried off the volume accordingly, and retreated with it to his den. It contained the Faust, and, I believe, in a more

110

complete shape than he had before seen that masterpiece of his old favorite. When we met at breakfast, a couple of hours after, he was full of the poem—dwelt with enthusiasm on the airy beauty of its lyrics, the terrible pathos of the scene before the *Mater Dolorosa*, and the deep skill shown in the various subtle shadings of character between Mephistopheles and poor Margaret. He remarked, however, of the Introduction (which I suspect was new to him), that blood would out—that, consummate artist as he was, Goethe was a German, and that nobody but a German would ever have provoked a comparison with the Book of Job, "the grandest poem that ever was written." He added, that he suspected the end of the story had been left *in obscuro*, from despair to match the closing scene of our own Marlowe's Doctor Faustus. Mr. Wilson mentioned a report that Coleridge was engaged on a translation of the Faust. "I hope it is so," said Scott; "Coleridge made Schiller's Wallenstein far finer than he found it, and so he will do by this. No man has all the resources of poetry in such profusion, but he cannot manage them so as to bring out anything of his own on a large scale at all worthy of his genius. He is like a lump of coal rich with gas, which lies expending itself in puffs and gleams, unless some shrewd body will clap it into a cast-iron box, and compel the compressed element to do itself justice. His fancy and diction would have long ago placed him above all his contemporaries, had they been under the direction of a sound judgment and a steady will.[117] I don't now expect a great original poem from Coleridge, but he might easily make a sort of fame for himself as a poetical translator,—that would be a thing completely unique and *sui generis*."

While this criticism proceeded, Scott was cutting away at his brown loaf and a plate of kippered salmon, in a style which strongly reminded me of Dandie Dinmont's luncheon at Mump's Hall; nor was his German topic at all the predominant one. On the contrary, the sentences which have dwelt on my memory dropt from him now and then, in the pauses, as it were, of his main talk;—for though he could not help recurring, ever and anon, to the subject, it would have been quite out of his way to make any literary matter the chief theme of his conversation, when there was a single person present who was not likely to feel much interested in its discussion.—How often have I heard him quote on such occasions Mr. Vellum's advice to the butler in Addison's excellent play of The Drummer: "Your conjuror, John, is indeed a twofold personage—but he *eats and drinks like other people*!"

I may, however, take this opportunity of observing, that nothing could have been more absurdly unfounded than the statement which I have seen repeated in various sketches of his Life and Manners, that he habitually abstained from conversation on literary topics. In point of fact, there were no topics on which he talked more openly or more earnestly; but he, when in society, lived and talked for the persons with whom he found himself surrounded, and if he did not always choose to enlarge upon the subjects which his companions for the time suggested, it was simply because he thought or fancied that these had selected, out of deference or flattery, subjects about which they really cared little more than they knew. I have already repeated, over and again, my conviction that Scott considered literature, *per se*, as a thing of far inferior importance to the high concerns of political or practical life; but it would be too ridiculous to question that literature nevertheless engrossed, at all times and seasons, the greater part of his own interest and reflection: nor can it be doubted that his general preference of the society of men engaged in the active business of the world, rather than that of, so-called, literary people, was grounded substantially on his feeling that literature, worthy of the name, was more likely to be fed and nourished by the converse of the former than by that of the latter class.

Before breakfast was over, the post-bag arrived, and its contents were so numerous, that Lord Melville asked Scott what election was on hand—not doubting that there must be some very particular reason for such a shoal of letters. He answered that it was much the same most days, and added, "though no one has kinder friends in the franking line, and though Freeling and Croker especially are always ready to stretch the point of privilege in my favor, I am nevertheless a fair contributor to the revenue, for I think my bill for letters seldom comes under £150 a year; and as to coach-parcels, they are a perfect ruination." He then told with high merriment a disaster that had lately befallen him. "One morning last spring," he said, "I opened a huge lump of a despatch, without looking how it was addressed, never doubting that it had travelled under some omnipotent frank like the First Lord of the

Admiralty's, when, lo and behold, the contents proved to be a MS. play, by a young lady of New York, who kindly requested me to read and correct it, equip it with prologue and epilogue, procure for it a favorable reception from the manager of Drury Lane, and make Murray or Constable bleed handsomely for the copyright; and on inspecting the cover, I found that I had been charged five pounds odd for the postage. This was bad enough—but there was no help, so I groaned and submitted. A fortnight or so after, another packet, of not less formidable bulk, arrived, and I was absent enough to break its seal, too, without examination. Conceive my horror when out jumped the same identical tragedy of The Cherokee Lovers, with a second epistle from the authoress, stating that, as the winds had been boisterous, she feared the vessel entrusted with her former communication might have foundered, and therefore judged it prudent to forward a duplicate."

Scott said he must retire to answer his letters, but that the sociable and the ponies would be at the door by one o'clock, when he proposed to show Melrose and Dryburgh to Lady Melville and any of the rest of the party that chose to accompany them; adding that his son Walter would lead anybody who preferred a gun to the likeliest place for a blackcock, and that Charlie Purdie (Tom's brother) would attend upon Mr. Wilson, and whoever else chose to try a cast of the salmon-rod. He withdrew when all this was arranged, and appeared at the time appointed, with perhaps a dozen letters sealed for the post, and a coach-parcel addressed to James Ballantyne, which he dropt at the turnpike-gate as we drove to Melrose. Seeing it picked up by a dirty urchin, and carried into a hedge pot-house, where half-a-dozen nondescript wayfarers were smoking and tippling, I could not but wonder that it had not been the fate of some one of those innumerable packets to fall into unscrupulous hands, and betray the grand secret. That very morning we had seen two post-chaises drawn up at his gate, and the enthusiastic travellers, seemingly decent tradesmen and their families, who must have been packed in a manner worthy of Mrs. Gilpin, lounging about to catch a glimpse of him at his going forth. But it was impossible in those days to pass between Melrose and Abbotsford without encountering some odd figure, armed with a sketch-book, evidently bent on a peep at the Great Unknown; and it must be allowed that many of these pedestrians looked as if they might have thought it very excusable to make prize, by hook or by crook, of a MS. chapter of the Tales of my Landlord.

Scott showed us the ruins of Melrose in detail; and as we proceeded to Dryburgh, descanted learnedly and sagaciously on the good effects which must have attended the erection of so many great monastic establishments in a district so peculiarly exposed to the inroads of the English in the days of the Border wars. "They were now and then violated," he said, "as their aspect to this hour bears witness; but for once that they suffered, any lay property similarly situated must have been *harried* a dozen times. The bold Dacres, Liddells, and Howards, that could get easy absolution at York or Durham for any ordinary breach of a truce with the Scots, would have had *to dree a heavy dole* had they confessed plundering from the fat brothers, of the same order perhaps, whose lines had fallen to them on the wrong side of the Cheviot." He enlarged, too, on the heavy penalty which the Crown of Scotland had paid for its rash acquiescence in the wholesale robbery of the Church at the Reformation. "The proportion of the soil in the hands of the clergy had," he said, "been very great—too great to be continued. If we may judge by their share in the public burdens, they must have had nearly a third of the land in their possession. But this vast wealth was now distributed among a turbulent nobility, too powerful before; and the Stuarts soon found, that in the bishops and lord abbots they had lost the only means of balancing their factions, so as to turn the scale in favor of law and order; and by and by the haughty barons themselves, who had scrambled for the worldly spoil of the church, found that the spiritual influence had been concentrated in hands as haughty as their own, and connected with no feelings likely to buttress their order any more than the Crown—a new and sterner monkery, under a different name, and essentially plebeian. Presently the Scotch were on the verge of republicanism, in state as well as kirk, and I have sometimes thought it was only the accession of King Jamie to the throne of England that could have given monarchy a chance of prolonging its existence here." One of his friends asked what he supposed might have been the annual revenue of the abbey of Melrose in its best day. He answered that he suspected, if all the sources of their income were now in clever hands, the produce could hardly be under £100,000 a year; and added: "Making every allowance for modern improvements, there can be no question that the sixty brothers of Melrose divided a princely rental. The superiors were often men of very high birth, and the great majority of the rest were younger brothers of gentlemen's families. I fancy they may have been, on the whole, pretty near akin to your Fellows of All Souls—who, according to their statute, must be *bene nati, bene vestiti, et mediocriter docti.* They had a good house in Edinburgh, where, no doubt, my lord abbot and his chaplains maintained a hospitable table during the sittings of Parliament." Some one regretted that we had no lively picture of the enormous revolution in manners that must have followed the downfall of the ancient Church in Scotland. He observed that there were, he fancied, materials enough for constructing such a one, but that they were mostly scattered in records—"of which," said he, "who knows anything to the purpose except Tom Thomson and John Riddell? It is common to laugh at such researches, but they pay the good brains that meddle with them;—and had Thomson been as diligent in setting down his discoveries as he has been in making them, he might, long before this time of day, have placed himself on a level with Ducange or Camden. The change in the country-side," he continued, "must indeed have been terrific; but it does not seem to have been felt very severely by a certain Boniface of St. Andrews, for when somebody asked him, on the subsidence of the storm, what he thought of all that had occurred,—'Why,' answered mine host, 'it comes to this, that the moder*au*tor sits in my meikle chair, where the dean sat before, and in place of calling for the third stoup of Bordeaux, bids Jenny bring ben anither bowl of toddy.'"

At Dryburgh, Scott pointed out to us the sepulchral aisle of his Haliburton ancestors, and said he hoped, in God's appointed time, to lay his bones among their dust. The spot was, even then, a sufficiently interesting and impressive one; but I shall not say more of it at present.

On returning to Abbotsford, we found Mrs. Scott and her daughters doing penance under the merciless curiosity of a couple of tourists who had arrived from Selkirk soon after we set out for Melrose. They were rich specimens—tall, lanky young men, both of them rigged out in new jackets and trousers of the Macgregor tartan; the one, as they had revealed, being a lawyer, the other a Unitarian preacher, from New England. These gentlemen, when told on their arrival that Mr. Scott was not at home, had shown such signs of impatience, that the servant took it for granted they must have serious business, and asked if they would wish to speak a word with his lady. They grasped at this, and so conducted themselves in the interview, that Mrs. Scott never doubted they had brought letters of introduction to her husband, and invited them accordingly to partake of her luncheon. They had been walking about the house and grounds with her and her daughters ever since that time, and appeared at the porch, when the Sheriff and his party returned to dinner, as if they had been already fairly enrolled on his visiting list. For the moment, he too was taken in—he fancied that his wife must have received and opened their credentials—and shook hands with them with courteous cordiality. But Mrs. Scott, with all her overflowing good-nature, was a sharp observer; and she, before a minute had elapsed, interrupted the ecstatic compliments of the strangers, by reminding them that her husband would be glad to have the letters of the friends who had been so good as to write by them. It then turned out that there were no letters to be produced—and Scott, signifying that his hour for dinner approached, added, that as he supposed they meant to walk to Melrose, he could not trespass further on their time. The two lion-hunters seemed quite unprepared for this abrupt escape. But there was about Scott, in perfection, when he chose to exert it, the power of civil repulsion; he bowed the overwhelmed originals to his door, and on reëntering the parlor, found Mrs. Scott complaining very indignantly that they had gone so far as to pull out their note-book, and beg an exact account, not only of his age—but of her own. Scott, already half relenting, laughed heartily at this misery. He observed, however, that, "if he were to take in all the world, he had better put up a sign-post at once,—

'Porter, ale, and British spirits,
Painted bright between twa trees;'[118]

and that no traveller of respectability could ever be at a loss for such an introduction as would insure his best hospitality." Still he was not quite pleased with what had happened—and as we were about to pass, half an hour afterwards, from the drawing-room to the dining-room, he said to his wife, "Hang the Yahoos, Charlotte—but we should have bid them stay dinner." "Devil a bit," quoth Captain John Ferguson, who had again come over from Huntly Burn, and had been latterly assisting the lady to amuse her Americans, "Devil a bit, my dear,—they were quite in a mistake, I could see. The one asked Madame whether she deigned to call her new house Tully-Veolan or Tillietudlem; and the other, when Maida happened to lay his nose against the window, exclaimed *pro-di-gi-ous*! In short, they evidently meant all their humbug not for you, but for the culprit of Waverley, and the rest of that there rubbish." "Well, well, Skipper," was the reply, "for a' that, the loons would hae been nane the waur o' their kail."

From this banter it may be inferred that the younger Ferguson had not as yet been told the Waverley secret—which to any of that house could never have been any mystery. Probably this, or some similar occasion soon afterwards, led to his formal initiation; for during the many subsequent years that the veil was kept on, I used to admire the tact with which, when in their topmost high-jinks humor, both "Captain John" and "The Auld Captain" eschewed any the most distant allusion to the affair.

And this reminds me, that at the period of which I am writing, none of Scott's own family, except of course his wife, had the advantage in that matter of the Skipper. Some of them, too, were apt, like him, so long as no regular confidence had been reposed in them, to avail themselves of the author's reserve for their own sport among friends. Thus one morning, just as Scott was opening the door of the parlor, the rest of the party being already seated at the breakfast-table, the Dominie was in the act of helping himself to an egg, marked with a peculiar hieroglyphic by Mrs. Thomas Purdie, upon which Anne Scott, then a lively rattling girl of sixteen, lisped out, "That's a mysterious-looking egg, Mr. Thomson—what if it should have been meant for *the Great Unknown*?" Ere the Dominie could reply, her father advanced to the foot of the table, and having seated himself and deposited his stick on the carpet beside him, with a sort of whispered whistle—"What's that Lady Anne's[119] saying?" quoth he; "I thought it had been well known that the *keelavined* egg must be a soft one for *the Sherra*." And so he took his egg, and while all smiled in silence, poor Anne said gayly, in the midst of her blushes, "Upon my word, papa, I thought Mr. John Ballantyne might have been expected." This allusion to Johnny's glory in being considered as the accredited representative of Jedediah Cleishbotham produced a laugh,—at which the Sheriff frowned—and then laughed too.

I remember nothing particular about our second day's dinner, except that it was then I first met my dear and honored friend William Laidlaw. The evening passed rather more quietly than the preceding one. Instead of the dance in the new dining-room, we had a succession of old ballads sung to the harp and guitar by the young ladies of the house; and Scott, when they seemed to have done enough, found some reason for taking down a volume of Crabbe, and read us one of his favorite tales,—

"Grave Jonas Kindred, Sibyl Kindred's sire,
Was six feet high, and looked six inches higher," etc.

But jollity revived in full vigor when the supper-tray was introduced; and to cap all merriment, Captain Ferguson dismissed us with The Laird of Cockpen. Lord and Lady Melville were to return to Melville Castle next morning, and Mr. Wilson and I happened to mention that we were engaged to dine and sleep at the seat of my friend and relation, Mr. Pringle of Torwoodlee, on our way to Edinburgh. Scott immediately said that he would send word in the morning to the Laird, that he and Adam Ferguson meant to accompany us—such being the unceremonious style in which country neighbors in Scotland visit each other. Next day, accordingly, we all rode over together to Mr. Pringle's beautiful seat—the "distant Torwoodlee" of The Lay of the Last Minstrel, but distant not above five or six miles from Abbotsford—coursing hares as we proceeded, but inspecting the antiquities of the *Catrail* to the interruption of our sport. We had another joyous evening at Torwoodlee. Scott and Ferguson returned home at night, and the morning after, as Wilson and I mounted for Edinburgh, our kind old host, his sides still sore with laughter, remarked that "the Sheriff and the Captain together were too much for any company."

There was much talk between the Sheriff and Mr. Pringle about the Selkirkshire Yeomanry Cavalry, of which the latter had been the original commandant. Young Walter Scott had been for a year or more Cornet in the corps, and his father was consulting Torwoodlee about an entertainment which he meant to give them on his son's approaching birthday. It was then that the new dining-room was to be first *heated* in good earnest; and Scott very kindly pressed Wilson and myself, at parting, to return for the occasion—which, however, we found it impossible to do. The reader must therefore be satisfied with what is said about it in one of the following letters:—

TO J. B. S. MORRITT, ESQ., M. P., ROKEBY.

ABBOTSFORD, 5th November, 1818.

MY DEAR MORRITT,—Many thanks for your kind letter of 29th October. The matter of the colts being as you state, I shall let it lie over until next year, and then avail myself of your being in the neighborhood to get a good pair of four-year-olds, since it would be unnecessary to buy them a year younger, and incur all the risks of disease and accident, unless they could have been had at a proportional under-value.

* * * * * * leaves us this morning after a visit of about a week. He improves on acquaintance, and especially seems so pleased with everything, that it would be very hard to quarrel with him. Certainly, as the Frenchman said, *il a un grand talent pour le silence*. I take the opportunity of his servant going direct to Rokeby to charge him with this letter, and a plaid which my daughters entreat you to accept of as a token of their *warm* good wishes. Seriously you will find it a good bosom friend in an easterly wind, a black frost, or when your country avocations lead you to face a *dry wap of snow*. I find it by far the lightest and most comfortable integument which I can use upon such occasions.

We had a grand jollification here last week;—the whole troop of Forest Yeomanry dining with us. I assure you the scene was gay and even grand, with glittering sabres, waving standards, and screaming bagpipes; and that it might not lack spectators of taste, who should arrive in the midst of the hurricane, but Lord and Lady Compton, whose presence gave a great zest to the whole affair. Everything went off very well, and as cavalry have the great advantage over infantry, that their *legs* never get drunk, they retired in decent disorder about ten o'clock. I was glad to see Lord and Lady Compton so very comfortable, and surrounded with so fine a family, the natural bond of mutual regard and affection. She has got very jolly, but otherwise has improved on her travels. I had a long chat with her, and was happy to find her quite contented and pleased with the lot she has drawn in life. It is a brilliant one in many respects, to be sure; but still I have seen the story of the poor woman, who, after all rational subjects of distress had been successively remedied, tormented herself about the screaming of a neighbor's peacock—I say, I have seen this so often realized in actual life, that I am more afraid of my friends making themselves uncomfortable, who have only imaginary evils to indulge, than I am for the peace of those who, battling magnanimously with real inconvenience and danger, find a remedy in the very force of the exertions to which their lot compels them.

I sympathize with you for the *dole* which you are *dreeing* under the inflictions of your honest proser. Of all the boring machines ever devised, your regular and determined story-teller is the most peremptory and powerful in his operations. This is a rainy day, and my present infliction is an idle cousin, a great amateur of the pipes, who is performing incessantly in the next room for the benefit of a probationary minstrel, whose pipes scream *à la distance*, as the young hoarse cock-chicken imitates the gallant and triumphant screech of a veteran Sir Chanticleer. Yours affectionately,

W. SCOTT.[BACK TO CONTENTS]

APPENDIX

THE DURHAM GARLAND

IN THREE PARTS

[The following is the *Garland* referred to at pages 4 and 26, in connection with the novel of Guy Mannering. The ballad was taken down from the recitation of Mrs. Young of Castle-Douglas, who, as her family informed Mr. Train, had long been in the habit of repeating it over to them once in the year, in order that it might not escape from her memory.]

PART I

1

A worthy Lord of birth and state,
Who did in Durham live of late—
But I will not declare his name,
By reason of his birth and fame.

2

This Lord he did a-hunting go;
If you the truth of all would know,
He had indeed a noble train,
Of Lords and Knights and Gentlemen.

3

This noble Lord he left the train
Of Lords and Knights and Gentlemen;
And hearing not the horn to blow,
He could not tell which way to go.

4

But he did wander to and fro,
Being weary, likewise full of woe:
At last Dame Fortune was so kind
That he the Keeper's house did find.

5

He went and knocked at the door,
He thought it was so late an hour.
The Forester did let him in,
And kindly entertained him.

6

About the middle of the night,
When as the stars did shine most bright,
This Lord was in a sad surprise,
Being wakened by a fearful noise.

7

Then he did rise and call with speed,
To know the reason then indeed,
Of all that shrieking and those cries
Which did disturb his weary eyes.

8

"I'm sorry, Sir," the Keeper said,
"That you should be so much afraid;
But I do hope all will be well,
For my wife she is in travail."

9

The noble Lord was learned and wise,
To know the Planets in the skies.
He saw one evil Planet reign,
He called the Forester again.

10

He gave him then to understand,
He'd have the Midwife hold her hand;
But he was answered by the maid,
"My Mistress is delivered."

11

At one o'clock that very morn,
A lovely infant there was born;
It was indeed a charming boy,
Which brought the man and wife much joy.

12
The Lord was generous, kind, and free,
And proffered Godfather to be;
The Goodman thanked him heartily
For his goodwill and courtesy.
13
A parson was sent for with speed,
For to baptize the child indeed;
And after that, as I heard say,
In mirth and joy they spent the day.
14
This Lord did noble presents give,
Which all the servants did receive.
They prayed God to enrich his store,
For they never had so much before.
15
And likewise to the child he gave
A present noble, rich, and brave;
It was a charming cabinet,
That was with pearls and jewels set.
16
And within it was a chain of gold,
Would dazzle eyes for to behold;
A richer gift, as I may say,
Was not beheld this many a day.
17
He charged his father faithfully,
That he himself would keep the key,
Until the child could write and read—
And then to give him it indeed;—
18
"Pray do not open it at all
Whatever should on you befall;
For it may do my godson good,
If it be rightly understood."
19
This Lord did not declare his name,
Nor yet the place from whence he came,
But secretly he did depart,
And left them grieved to the heart.
PART II
1
The second part I now unfold,
As true a story as e'er was told,
Concerning of a lovely child,
Who was obedient, sweet, and mild.
2
This child did take his learning so,
If you the truth of all would know,
At eleven years of age indeed,
Both Greek and Latin he could read.
3
Then thinking of his cabinet,
That was with pearls and jewels set,
He asked his father for the key,
Which he gave him right speedily;

117

4

And when he did the same unlock,
He was with great amazement struck
When he the riches did behold,
And likewise saw the chain of gold.

5

But searching farther he did find
A paper which disturbed his mind,
That was within the cabinet,
In Greek and Latin it was writ.

6

My child, serve God that is on high,
And pray to him incessantly;
Obey your parents, love your king,
That nothing may your conscience sting.

7

At seven years hence your fate will be,
You must be hanged upon a tree;
Then pray to God both night and day,
To let that hour pass away.

8

When he these woeful lines did read,
He with a sigh did say indeed,
"If hanging be my destiny,
My parents shall not see me die;

9

"For I will wander to and fro,
I'll go where I no one do know;
But first I'll ask my parents' leave,
In hopes their blessing to receive."

10

Then locking up his cabinet,
He went from his own chamber straight
Unto his only parents dear,
Beseeching them with many a tear

11

That they would grant what he would have—
"But first your blessing I do crave,
And beg you'll let me go away,
'T will do me good another day."

12

*****
*****

"And if I live I will return,
When seven years are past and gone."

13

Both man and wife did then reply,
"I fear, my son, that we shall die;
If we should yield to let you go,
Our aged hearts would break with woe."

14

But he entreated eagerly,
While they were forced to comply,
And give consent to let him go,
But where, alas! they did not know.

15

In the third part you soon shall find,
That fortune was to him most kind,
And after many dangers past,
He came to Durham at the last.

PART III

1

He went by chance, as I heard say,
To that same house that very day
In which his Godfather did dwell;
But mind what luck to him befell—

2

This child did crave a service there,
On which came out his Godfather,
And seeing him a pretty youth,
He took him for his Page in truth.

3

Then in this place he pleased so well,
That 'bove the rest he bore the bell;
This child so well the Lord did please,
He raised him higher by degrees.

4

He made him Butler sure indeed,
And then his Steward with all speed,
Which made the other servants spite,
And envy him both day and night.

5

He was never false unto his trust,
But proved ever true and just;
And to the Lord did hourly pray
To guide him still both night and day.

6

In this place, plainly it appears,
He lived the space of seven years;
His parents then he thought upon,
And of his promise to return.

7

Then humbly of his Lord did crave,
That he his free consent might have
To go and see his parents dear,
He had not seen this many a year.

8

Then having leave, away he went,
Not dreaming of the false intent
That was contrived against him then
By wicked, false, deceitful men.

9

They had in his portmanteau put
This noble Lord's fine golden cup;
That when the Lord at dinner was,
The cup was missed as come to pass.

10

"Where can it be?" this Lord did say,
"We had it here but yesterday."
The Butler then replied with speed,
"If you will hear the truth indeed.

11

"Your darling Steward which is gone,
With feathered nest away is flown;
I'll warrant you he has that, and more
That doth belong unto your store."

12

"No," says this Lord, "that cannot be,
For I have tried his honesty;"
"Then," said the Cook, "my Lord, I die
Upon a tree full ten feet high."

13

Then hearing what these men did say,
He sent a messenger that day,
To take him with a hue and cry,
And bring him back immediately.

14

They searched his portmanteau with speed,
In which they found the cup indeed;
Then was he struck with sad surprise,
He could not well believe his eyes.

15

The assizes then were drawing nigh,
And he was tried and doomed to die;
And his injured innocence
Could nothing say in his defense.

16

But going to the Gallows tree,
On which he thought to hanged be
He clapped his hands upon his breast,
And thus in tears these words exprest:—

17

"Blind Fortune will be Fortune still,
I see, let man do what he will;
For though this day I needs must die,
I am not guilty—no, not I."

18

This noble Lord was in amaze,
He stood and did with wonder gaze;
Then he spoke out with words so mild,—
"What mean you by that saying, Child?"

19

"Will that your Lordship," then said he,
"Grant one day's full reprieve for me,
A dismal story I'll relate,
Concerning of my wretched fate."

20

"Speak up, my Child," this Lord did say,
"I say you shall not die this day—
And if I find you innocent,
I'll crown your days with sweet content."

21

He told him all his dangers past,
He had gone through from first to last,
He fetched the chain and cabinet,
Likewise the paper that was writ.

22

When that this noble Lord did see,
He ran to him most eagerly,
And in his arms did him embrace,
Repeating of those words in haste.—

23

"My Child, my Child, how blessed am I
Thou art innocent, and shalt not die;
For I'm indeed thy Godfather,
And thou wast born in fair Yorkshire.

24

"I have indeed one daughter dear,
Which is indeed my only heir;
And I will give her unto thee,
And crown you with felicity."

25

So then the Butler and the Cook
('Twas them that stole the golden cup)
Confessed their faults immediately,
And for it died deservedly.

26

This goodly youth, as I do hear,
Thus raised, sent for his parents dear,
Who did rejoice their Child to see—
And so I end my Tragedy.[Back to Contents]

NARRATIVE OF THE LIFE OF JAMES ANNESLEY.

(See NOTE, p. 26.)

"Lord and Lady Altham, of Dunmain, in the county of Wexford, had been for many years married and childless, when, in the year 1715, their warmest hopes and wishes were realized by the birth of an heir to their estates and title. On that joyful evening the hospitality of the house of Dunmain was claimed by a young gentleman travelling from Dublin, named 'Master Richard Fitzgerald,' who joined Lord Altham and his household in drinking the healths of the 'lady in the straw,' and the long expected heir, in the customary groaning drink. It does not appear that Master Fitzgerald was learned in astrology, or practised any branch of the 'Black art,' or that he used any spell with reference to the infant more potent than these hearty libations and sincere good wishes for his future prosperity. Next day, before leaving the hospitable mansion, the little hero of this tale was presented to the stranger, who 'kissed him, and gave the nurse half-a-guinea.'

"Of Fitzgerald we have only to add, that he entered the army and became a distinguished officer in the service of the queen of Hungary, and that twenty-eight years afterwards he returned to Ireland to assist in recovering for his former infantile friend the estates and titles of his ancestors, which had been for many years iniquitously withheld from him.

"Lord and Lady Altham lived unhappily together, and a separation took place soon after the birth of their son. Her Ladyship, shamefully neglected by her husband, resided in England during the remainder of her life, and from disease and poverty was reduced to a state of extreme imbecility both of body and mind.

"James Annesley, the infant son of this unhappy mother, was entrusted, by Lord Altham, to the charge of a woman of indifferent character, named Joan or Juggy Landy. Juggy was a dependent of the family, and lived in a cabin on the estate, about a quarter of a mile from the house of Dunmain. This hut is described as a 'despicable place, without any furniture except a pot, two or three trenchers, a couple of straw beds on the floor,' and 'with only a bush to draw in and out for a door.' Thus humbly and inauspiciously was the boy reared under the care of a nurse, who, however unfortunate or guilty, appears to have lavished upon her young charge the most affectionate attention. From some unexplained cause, however, Juggy Landy incurred the displeasure of Lord Altham, who took the boy from her, and ordered his groom to 'horsewhip her,' and 'to set the dogs upon her,' when she persisted in hovering about the premises to obtain a sight of her former charge.

"Lord Altham now removed with his son to Dublin where he appears to have entered upon a career of the most dissipated and profligate conduct. We find him reduced to extreme pecuniary embarrassment, and his property became a prey to low and abandoned associates; one of whom, a Miss Kennedy, he ultimately endeavored to introduce to society as his wife. This worthless woman must have obtained great ascendancy over his Lordship, as she was enabled to drive James Annesley from his father's protection, and the poor boy became a houseless vagabond, wandering about the streets of Dublin, and procuring a scanty and precarious subsistence 'by running of errands and holding gentlemen's horses.'

"Meantime Lord Altham's pecuniary difficulties had so increased as to induce him to endeavor to borrow money on his reversionary interest in the estates of the Earl of Anglesey, to whom he was heir-at-law. In this scheme he was joined by his brother Captain Annesley, and they jointly succeeded in procuring several small sums of money. But as James Annesley would have proved an important legal impediment to these transactions, he was represented to some parties to be dead; and where his existence could not be denied, he was asserted to be the natural son of his Lordship and of Juggy Landy.

"Lord Altham died in the year 1727, 'so miserably poor that he was actually buried at the public expense.' His brother Captain Annesley attended the funeral as chief mourner, and assumed the title of Baron Altham, but when he claimed to have this title registered he was refused by the king-at-arms, 'on account of his nephew being reported still alive, and for want of the honorary fees.' Ultimately, however, by means which are stated to have been 'well known and obvious,' he succeeded in procuring his registration.

"But there was another and a more sincere mourner at the funeral of Lord Altham than the successful inheritor of his title: a poor boy of twelve years of age, half naked, bareheaded and barefooted, and wearing, as the most important part of his dress, an old yellow livery waistcoat,[120] followed at a humble distance, and wept over his father's grave. Young Annesley was speedily recognized by his uncle, who forcibly drove him from the place, but not before the boy had made himself known to several old servants of his father, who were attending the corpse of their late lord to the tomb.

"The usurper now commenced a series of attempts to obtain possession of his nephew's person, for the purpose of transporting him beyond seas, or otherwise ridding himself of so formidable a rival. For some time, however, these endeavors were frustrated, principally through the gallantry of a brave and kind-hearted butcher, named Purcel, who, having compassion upon the boy's destitute state, took him into his house and hospitably maintained him for a considerable time; and on one occasion, when he was assailed by a numerous party of his uncle's emissaries, Purcel placed the boy between his legs, and stoutly defending him with his cudgel, resisted their utmost efforts, and succeeded in rescuing his young charge.

"After having escaped from many attempts of the same kind, Annesley was at length kidnapped in the streets of Dublin, dragged by his uncle and a party of hired ruffians to a boat, and carried on board a vessel in the river, which immediately sailed with our hero for America, where, on his arrival, he was apprenticed as a plantation slave, and in this condition he remained for the succeeding thirteen years.

"During his absence his uncle, on the demise of the Earl of Anglesey, quietly succeeded to that title and immense wealth.

"While forcibly detained in the plantations, Annesley suffered many severe hardships and privations, particularly in his frequent unsuccessful attempts to escape. Among other incidents which befell him, he incurred the deadly hatred of one master, in consequence of a suspected intrigue with his wife—a charge from which he was afterwards honorably acquitted. The daughter of a second master became affectionately attached to him; but it does not appear that this regard was reciprocal. And finally, in effecting his escape, he fell into the hands of some hostile negroes, who stabbed him severely in various places; from the effects of which cruelty he did not recover for several months.

"At the end of thirteen years, Annesley, who had now attained the age of twenty-five, succeeded in reaching Jamaica in a merchant vessel, and he immediately volunteered himself as a private sailor on board a man-of-war. Here he was at once identified by several officers; and Admiral Vernon, who was then in command of the British West India fleet, wrote home an account of the case to the Duke of Newcastle (the Premier), and, 'in the mean time, supplied him with clothes and money, and treated him with the respect and attention which his rank demanded.'

"The Earl of Anglesey no sooner heard of these transactions on board the fleet, than he used every effort to keep possession of his usurped title and property, and 'the most eminent lawyers within the English and Irish bars were retained to defend a cause, the prosecution of which was not as yet even threatened.'

"On Annesley's arrival in Dublin, 'several servants who had lived with his father came from the country to see him. They knew him at first sight, and some of them fell on their knees to thank heaven for his preservation,—embraced his legs, and shed tears of joy for his return.'

"Lord Anglesey became so much alarmed at the probable result of the now threatened trial, that he expressed his intention to make a compromise with the claimant, renounce the title, and retire into France; and with this view he commenced learning the French language. But this resolution was given up, in consequence of an occurrence which encouraged the flattering hope that his opponent would be speedily and most effectually disposed of.

"After his arrival in England, Annesley unfortunately occasioned the death of a man by the accidental discharge of a fowling-piece which he was in the act of carrying. Though there could not exist a doubt of his innocence from all intention of such a deed, the circumstance offered too good a chance to be lost sight of by his uncle, who employed an attorney named Gifford, and with his assistance used every effort at the coroner's inquest, and the subsequent trial, to bring about a verdict of murder. In this, however, he did not succeed, although 'he practised all the unfair means that could be invented to procure the removal of the prisoner from the healthy gaol to which he had been at first committed;' and 'the Earl even appeared in person on the bench, endeavoring to intimidate and browbeat the witnesses, and to inveigle the prisoner into destructive confessions.' Annesley was honorably acquitted, after his uncle had expended nearly one thousand pounds on the prosecution.

"The trial between James Annesley, Esq., and Richard, Earl of Anglesey, before the Right Honorable the Lord Chief Justice and other Barons of the Exchequer, commenced on the 11th November, 1743, and was continued for thirteen days. The defendant's counsel examined an immense number of witnesses in an attempt to prove that Annesley was the illegitimate son of the late Baron Altham. The Jury found for the plaintiff; but it did not prove sufficient to recover his title and estates: for his uncle 'had recourse to every device the law allowed, and his powerful interest procured a writ of error which set aside the verdict.' Before another trial could be brought about, Annesley died without male issue, and Lord Anglesey consequently remained in undisturbed possession.

"It is presumed that the points of resemblance between the leading incidents in the life of this unfortunate young nobleman and the adventures of Henry Bertram in Guy Mannering, are so evident as to require neither comment nor enumeration to make them apparent to the most cursory reader of the Novel. The addition of a very few other circumstances will, it is believed, amount to a proof of the identity of the two stories.[Back to Contents]

END OF VOLUME FIVE

Footnote 1: The Mull of Cantyre.[Back to Main Text]

Footnote 2: [Joseph Train was born in 1779, at Gilminscroft, Sorn, Ayrshire, where his father was grieve and land-steward. The boy was apprenticed at an early age to a weaver in Ayr, but, notwithstanding the narrowness of his circumstances, and a very imperfect education, he even then showed a love of learning and a passion for antiquarian lore. From 1799 to 1802 he served in the Ayrshire militia. While the regiment was stationed at Inverness, he became a subscriber to Currie's edition of Burns, and his colonel, Sir David Hunter-Blair, seeing the volumes at the bookseller's, was surprised to learn that they had been ordered by one of his men. Greatly pleased thereat, Sir David had the books handsomely bound and sent to Train, free of charge; and later obtained for him an appointment in the Excise in the Ayr district. He was a faithful and efficient officer, but owing to the then prevalent custom of giving the higher places in the Excise to Englishmen, all Scott's efforts for the advancement of his friend were unavailing; he remained supervisor till he went on the retired list in 1836. In 1829 Train was admitted a member of the Scottish Society of Antiquaries. Though the death of Scott made a sad blank in his life, his interest in his favorite studies continued to the end. The latter part of his life was spent in a cottage at Castle Douglas, where he was visited shortly before his death by James Hannay, who found him in a little parlor, crowded with antiquities of interest and value,—the antiquary, "a tall old man, with an autumnal red in his face, hale looking, and of simple, quaint manners." (See *Household Words*, July 10, 1853.) Train's last extended works were an *Historical and Statistical Account of the Isle of Man, with a view of its peculiar customs and popular superstitions* (1845); and a study of a local religious sect in *The Buchanites from First to Last* (1846); but he was an occasional contributor to various periodicals. He died December 1, 1852.][Back to Main Text]

Footnote 3: "*The Voyages, Dangerous Adventures, and Imminent Escapes of Capt. Rich. Falconer.*Containing the Laws, Customs, and Manners of the Indians in America; his shipwrecks; his marrying an Indian wife; his narrow escape from the Island of Dominico, etc. Intermixed with the Voyages and Adventures of Thomas Randal, of Cork, Pilot; with his Shipwreck in the Baltick, being the only man that escap'd. His being taken by the Indians of Virginia, etc. And an Account of his Death. The Fourth Edition. London. Printed for J. Marshall, at the Bible in Gracechurch Street. 1734."

On the fly-leaf is the following note, in Scott's handwriting: "This book I read in early youth. I am ignorant whether it is altogether fictitious and written upon De Foe's plan, which it greatly resembles, or whether it is only an exaggerated account of the adventures of a real person. It is very scarce, for, endeavoring to add it to the other favorites of my infancy, I think I looked for it ten years to no purpose, and at last owed it to the active kindness of Mr. Terry. Yet Richard Falconer's adventures seem to have passed through several editions."[Back to Main Text]

Footnote 4: "*The Travels and Adventures of William Bingfield, Esq.*, containing, as surprizing a Fluctuation of Circumstances, both by Sea and Land, as ever befel one man. With an Accurate Account of the Shape, Nature, and Properties of that most furious, and amazing Animal, the Dog-Bird. Printed from his own Manuscript. With a beautiful Frontispiece. 2 vols. 12mo. London: Printed for E. Withers, at the Seven Stars, in Fleet Street. 1753." On the fly-leaf of the first volume Scott has written as follows: "I read this scarce little *Voyage Imaginaire* when I was about ten years old, and long after sought for a copy without being able to find a person who would so much as acknowledge having heard of William Bingfield or his Dog-birds, until the indefatigable kindness of my friend Mr. Terry, of the Haymarket, made me master of this copy. I am therefore induced to think the book is of very rare occurrence." [In consequence of these Notes, both Falconer and Bingfield have been recently reprinted in London.—(1839.)][Back to Main Text]

Footnote 5: Johnson's *Vanity of Human Wishes*.[Back to Main Text]

Footnote 6: Francis, Lord Seaforth, died 11th January, 1815, in his 60th year, having outlived four sons, all of high promise. His title died with him, and he was succeeded in his estates by his daughter, Lady Hood, now the Hon. Mrs. Stewart-Mackenzie of Seaforth.— See some verses on Lord Seaforth's death, in Scott's *Poetical Works*, vol. viii. p. 392 [Cambridge Ed. p. 419]. The Celtic designation of the chief of the clan MacKenzie, *Caberfae*, means *Staghead*, the bearing of the family. The prophecy which Scott alludes to in this letter is also mentioned by Sir Humphry Davy in one of his Journals (see his *Life*, by Dr. Davy, vol. ii. p. 72),—and it was, if the account be correct, a most extraordinary one, for it connected the fall of the house of Seaforth not only with the appearance of a deaf *Caberfae*, but with the contemporaneous appearance of various different physical misfortunes in several of the other great Highland chiefs; all of which are said—and were certainly believed both by Scott and Davy—to have actually occurred within the memory of the generation that has not yet passed away. Mr. Morritt can testify thus far—that he "heard the prophecy quoted in the Highlands at a time when Lord Seaforth had two sons both alive and in good health—so that it certainly was not made *après coup*." [Mrs. Stewart-Mackenzie died at Brahan Castle in 1862, in her 79th year. "Her funeral was one of the largest ever witnessed in the North." The Seaforth estates passed to the eldest of her three sons.][Back to Main Text]

Footnote 7: John Ballantyne put forth the following paragraph in the *Scots Magazine* of December, 1814:—

"Mr. Scott's poem of *The Lord of the Isles* will appear early in January. The Author of *Waverley* is about to amuse the public with a new novel, in three volumes, entitled *Guy Mannering*."[Back to Main Text]

Footnote 8: He was not forty-four till August, 1815.[Back to Main Text]

Footnote 9: E. G. "If they want to depose Scott, I only wish they would not set me up as a competitor. I like the man—and admire his works to what Mr. Braham calls *Entusymusy*. All such stuff can only vex him, and do me no good."—Byron (1813), vol. ii. p. 259.

"Scott is certainly the most wonderful writer of the day. His novels are a new literature in themselves, and his poetry as good as any—if not better (only on an erroneous system), and only ceased to be popular, because the vulgar learned were tired of hearing 'Aristides called the Just,' and Scott the Best, and ostracized him."—Byron (1821), vol. v. p. 72.[Back to Main Text]

Footnote 10: I leave my text as it stood in the former editions; but since the last of these appeared, a writer in *The Gentleman's Magazine* (July, 1840) has pointed out some very remarkable coincidences between the narrative of *Guy Mannering* and the very singular history of James Annesley, claimant in 1743 of the honors and estates of the Earls of Anglesey, in Ireland. That Sir Walter must have read the records of this celebrated trial, as well as Smollett's edition of the story in *Peregrine Pickle*, there can be no doubt. How the circumstance had not recurred to his memory when writing the explanatory Introduction to his Novel, I can offer no conjecture. Very possibly the *Garland* itself may have been framed after the Annesley trial took place.—(1841.) [The paper in *The Gentleman's Magazine*, referred to above, will be found in the Appendix to this volume.][Back to Main Text]

Footnote 11: *Lord of the Isles*, Canto vi.[Back to Main Text]

Footnote 12: [John Murray—the third of the name—gives some interesting notes of his recollections of these meetings in Albemarle Street, in the *Memoirs* of his father (vol. i. p. 267).][Back to Main Text]

Footnote 13: Mr. Murray had, at the time of giving the vase, suggested to Lord Byron, that it would increase the value of the gift to add some such inscription; but the noble poet answered modestly,—

"April 9, 1815. DEAR MURRAY,—I have a great objection to your proposition about inscribing the vase—which is, that it would appear *ostentatious* on my part; and of course I must send it as it is, without any alteration. Yours ever, BYRON."[Back to Main Text]

Footnote 14: This most amiable and venerable gentleman, my dear and kind friend, died at Edinburgh on the 17th February, 1839, in the 80th year of his age. He retained his strong mental faculties in their perfect vigor to the last days of this long life, and with them all the warmth of social feelings which had endeared him to all who were so happy as to have any opportunity of knowing him. The reader will find an affectionate tribute to his worth, from Sir Walter Scott's Diary, in a subsequent volume of these Memoirs.—(March, 1839.)[Back to Main Text]

Footnote 15: Since this narrative was first published, I have been told by two gentlemen who were at this dinner, that, according to their recollection, the Prince *did not* on that occasion run so "near the wind" as my text represents; and I am inclined to believe that a scene at Dalkeith, in 1822, may have been unconsciously blended with a gentler rehearsal of Carlton House, 1815. The Chief Commissioner had promised to revise my sheets for the present edition; but alas, he never did so—and I must now leave the matter as it stands.— (1839.)[Back to Main Text]

Footnote 16: [*The Search after Happiness.*][Back to Main Text]

Footnote 17: Scott's *Poetical Works*, vol. xi. p. 353 [Cambridge Ed. p. 431].[Back to Main Text]

Footnote 18: Mechlin—the Highlander gave it the familiar pronunciation of a Scotch village, Mauchline, celebrated in many of Burns's poems.[Back to Main Text]

Footnote 19: See Major Gordon's *Personal Memoirs* (1830), vol. ii. pp. 325-338.[Back to Main Text]

Footnote 20: The skull of Shaw is now in the Museum at Abbotsford.[Back to Main Text]

Footnote 21: Scott acknowledges, in a note to *St. Ronan's Well* (chap. xv.), that he took from Platoff this portrait of Mr. Touchwood: "His face, which at the distance of a yard or two seemed hale and smooth, appeared, when closely examined, to be seamed with a million of wrinkles, crossing each other in every direction possible, but as fine as if drawn by the point of a very small needle." Thus did every little peculiarity remain treasured in his memory, to be used in due time for giving the air of minute reality to some imaginary personage.[Back to Main Text]

Footnote 22: See *Poetical Works* (Edin. Ed.), vol. xi. p. 295 [Cambridge Ed. p. 420].[Back to Main Text]

Footnote 23: John Scott, Esq., of Gala, died at Edinburgh, 19th April, 1840.— (1842.)[Back to Main Text]

Footnote 24: I think it very probable that Scott had his own first interview with the Duke of Wellington in his mind when he described the introduction of Roland Græme to the Regent Murray, in the novel of *The Abbot*, chap. xviii.:—"Such was the personage before whom Roland Græme now presented himself with a feeling of breathless awe, very different from the usual boldness and vivacity of his temper. In fact, he was, from education and nature, ... much more easily controlled by the moral superiority arising from the elevated talents and renown of those with whom he conversed, than by pretensions founded only on rank or external show. He might have braved with indifference the presence of an Earl merely distinguished by his belt and coronet; but he felt overawed in that of the eminent soldier and statesman, the wielder of a nation's power, and the leader of her armies."[Back to Main Text]

Footnote 25: This was published in the *Edinburgh Annual Register* in 1815.— See *Poetical Works*(Ed. 1834), vol. xi. p. 297 [Cambridge Ed. p. 421].[Back to Main Text]

Footnote 26: See *Poetical Works* (Ed. 1834), vol. xi. p. 312 [Cambridge Ed. p. 424].[Back to Main Text]

Footnote 27: Irving's *Abbotsford and Newstead*, 1835, p. 40.[Back to Main Text]

Footnote 28: A *birse*, or bunch of hog's *bristles*, forms the cognizance of the Sutors. When a new burgess is admitted into their community, *the birse* passes round with the cup of welcome, and every elder brother dips it into the wine, and draws it through his mouth, before it reaches the happy neophyte, who of course pays it similar respect.[Back to Main Text]

Footnote 29: [A touching letter from Morritt, written shortly before his wife's death, and one of Scott's, written after that event, will be found in *Familiar Letters*, vol. i. pp. 352-354.][Back to Main Text]

Footnote 30: See Scott's *Poetical Works* (Ed. 1834), vol. xi. p. 317 [Cambridge Ed. p. 425].[Back to Main Text]

Footnote 31: This Mr. Campbell was the same whom the poet's mother employed to teach her boys to sing, as recorded in the Autobiographical Fragment—*ante*, vol. i. p. 44. I believe he was also the "litigious Highlander" of a story told in Irving's *Abbotsford and Newstead*, p. 57.

[In the November of this year, Scott writes to Lady Abercorn: "The only thing I have been doing of late is to write two or three songs for a poor man called Campbell.... He has made an immense collection of Highland airs, and I have given him words for some of them. One of them is the only good song I ever wrote—it is a fine Highland Gathering tune called *Pibroch an Donuil Dhu*, that is, the Pibroch of Donald the Black."—*Familiar Letters*, vol. i. p. 374.][Back to Main Text]

Footnote 32: [In the letter accompanying his gift, Glengarry says: "His name is Maida, out of respect for that action in which my brother had the honor to lead the 78th Highlanders to victory." Writing to Joanna Baillie, April 12, Scott describes his new friend as

126

"the finest dog of the kind in Scotland.... He is between the deer greyhound and mastiff, with a shaggy mane like a lion; he always sits beside me at dinner, his head as high as the back of my chair; yet it will gratify you to know that a favorite cat keeps him in the greatest possible order, and insists upon all rights of precedence, and scratches with impunity the nose of an animal who would make no bones of a wolf, and pulls down a red deer without fear or difficulty. I heard my friend set up some most piteous howls, and I assure you the noise was no joke, all occasioned by his fear of passing puss, who had stationed himself on the stairs."—*Familiar Letters*, vol. i. p. 358.][Back to Main Text]

Footnote 33: Coleridge—*Ancient Mariner.*[Back to Main Text]

Footnote 34: The late Mr. Hay Donaldson, W. S.,—an intimate friend of both Thomas and Walter Scott,—and Mr. Macculloch of Ardwell, the brother of Mrs. Thomas Scott.[Back to Main Text]

Footnote 35: Shortly after Beau Brummell (immortalized in *Don Juan*) fell into disgrace with the Prince Regent, and was dismissed from the society of Carlton House, he was riding with another gentleman in the Park, when the Prince met them. His Royal Highness stopt to speak to Brummell's companion—the Beau continued to jog on—and when the other dandy rejoined him, asked with an air of sovereign indifference, "Who is your fat friend?" Such, at least, was the story that went the round of the newspapers at the time, and highly tickled Scott's fancy. I have heard that nobody enjoyed so much as the Prince of Wales himself an earlier specimen of the Beau's assurance. Taking offence at some part of His Royal Highness's conduct or demeanor, "Upon my word," observed Mr. Brummell, "if this kind of thing goes on, I shall be obliged to cut Wales, and bring the old King into fashion."[Back to Main Text]

Footnote 36: See *Hudibras.*[Back to Main Text]

Footnote 37: In February, 1816, when James Ballantyne married, it is clearly proved by letters in his handwriting, that he owed to Scott more than £3000 of personal debt.—(1839.)[Back to Main Text]

Footnote 38: James Ballantyne's dwelling-house was then in this street, adjoining the Canongate of Edinburgh.[Back to Main Text]

Footnote 39: *May,* 1839. Since this book was first published, I have received from the representatives of Mr. Blackwood several documents which throw light on the transaction here mentioned. It will be apparent from one of those I am about to quote, that Blackwood, before he sent his message to Jedediah Cleishbotham, had ascertained that no less a person than Mr. Gifford concurred in his opinion—nay, that James Ballantyne himself took the same view of the matter. But the reader will be not less amused in comparing the "Black Hussar's" missive in the text, with the edition of it which actually reached Blackwood—and which certainly justifies the conjecture I had ventured to express.

TO WILLIAM BLACKWOOD, ESQ.

EDINBURGH, 4th October, 1816.

MY DEAR SIR,—Our application to the author of *Tales of my Landlord* has been anything but successful; and in order to explain to you the reason why I must decline to address him in this way in future, I shall copy his answer *verbatim:*—

"My respects to our friends the Booksellers. I belong to the Death-head Hussars of Literature, who neither *take* nor *give* criticism. I am extremely sorry they showed my work to Gifford, nor would I cancel a leaf to please all the critics of Edinburgh and London; and so let that be as it is: They are mistaken if they think I don't know when I am writing ill, as well as Gifford can tell me. I beg there may be no more communications with critics."

Observe—that I shall at all times be ready to convey anything from you to the author in a written form, but I do not feel warranted to interfere farther.

Yours very truly,

J. BALLANTYNE.

TO JAMES BALLANTYNE, ESQ.

EDINBURGH, 5th October, 1816.

MY DEAR SIR,—I am not a little vexed at having ventured to suggest anything to the author of the *Tales of my Landlord*, since I find he considers it in the light of *sutor ultra crepidam.* I never had for one moment the vanity to think, that from any poor remark of mine, or indeed of any human being, he would be induced to blot one line or alter a single incident, unless the same idea occurred to his own powerful mind. On stating to you what struck me, and finding that your opinion coincided with mine, I was induced to request of you to state it to the author, in order that he might be aware that the expense of cancelling the sheets was no object to me. I was the more anxious to do this, in case the author should have given you the MS. of this portion of the work sooner than he intended, in order to satisfy the clamoring for it which I teased you with. I trust the author will do me the justice to believe that it is quite impossible for any one to have a higher admiration of his most extraordinary talents; and speaking merely as a bookseller, it would be quite unnecessary to be at the expense of altering even one line, although the author himself (who alone can be the proper judge) should wish it, as the success of the work must be rapid, great, and certain.

With regard to the first volume having been shown to Mr. Gifford, I must state in justification of Mr. Murray, that Mr. G. is the only friend whom he consults on all occasions, and to whom his most secret transactions are laid open. He gave him the work, not for the purpose of criticism, but that as a friend he might partake of the enjoyment he had in such an extraordinary performance. No language could be stronger than Mr. Gifford's, as I mentioned to you; and as the same thing had occurred to Mr. G. as to you and me, you thought there would be no harm in stating this to the author.

I have only again to express my regret at what has taken place, and to beg you will communicate this to the author in any way you may think proper.

Yours, etc.,

W. BLACKWOOD.

[A much fuller and more accurate knowledge of this whole transaction, than that possessed by Lockhart, can be gathered from the annals of the two great publishing houses concerned in it;—Smiles's *Memoir of John Murray* (vol. i. chap. xviii.), and Mrs. Oliphant's *William Blackwood and his Sons* (vol. i. pp. 56-92), especially from the latter work, in which the whole incident is set in its proper light. Notwithstanding the heavy preliminary tax for unsalable books from the Ballantynes' "wretched stock," neither publisher seems to have had a moment's doubt as to the acceptance of the offer of the ostensibly anonymous Work of Fiction, though they were much fretted by the delays, uncertainties, and mysteries attending the matter. "One in business must submit to many things, and swallow many a bitter pill, when such a man as Walter Scott is the object in view," writes Blackwood to Murray,—the bitterness being largely the dealing with James Ballantyne. "John I always considered as no better than a swindler, but James I put some trust and confidence in. You judged him more accurately." ... And on another occasion,—"Except my wife, there is not a friend whom I dare advise with. I have not ventured to mention the business to my brother on account of the cursed mysteries and injunctions of secrecy connected with it. I know he would blame me for engaging in it, for he has a very small opinion of the Ballantynes." Apart from the vexations attending their office as intermediaries, for which the Ballantynes were only partially responsible, this shrewd, if irritated, observer appears to have formed opinions of the brothers as business men, in some respects not differing greatly from those held by Lockhart in later days.

The delight of the two publishers in at last receiving the MS. of *The Black Dwarf* and the manner in which it passed into the hands of Constable, even before the stipulated 6000 copies were disposed of,—it must be owned he treated his rivals somewhat unhandsomely, finally severing them from Scott's literary career,—are fully set forth by the historian of the House of Blackwood. With her "one cannot but feel that this was one of those tragically insignificant circumstances which so often shape life apart from any consciousness of ours. Probably ruin would never have overtaken Sir Walter had he been in the steady and careful hands of Murray and Blackwood, for it is unlikely that even the glamour of the great Magician would have turned heads so reasonable and sober."][Back to Main Text]

Footnote 40: The sister of Miss Jane Nicolson.—See *ante*, vol. i. p. 248. Vol. ii. p. 82.[Back to Main Text]

Footnote 41: [Referring to the edition of 1839, in ten volumes.][Back to Main Text]

Footnote 42: [Scott says in a letter to John Murray, written October 20, 1814: "In casting about how I might show you some mark of my sense of former kindness, a certain

MS. History of Scotland in *Letters to my Children* has occurred to me, which I consider as a desideratum; it is upon the plan of *Lord Lyttelton's Letters*, as they are called." Nearly a year later he returns to the subject, and says: "I intend to revise my letters on Scottish History for you, but I will not get to press till November, for the country affords no facilities for consulting the necessary authorities. I hope it may turn out a thing of some interest, though I rather intend to keep to its original purpose as a book of instruction to children." These references seem to show that the work may have been further advanced than Lockhart supposed. The announcement of the proposed book by Constable and Longman naturally excited the indignation of Blackwood and Murray, as is shown in a vigorous letter from the Edinburgh to the London publisher, blaming equally the Ballantynes and Constable.— See *Memoirs of John Murray*, vol. i. pp. 245, 246, 462.][Back to Main Text]

Footnote 43: A cast from the monumental effigy at Stratford-upon-Avon—now in the library at Abbotsford—was the gift of Mr. George Bullock, long distinguished in London as a collector of curiosities. This ingenious man was, as the reader will see in the sequel, a great favorite with Scott.[Back to Main Text]

Footnote 44: Mrs. Terry had offered the services of her elegant pencil in designing some windows of painted glass for Scott's armory, etc.[Back to Main Text]

Footnote 45: The late James Boswell, Esq., of the Temple—second son of *Bozzy*.[Back to Main Text]

Footnote 46: The Honorable William Lamb—now Lord Melbourne.[Back to Main Text]

Footnote 47: [Even such keen observers as Murray and Blackwood had their intervals of doubt regarding the authorship of the Novels. In June, 1816, Blackwood writes: "There have been various rumors with regard to Greenfield being the author, but I never paid much attention to it; the thing appeared to me so very improbable.... But from what I have heard lately, and from what you state, I now begin to think that Greenfield may probably be the author." And only a month after the date of his letter to Scott, here given, Murray writes to Blackwood:—

"I can assure you, but *in the greatest confidence*, that I have discovered the author of all these Novels to be Thomas Scott, Walter Scott's brother. He is now in Canada. I have no doubt but that Mr. Walter Scott did a great deal to the first Waverley Novel, because of his anxiety to save his brother, and his doubt about the success of the work. This accounts for the many stories about it. Many persons had previously heard from Mr. Scott, but you may rely upon the certainty of what I have told you." By this time Blackwood is firm in the faith of Scott's authorship; but Bernard Barton writes to Murray that he has heard that James Hogg is the author of *Tales of my Landlord*, and that he has had intimation from himself to that effect; while Lady Mackintosh is informed on excellent authority that the writer is Mrs. Thomas Scott. Writing to Blackwood in February, 1817, Murray avers,—"I will believe, till within an inch of my life, that the author of *Tales of my Landlord* is Thomas Scott."—See Smiles's *Memoir of John Murray*, vol. i. pp. 461, 473, 474.][Back to Main Text]

Footnote 48: *Parisina—The Dream*—and the "Domestic Pieces," had been recently published.[Back to Main Text]

Footnote 49: [On November 27 Scott had written to Joanna Baillie, who had just returned from a tour on the Continent:—

"All I ever longed for on the Continent was their light wines, which you do not care about, and their fine climate, which we should both value equally; and to say truth, I never saw scene or palace which shook my allegiance to Tweedside and Abbotsford, though so inferior in every respect, and though the hills, or rather braes, are just high enough 'to lift us to the storm' when the storms are not so condescending as to sweep both crest and base, which, to do them justice, is seldom the case. What have I got to send you?... Alas, nothing but the history of petty employments and a calendar of increasing bad weather. The latter was much mitigated by enjoying for a good portion of the summer the society of John Morritt, of Rokeby, who has so much of that which is delightful, both in his grave and gay moods, that he can make us forget the hillside while sitting by the fireside. His late loss has cast a general shade of melancholy over him, which renders him yet dearer to his friends, by the gentle and unaffected manner in which his natural gayety of temper gleams through it and renders it still more interesting....

"A far different object of interest, yet still of interest, checkered with pity and disapprobation, is Lord Byron, whose present situation seems to rival all that ever has been said and sung of the misfortunes of a too irritable imagination. The last part of *Childe Harold* intimates a terrible state of mind, and with all the power and genius which characterized his former productions, the present seems to indicate a more serious and desperate degree of misanthropy. I own I was not much moved by the scorn of the world which his first poems implied, because I know it is a humor of mind which those whom fortune has spoilt by indulgence, or irritated by reverses, are apt to assume, because it looks melancholy and gentlemanlike, and becomes a bard as well as being desperately in love, or very fond of the sunrise, though he lies in bed till noon, or anxious in recommending to others to catch cold by visiting old abbeys by moonlight, which he never happened to see under the chaste moonbeam himself; but this strange poem goes much deeper, and either the Demon of Misanthropy is in full possession of him, or he has already invited ten guests, equally desperate, to the swept and garnished mansion of Harold's understanding."—*Familiar Letters*, vol. i. p. 369.][Back to Main Text]

Footnote 50: [This is probably the "expression of kindness" which encouraged Murray to beg Scott to review in the *Quarterly* Byron's recently published volumes, *Childe Harold, Canto III.*, and *The Prisoner of Chillon, a Dream, and Other Poems.* The request was promptly complied with, and the article appeared in the next number issued (*dated* October, 1816),—a review full of generous, and also judicious, appreciation. For some reason, hard now to discover, unless it were the kindliness of the writer's tone towards the younger poet, some of Lady Byron's friends, among whom was Joanna Baillie, seem to have taken strong exception to the paper, and Miss Baillie wrote to Scott at some length on the matter, even animadverting upon the purely literary criticism of the reviewer. Much of the correspondence which ensued, including a characteristic letter from Lady Byron, can be found in the *Familiar Letters* (vol. i. pp. 413-422).

Of the review, Byron writes to Murray (March 3, 1817):—

... "It seems to me (as far as the subject of it may be permitted to judge) to be *very well* written as a composition, and ... even those who may condemn its partiality, must praise its generosity. The temptations to take another and less favorable view of the question have been so great and numerous, that, what with public opinion, politics, etc., he must be a gallant as well as a good man, who has ventured in that place and at this time to write such an article even anonymously. Such things, however, are their own reward; and I even flatter myself that the writer, whoever he may be (and I have no guess), will not regret that the perusal of this has given me as much gratification as any composition of that nature could give, and more than any other has ever given,—and I have had a good many in my time of one kind or the other. It is not the mere praise, but there is a tact and a delicacy throughout, not only with regard to me, but to others, which, as it has not been observed elsewhere, I had till now doubted, whether it could be observed anywhere." He writes a few weeks later, on learning that Scott wrote the article: ... "It cannot add to my good opinion of him, but it adds to that of myself."—*Letters and Journals of Lord Byron* (1900), vol. iv. pp. 63, 85.][Back to Main Text]

Footnote 51: Since I have mentioned this reviewal, I may as well, to avoid recurrence to it, express here my conviction, that Erskine, not Scott, was the author of the critical estimate of the Waverley Novels which it embraces—although, for the purpose of mystification, Scott had taken the trouble to transcribe the paragraphs in which that estimate is contained. At the same time I cannot but add that, had Scott really been the sole author of this reviewal, he need not have incurred the severe censure which has been applied to his supposed conduct in the matter. After all, his judgment of his own works must have been allowed to be not above, but very far under the mark; and the whole affair would, I think, have been considered by every candid person exactly as the letter about Solomon and the rival mothers was by Murray, Gifford, and the "four o'clock visitors" of Albemarle Street— as a good joke. A better joke, certainly, than the allusion to the report of Thomas Scott being the real author of Waverley, at the close of the article, was never penned; and I think it includes a confession over which a misanthrope might have chuckled: "We intended here to conclude this long article, when a strong report reached us of certain Transatlantic confessions, which, if genuine (though of this we know nothing), assign a different author to these volumes than the party suspected by our Scottish correspondents. Yet a critic may be excused seizing upon the nearest suspicious person, on the principle happily expressed by Claverhouse, in a letter to the Earl of Linlithgow. He had been, it seems, in search of a gifted weaver, who used to hold forth at conventicles: 'I sent for the webster (weaver), they brought in his *brother* for him: though he, maybe, cannot preach like his brother, I doubt not but he is as well-principled as he, wherefore I thought it would be no great fault to give him the trouble to go to jail with the rest!'"—*Miscellaneous Prose Works*, vol. xix. pp. 85, 86.[Back to Main Text]

Footnote 52: [On reading *The Black Dwarf*, Mrs. Leigh believed her brother to be the author, and wrote to him to that effect. Byron had not yet seen the book, and says in his reply: "I am not P. P. [Peter Pattieson], I assure you on my honor, and do not understand to what book you allude, so that all your compliments are quite thrown away."—Byron's *Letters and Journals* (1900), vol. iv. p. 56.][Back to Main Text]

Footnote 53: [Lady Louisa Stuart, whose approbation Scott writes he values "beyond a whole wilderness of critics," says in a letter of December 5, 1816:

"[Old Mortality] is super-excellent in all its points; it breaks up fresh ground, and has all the raciness of originality. I cannot help thinking it will bear down the world before it triumphantly. As usual it makes its personages our intimate acquaintance, and its scenes so present to the eye, that, last night, after sitting up unreasonably late over it, I got no sleep, from a kind of fever of mind it had occasioned. It seemed as if I had been an eye and ear witness of all the passages, and I could not lull the agitation into calmness. Mause and Cuddie hurried my spirits in another way; they forced me to laugh out aloud, which one seldom does alone. On a second slower reading I expect to be still better pleased, and then also I suppose I shall find out the faults. At present it has, in the Scotch phrase, 'taken me off my feet,' and I do not criticise, though I think you will believe me when I say I do not and will not flatter. One thing I regret, that like the author of *The Antiquary*, Jedediah did not add a glossary; because even I, a mongrel, occasionally paying long visits to Scotland, and hearing Girsy at Bothwell gate and Peggy Macgowan hold forth in the village,—even I, thus qualified, have found a great many words absolute Hebrew to me, and I fear the altogether English will find many more beyond their comprehension or conjecture. But this may be remedied in another edition. I have as yet only one great attack to make, and that upon a single word; but such a word! such an anachronism! Claverhouse says he has no time to hear *sentimental* speeches. My dear sir! tell Jedediah that Claverhouse never heard the sound of those four syllables in his life. We are used to them; but *sentiment* and *sentimental* were, I believe, first introduced into the language by Sterne, and are hardly as old as I am. Let alone the Covenanters' days, I am persuaded you would look in vain for them in the works of Richardson and Fielding. Nay, the French, from whom they were borrowed, did not talk of *le sentiment* in that sense till long after Louis XIV.'s reign. No such thing is to be found in Madame de Sévigné, la Bruyère, etc., etc., etc. At home or abroad I defy Lord Dundee ever to have met with the expression. Mr. Peter Pattieson had been reading the *Man of Feeling*, and it was a slip of his tongue, which I am less inclined to excuse than Mause's abstruse Scotch, which I duly reverence, as she did Kettledrummle's sermons, because I do not understand it. Once more I shall be much disappointed if this work does not quickly acquire a very great reputation. I fancy Mr. Morritt is in the secret; yet, as I am not certain, I will keep on the secure side and not mention it when I write to him, however one may long to *intercommune* on such subjects with those likely to hold the same faith."

At the close of his reply, Scott says: "I must not forget to thank your Ladyship for your acute and indisputable criticism on the application of the word *sentimental*. How it escaped my pen I know not, unless that the word owed me a grudge for the ill will I have uniformly borne it, and was resolved to slip itself in for the express purpose of disgracing me. I will certainly turn it out the first opportunity." This was done in the second edition.—*Familiar Letters*, vol. i. pp. 394, 400.][Back to Main Text]

Footnote 54: [Scott's old friend, John Richardson, who was from the first in the secret of the Waverley Novels, was a stanch Whig, as beseemed the descendant of an old Covenanting family. Some of his ancestral traditions suggested certain passages in *Old Mortality*, and he has recorded that during a visit to Abbotsford Scott gave him the proof sheets of the first volume to read, and how he lost a night's sleep in doing it. Twelve years later, in writing to Scott regarding *The Tales of a Grandfather*, he says that in this work,—"You have paid a debt which you owed to the manes of the Covenanters for the flattering picture which you drew of Claverhouse in *Old Mortality*."

Scott says in his reply (December, 1828): "As to Covenanters and Malignants, they were both a set of cruel and bloody bigots, and had, notwithstanding, those virtues with which bigotry is sometimes allied. Their characters were of a kind much more picturesque than beautiful; neither had the least idea either of toleration or humanity, so that it happens that, so far as they can be distinguished from each other, one is tempted to hate most the party which chances to be uppermost for the time."—See *Journal*, note, vol. ii. p. 404.][Back to Main Text]

Footnote 55: Joanna Baillie's *Orra*.[Back to Main Text]

Footnote 56: *Twelfth Night*, Act II. Scene 3.[Back to Main Text]

Footnote 57: The late Right Honorable Robert Dundas of Arniston, Chief Baron of the Scotch Exchequer; one of Scott's earliest and kindest friends in that distinguished family.[Back to Main Text]

Footnote 58: This young gentleman is now an officer in the East India Company's army.—(1837.) Mr. W. S. Terry lived to distinguish himself as a soldier, and fell in action against the Afghans.—(1848.)[Back to Main Text]

Footnote 59: Sir Archy Mac-Sarcasm and Sir Pertinax Mac-Sycophant.[Back to Main Text]

Footnote 60: [On the 17th of March, Scott had written to Joanna Baillie: "Two *remarkables* struck me in my illness: the first was, that my great wolf-dog clamored wildly and fearfully about my bed when I was very ill, and would hardly be got out of the room; the other, that when I was recovering, all acquired and factitious tastes seemed to leave me, and I could eat nothing but porridge, and listen to no better reading than a stupid Scottish diary which would have made a whole man sick."—*Familiar Letters*, vol. i. p. 421.][Back to Main Text]

Footnote 61: See *Poetical Works*, vol. xi. p. 348 [Cambridge Ed. p. 436]. Scott's farewell for Kemble first appeared in *The Sale-Room* for April 5, 1817; and in the introductory note James Ballantyne says: "The character fixed upon, with happy propriety, for Kemble's closing scene, was Macbeth. He had labored under a severe cold for a few days before, but on the memorable night the physical annoyance yielded to the energy of his mind. 'He was,' he said in the Green-room, immediately before the curtain rose, 'determined to leave behind him the most perfect specimen of his art which he had ever shown;' and his success was complete. At the moment of the tyrant's death, the curtain fell by the universal acclamation of the audience. The applauses were vehement and prolonged; they ceased—were resumed—rose again—were reiterated—and again were hushed. In a few minutes the curtain ascended, and Mr. Kemble came forward, in the dress of Macbeth (the audience by a consentaneous movement rising to receive him), to deliver his *farewell*." ... "Mr. Kemble delivered the lines with exquisite beauty, and with an effect that was evidenced by the tears and sobs of many of the audience. His own emotions were very conspicuous. When his farewell was closed, he lingered long on the stage, as if unable to retire. The house again stood up, and cheered him with the waving of hats and long shouts of applause."[Back to Main Text]

Footnote 62: Mr. Laidlaw has not published many verses; but his song of *Lucy's Flitting*—a simple and pathetic picture of a poor Ettrick maiden's feelings in leaving a service where she had been happy—has long been, and must ever be, a favorite with all who understand the delicacies of the Scottish dialect, and the manners of the district in which the scene is laid.[Back to Main Text]

Footnote 63: These anecdotes were subsequently inserted in the Introduction to *Guy Mannering*.[Back to Main Text]

Footnote 64: Scott's meeting with this Mr. Smith occurred at the table of his friend and colleague, Hector Macdonald Buchanan. The company, except Scott and Smith, were all, like their hospitable landlord, Highlanders.[Back to Main Text]

Footnote 65: Lady Montagu was the daughter of the late Lord Douglas by his first marriage with Lady Lucy Graham, daughter of the second Duke of Montrose.[Back to Main Text]

Footnote 66: Lord Montagu's house at Ditton Park, near Windsor, had recently been destroyed by fire—and the ruins revealed some niches with antique candlesticks, etc., belonging to a domestic chapel that had been converted to other purposes from the time, I believe, of Henry VIII.[Back to Main Text]

Footnote 67: Mr. Atkinson, of St. John's Wood, was the architect of Lord Montagu's new mansion at Ditton, as well as the artist ultimately employed in arranging Scott's interior at Abbotsford.[Back to Main Text]

Footnote 68: Shakespeare's Poems—*Venus and Adonis.*[Back to Main Text]

Footnote 69: [A misprint of some earlier date, possibly the *16th.* See the more detailed account of Scott's movements at this time, to be found in *Familiar Letters*, vol. i. pp. 432-436.][Back to Main Text]

Footnote 70: On completing this purchase, Scott writes to John Ballantyne:—"DEAR JOHN,—I have closed with Usher for his beautiful patrimony, which makes me a great laird. I am afraid the people will take me up for coining. Indeed, these novels, while their attractions last, are something like it. I am very glad of *your* good prospects. Still I cry, *Prudence! Prudence!*—Yours truly,

W. S."[Back to Main Text]

Footnote 71: [On August 1, 1817, Jeffrey writes to Scott, asking if he could not be induced to write a notice of Mr. C. K. Sharpe's edition of Kirkton's *Secret and True History of the Church of Scotland*, for the *Edinburgh Review*, to which Scott replies, August 5:—

"I flatter myself it will not require many protestations to assure you with what pleasure I would undertake any book that can give you pleasure; but in the present case I am hampered by two circumstances: one, that I promised Gifford a review of this very Kirkton for the *Quarterly*; the other that I shall certainly be unable to keep my word with him. I am obliged to take exercise three or four hours in the forenoon and two after dinner, to keep off the infernal spasms which since last winter have attacked me with such violence, as if all the imps that used to plague poor Caliban were washing, wringing, and ironing the unshapely but useful bag which Sir John Sinclair treats with such distinction—my stomach, in short. Now, as I have much to do of my own, I fear I can hardly be of use to you in the present case, which I am very sorry for, as I like the subject, and would be pleased to give my own opinion respecting the Jacobitism of the editor, which, like my own, has a good spice of affectation in it, mingled with some not unnatural feelings of respect for a cause which, though indefensible in common sense and ordinary policy, has a great deal of high-spirited Quixotry about it.

"Can you not borrow from your briefs and criticism a couple of days to look about you here? I dare not ask Mrs. Jeffrey till next year, when my hand will be out of the mortar-tub; and at present my only spare bed was till of late but accessible by the feudal accommodation of a drawbridge made of two deals, and still requires the clue of Ariadne.... I am like one of Miss Edgeworth's heroines, master of all things in miniature—a little hill, and a little glen, and a little horse-pond of a loch, and a little river, I was going to call it,—the Tweed; but I remember the minister was mobbed by his parishioners for terming it, in his statistical report, an inconsiderable stream. So pray do come and see me, and if I can stead you, or pleasure you, in the course of the winter, you shall command me."—Cockburn's *Life of Jeffrey*, vol. i p. 417.][Back to Main Text]

Footnote 72: I have before me two letters of Mr. Irving's to Scott, both written in September, 1817, from Edinburgh, and referring to his visit (which certainly was his only one at Abbotsford) as immediately preceding. There is also in my hands a letter from Scott to his friend John Richardson, of Fludyer Street, dated 22d September, 1817, in which he says, "When you see Tom Campbell, tell him, with my best love, that I have to thank him for making me known to Mr. Washington Irving, who is one of the best and pleasantest acquaintances I have made this many a day."[Back to Main Text]

Footnote 73: [From the journal of three English ladies, travellers in Scotland in the summer of 1817, we get another glimpse of Johnnie Bower, and a pleasant sketch of Sophia Scott:—

"In the chancel Miss Scott, a very charming, lively girl of seventeen, pointed out to us 'The Wizard's Grave,' and then the black stone in the form of a coffin, to which the allusion is made in the poem, 'A Scottish monarch sleeps below,'—said to be the tomb of Alexander II. 'But I will tell you a secret,' she half whispered; 'only don't you tell Johnnie Bower. There is no Scottish monarch there at all, nor anybody else, for papa had the stone taken up, not long ago, and no coffin nor anything was to be found. And then Johnnie came and begged me not to tell people so. "For what wull I do, Miss Scott, when I show the ruins, if I canna point to this bit, and say, 'A Scottish monarch sleeps below'?"' As, however, he had the pleasure of saying this to us the evening before, Miss Scott thought we might fairly have her secret....

"We now set out for Dryburgh, about five miles. Mr. Scott placed his daughter in our carriage, that she might point out the different places as we passed them. We could not have had a better director, nor a more lively, entertaining companion. Every spot was known to her, and in this fairyland her quick imagination seemed to delight in all the legendary lore she had heard, and could so promptly apply.... At the view of some distant mountains, Miss Scott suddenly exclaimed, 'Look, there are the Cheviots; are you not glad to see England again?' We assured her we were, though we should quit Scotland with so much regret. 'Well,' she said, 'I should not have liked you if you were not glad to return home.' Her father had taken her to London the year before, and she was delighted to get back again, and to hail the Cheviots on her return. It was plain to see she was her father's darling, and she talked of him with enthusiasm. She has a very natural, unaffected character, with a strong tincture of romantic feeling, which seemed judiciously kept in check by him, as she said he did not allow her to read much poetry, nor had she even read all his own poems, which were never to be found *in the way*, at their house. She spoke of her sister and her brothers, with a warmth of affection very pleasing. On asking what was become of Camp, she shook her head, and said he was dead. 'You must never come to Abbotsford when any of the dogs die, for there is a sad weeping amongst us all.'"—Lang's *Life of Lockhart*, vol. i. pp. 232-234.][Back to Main Text]

Footnote 74: ["His daughter Sophia and his son Charles were those of his family who seemed most to feel and understand his humors, and to take delight in his conversation. Mrs. Scott did not always pay the same attention, and would now and then make a casual remark which would operate a little like a damper. Thus, one morning at breakfast, when Dominie Thomson the tutor was present, Scott was going on with great glee to relate an anecdote of the laird of Macnab, 'who, poor fellow!' premised he, 'is dead and gone.' 'Why, Mr. Scott,' exclaimed the good lady, 'Macnab's not dead, is he?' 'Faith, my dear,' replied Scott, with humorous gravity, 'if he's not dead, they've done him a great injustice,—for they've buried him.'

"The joke passed harmless and unnoticed by Mrs. Scott, but hit the poor Dominie just as he had raised a cup of tea to his lips ... sending half its contents about the table."—Irving's *Abbotsford*.][Back to Main Text]

Footnote 75: [That this visit remained a vivid and delightful memory to the end of Irving's life is shown in some words spoken not long before his death: "Oh! Scott was a master spirit—as glorious in his conversation as in his writings. Jeffrey was delightful, and had *eloquent runs* in conversation; but there was a consciousness of talent with it. Scott had nothing of that. He spoke from the fulness of his mind, pouring out an incessant flow of anecdote, story, with dashes of humor, and then never monopolizing, but always ready to listen to and appreciate what came from others. I never felt such a consciousness of happiness as when under his roof."—*Washington Irving's Life and Letters*, vol. iv. p. 260.][Back to Main Text]

Footnote 76:

"Good-morrow to thy sable beak,
And glossy plumage dark and sleek,
Thy crimson moon, and azure eye,
Cock of the heath, so wildly shy!" etc.[Back to Main Text]

Footnote 77: The *flageolet* alludes to Mr. Alexander Ballantyne, the third of the brothers—a fine musician, and a most amiable and modest man, never connected with Scott in any business matters, but always much his favorite in private.[Back to Main Text]

Footnote 78: Mr. Magrath has now been long established in his native city of Dublin. His musical excellence was by no means the only merit that attached Scott to his society while he remained in Edinburgh.[Back to Main Text]

Footnote 79: This fine greyhound, a gift from Terry, had been sent to Scotland under the care of Mr. Magrath. Terry had called the dog *Marmion*, but Scott rechristened him *Hamlet*, in honor of his "inky coat."[Back to Main Text]

Footnote 80: Before the second and larger part of the present house of Abbotsford was built, the small room, subsequently known as the breakfast parlor, was during several years Scott's *sanctum*.[Back to Main Text]

Footnote 81: This alludes to certain pieces of painted glass, representing the heads of some of the old Scotch kings, copied from the carved ceiling of the presence-chamber in Stirling Castle. There are engravings of them in a work called *Lacunar Strevelinense*. Edinb. 4to, 1817.[Back to Main Text]

Footnote 82: Adam Paterson was the intelligent foreman of the company of masons then employed at Abbotsford.[Back to Main Text]

Footnote 83: Thomas Scott had sent his brother the horns and feet of a gigantic stag, shot by him in Canada. The feet were ultimately suspended to bell-cords in the armory at Abbotsford; and the horns mounted as drinking-cups.[Back to Main Text]

Footnote 84: They called Daniel Terry among themselves "The Grinder," in double allusion to the song of *Terry the Grinder*, and to some harsh under-notes of their friend's voice.[Back to Main Text]

Footnote 85: [On the 16th of February, Lady Louisa Stuart wrote:—

"I have read *Rob Roy* twice.... The scale with me would be *Waverley*, *Old Mortality*, *Guy Mannering*—so far I am sure. I am not sure which of the others I could positively prefer; there are striking beauties in each. In *Rob Roy* the painting of character is as vivid as in anything the author ever wrote. Rob himself, Die Vernon, Nicol Jarvie, Andrew Fairservice, not to speak of the Tory baronet and his cubs, or the Jesuit Rashleigh. The beginning and end, I am afraid, I quarrel with; ... but beginnings signify little; ends signify more. Now, I fear the end of this is huddled, as if the author were tired and wanted to get rid of his personages as fast as he could, knocking them on the head without mercy. Die Vernon has what a Lord Bellamont (famous in my day and before it for profligacy and affectation) used to call such 'a catastrophical countenance' that one cannot reconcile oneself to her being married and settled like her sober neighbors. It is almost as bad as if Flora MacIvor had married the Colonel's nephew.... You see I give my opinion (let it be worth something or nothing) as if I were writing to a person not supposed to be in any way sib to the mysterious Unknown; but it is because I believe you have too distinguishing a taste to relish all sugar and treacle. Goldsmith's metaphor was bad when he said, 'Who peppers the highest is surest to please,' for flattery resembles neither pepper nor salt. Apropos of the mystery, those who see far into a millstone are now sure that the *Tales of my Landlord* were written by a different person, and parts of them by different hands. When they give their reasons with a complacent delight in their own sagacity, I think to myself, how often must I have talked as much wise nonsense upon subjects which I knew nothing about."—*Familiar Letters*, vol. ii. p. 11.][Back to Main Text]

Footnote 86: *Collection of Inventories and other Records of the Royal Wardrobe and Jewel-House, etc.* Edin. 1815, 4to.[Back to Main Text]

Footnote 87: A stage-coach, so called, which ran betwixt Edinburgh and Jedburgh.[Back to Main Text]

Footnote 88: Slightly altered from Dr. Johnson's Prologue to the comedy of *A Word to the Wise*.

Footnote 89: Mr. Nicol Milne of Faldonside. This gentleman's property is a valuable and extensive one, situated immediately to the westward of Abbotsford; and Scott continued, year after year, to dream of adding it also to his own.[Back to Main Text]

Footnote 90: A sawmill had just been erected at Toftfield.[Back to Main Text]

Footnote 91: A cocklaird adjoining Abbotsford at the eastern side. His farm is properly *Lochbreist*; but in the neighborhood he was generally known as *Laird Lauchie*—or *Lauchie Langlegs*. Washington Irving describes him in his *Abbotsford*, with high gusto. He was a most absurd original.[Back to Main Text]

Footnote 92: An article in one of the early numbers of *Blackwood's Magazine*, entitled *The Chaldee MS.*, in which the literati and booksellers of Edinburgh were quizzed *en masse*—Scott himself among the rest. It was in this lampoon that Constable first saw himself designated in print by the *sobriquet* of "The Crafty," long before bestowed on him by one of his own most eminent Whig supporters; but nothing nettled him so much as the passages in which he and Blackwood are represented entreating the support of Scott for their respective Magazines, and waved off by "the Great Magician" in the same identical phrases of contemptuous indifference. The description of Constable's visit to Abbotsford may be worth transcribing—for Sir David Wilkie, who was present when Scott read it, says he was almost choked with laughter, and he afterwards confessed that the Chaldean author had given a sufficiently accurate version of what really passed on the occasion:—

"26. But when the Spirits were gone, he (The Crafty) said unto himself, I will arise and go unto a magician, which is of my friends: of a surety he will devise some remedy, and free me out of all my distresses.

"27. So he arose and came unto that great magician which hath his dwelling in the old fastness, hard by the River Jordan, which is by the Border.

"28. And the magician opened his mouth and said, Lo! my heart wisheth thy good, and let the thing prosper which is in thy hands to do it.

"29. But thou seest that my hands are full of working, and my labor is great. For, lo, I have to feed all the people of my land, and none knoweth whence his food cometh; but each man openeth his mouth, and my hand filleth it with pleasant things.

"30. Moreover, thine adversary also is of my familiars.

"31. The land is before thee: draw thou up thine hosts for the battle on the mount of Proclamation, and defy boldly thine enemy, which hath his camp in the place of Princes; quit ye as men, and let favor be shown unto him which is most valiant.

"32. Yet tarry ye silent; peradventure will I help thee some little.

"33. But the man which is Crafty saw that the magician loved him not. For he knew him of old, and they had had many dealings; and he perceived that he would not assist him in the day of his adversity.

"34. So he turned about, and went out of his fastness. And he shook the dust from his feet, and said, Behold I have given this magician much money, yet see now, he hath utterly deserted me. Verily, my fine gold hath perished."—Chap. iii.[Back to Main Text]

Footnote 93: [The story of the composition of *The Chaldee Manuscript*, its publication in the first number of the magazine, destined to so long and brilliant a career, and the extraordinary commotion caused thereby, is admirably told in the *Annals of a Publishing House*, which also gives the details regarding Laidlaw's brief connection with the new periodical, and the correspondence of Scott and Blackwood during its early months.—See Mrs. Oliphant's *William Blackwood and His Sons*, vol. i. chap. iii.][Back to Main Text]

Footnote 94: John Usher, the ex-proprietor of Toftfield, was eventually Scott's tenant on part of those lands for many years. He was a man of far superior rank and intelligence to the rest of the displaced lairds—and came presently to be one of Scott's trusty rural friends, and a frequent companion of his sports.[Back to Main Text]

Footnote 95: A yoke of oxen.[Back to Main Text]

Footnote 96: Scott's article on Kirkton's *History of the Church of Scotland*, edited by Mr. C. K. Sharpe, appeared in the 36th number of the *Quarterly Review*,—See *Miscellaneous Prose Works*, vol. xix. p. 213.[Back to Main Text]

Footnote 97: Scott expressed great satisfaction on seeing the *Lives of the Covenanters*—Cameron, Peden, Semple, Wellwood, Cargill, Smith, Renwick, etc.—reprinted without mutilation in the *Biographia Presbyteriana*. Edin. 1827. The publisher of this collection was the late Mr. John Stevenson, long chief clerk to John Ballantyne, and usually styled by Scott "True Jock," in opposition to one of his old master's many *aliases*—namely, "Leein' Johnnie."[Back to Main Text]

Footnote 98: See Scott's *Prose Miscellanies*, vol. xviii. p. 250.[Back to Main Text]

Footnote 99: The Letters of Horace Walpole to George Montagu.[Back to Main Text]

Footnote 100: *Anthony Hall* is only known as Editor of one of Leland's works. I have no doubt Scott was thinking of *John Hall Stevenson*, author of *Crazy Tales*, the friend, and (it is said) the *Eugenius* of Sterne.[Back to Main Text]

Footnote 101: I believe Mr. Rose's *Court and Parliament of Beasts* is here alluded to.[Back to Main Text]

Footnote 102: Bullock's manufactory was in this street.[Back to Main Text]

Footnote 103: A drama founded on the novel of *Rob Roy* had been produced, with great success, on the London stage.[Back to Main Text]

Footnote 104: Mr. Alexander Nasmyth, an eminent landscape painter of Edinburgh—the father of Mrs. Terry.[Back to Main Text]

Footnote 105: See *ante*, vol. iii. p. 220.[Back to Main Text]

Footnote 106:
"What beauties does Flora disclose,
How sweet are her smiles upon Tweed," etc.—*Crawford*.[Back to Main Text]

Footnote 107: The late Sir Patrick Murray of Ochtertyre, Bart.—one of the Scotch Barons of Exchequer.[Back to Main Text]

Footnote 108: [Of Hinse, Washington Irving writes in his *Abbotsford*:—
"Among the other important and privileged members of the household who figured in attendance at dinner, was a large gray cat, who, I observed, was regaled from time to time with titbits from the table. This sage grimalkin was a favorite of both master and mistress, and slept at night in their room, and Scott laughingly observed, that one of the least wise parts of their establishment was that the window was left open at night for puss to go in and out. The cat assumed a kind of ascendency among the quadrupeds—sitting in state in Scott's armchair, and occasionally stationing himself on a chair beside the door, as if to review his subjects as they passed, giving each dog a cuff beside the ears as he went by. This clapper-clawing was always taken in good part; it appeared to be, in fact, a mere act of sovereignty on the part of grimalkin to remind the others of their vassalage; which they acknowledged by the most perfect acquiescence. A general harmony prevailed between sovereign and subjects, and they would all sleep together in the sunshine."][Back to Main Text]

Footnote 109: See Croker's *Boswell* (edit. 1831), vol. iii p. 38.[Back to Main Text]

Footnote 110: George Hogarth, Esq., W. S., brother of Mrs. James Ballantyne. This gentleman is now well known in the literary world; especially by a History of Music, of which all who understand that science speak highly. [He was the father-in-law of Charles Dickens, and for many years a musical and dramatic critic in London.][Back to Main Text]

Footnote 111: "Now, John," cried Constable, one evening after he had told one of his best stories, "now, John, is that true?" His object evidently was, in Iago's phrase, *to let down the pegs*; but Rigdum answered gayly, "True, indeed! Not one word of it!—any blockhead may stick to truth, my hearty—but 't is a sad hamperer of genius."[Back to Main Text]

Footnote 112: [This letter was written August 11, by Lady Louisa Stuart, and it appears in its original and complete form in *Familiar Letters*, vol. ii. p. 18. To the end of her long life, the writer was somewhat influenced by the feeling prevailing in her youth as to the loss of caste suffered by women of good social position who appeared in print. Writing to Mrs. Lockhart after her father's death, and enclosing some of his letters, Lady Louisa says: "If Mr. Lockhart wishes to insert any of these, I will beg not to be named. It is not that I am not proud enough of having been honored with *his* regard, but I never yet saw my name in print, and hope I never shall." Mr. Lockhart evidently in part overcame this objection.][Back to Main Text]

Footnote 113: In 1827, Lady Louisa wrote for Caroline, Lady Scott, a great-granddaughter of the duke, *Some Account of John, Duke of Argyle, and his Family*. This delightful memoir was first printed (privately) in 1863. It was published in 1899, in *Selections from the Manuscripts of Lady Louisa Stuart*.[Back to Main Text]

Footnote 114: [Sheffield Place, the seat of Lord Sheffield, the friend and editor of Gibbon.][Back to Main Text]

Footnote 115: *Ebony* was Mr. Blackwood's own usual designation in the *jeux d'esprit* of his young Magazine, in many of which the persons thus addressed by Scott were conjoint culprits. They both were then, as may be inferred, sweeping the boards of the Parliament House as "briefless barristers."[Back to Main Text]

Footnote 116: I understand that this now celebrated soup was *extemporized* by M. Florence on Scott's first visit to Bowhill after the publication of *Guy Mannering*. Florence had *served*—and Scott having on some sporting party made his personal acquaintance, he used often afterwards to gratify the poet's military propensities by sending up magnificent representations in pastry, of citadels taken by the Emperor, etc.[Back to Main Text]

Footnote 117: In the Introduction to *The Lay of the Last Minstrel*, 1830, Sir Walter says: "Were I ever to take the unbecoming freedom of censuring a man of Mr. Coleridge's extraordinary talents, it would be on account of the caprice and indolence with which he has thrown from him, as in mere wantonness, those unfinished scraps of poetry, which, like the Torso of antiquity, defy the skill of his poetical brethren to complete them. The charming fragments which the author abandons to their fate are surely too valuable to be treated like the proofs of careless engravers, the sweepings of whose studios often make the fortune of some painstaking collector." And in a note to *The Abbot*, alluding to Coleridge's beautiful and tantalizing fragment of *Christabel*, he adds: "Has not our own imaginative poet cause to fear that future ages will desire to summon him from his place of rest, as Milton longed

'To call up him who left half told

The story of Cambuscan bold'?"[Back to Main Text]

Footnote 118: Macneill's *Will and Jean*.[Back to Main Text]

Footnote 119: When playing, in childhood, with the young ladies of the Buccleuch family, she had been overheard saying to her namesake Lady Anne Scott, "Well, I do wish I were Lady Anne too—it is so much prettier than Miss;" thenceforth she was commonly addressed in the family by the coveted title.[Back to Main Text]

Footnote 120: *Vide* "Green-breeks" in the General Introduction to the *Waverley Novels*. Surely *Yellow Waistcoat* was his prototype.[Back to Main Text]

Lightning Source UK Ltd.
Milton Keynes UK
UKHW021844070520
362943UK00018B/349